Thieving
Three-Fingered Jack

CRITICAL CARIBBEAN STUDIES

Series Editors: Yolanda Martínez-San Miguel, Michelle Stephens, and
Kathleen Lopez

Focused particularly in the twentieth and twenty-first centuries, although
attentive to the context of earlier eras, this series encourages interdisciplinary approaches and methods and is open to scholarship in a variety
of areas, including anthropology, cultural studies, diaspora and transnational studies, environmental studies, gender and sexuality studies,
history, and sociology. The series pays particular attention to the four
main research clusters of Critical Caribbean Studies at Rutgers University,
where the coeditors serve as members of the executive board: Caribbean
Critical Studies Theory and the Disciplines; Archipelagic Studies
and Creolization; Caribbean Aesthetics, Poetics, and Politics; and
Caribbean Colonialities.

Giselle Anatol, *The Things That Fly in the Night: Female Vampires in
Literature of the Circum-Caribbean and African Diaspora*

Frances R. Botkin, *Thieving Three-Fingered Jack: Transatlantic Tales of a
Jamaican Outlaw, 1780–2015*

Alaí Reyes-Santos, *Our Caribbean Kin: Race and Nation in the Neoliberal
Antilles*

Milagros Ricourt, *The Dominican Racial Imaginary: Surveying the
Landscape of Race and Nation in Hispaniola*

Katherine A. Zien, *Sovereign Acts: Performing Race, Space, and Belonging
in Panama and the Canal Zone*

Thieving Three-Fingered Jack

Transatlantic Tales of a Jamaican Outlaw, 1780–2015

Frances R. Botkin

RUTGERS UNIVERSITY PRESS

NEW BRUNSWICK, CAMDEN, AND NEWARK,
NEW JERSEY, AND LONDON

978-0-8135-8739-4
978-0-8135-8738-7
978-0-8135-8740-0
Cataloging-in-Publication data is available from the Library of Congress.

A British Cataloging-in-Publication record for this book is available from the British Library.

∞ The paper used in this publication meets the requirements of the American National Standard for Information Sciences—Permanence of Paper for Printed Library Materials, ANSI Z39.48–1992.

www.rutgersuniversitypress.org

Manufactured in the United States of America

Dedicated to Col. Frank Lumsden
of the Charles Town Maroons

Quashie, by Col. Frank Lumsden, 2009. Private collection.

Contents

Thieving
Three-Fingered Jack

Introduction

REPRESENTING
THREE-FINGERED JACK

The fugitive slave known as "Three-Fingered Jack" terrorized colonial Jamaica for almost two years, until he was captured and killed in 1781 by Maroons, self-emancipated Afro-Jamaicans, bound by treaty to police the island for insurgents and runaways.[1] A thief and a killer, Jack was also a freedom fighter who sabotaged the colonial machine until his grisly death at its behest. Early Jamaican accounts of Three-Fingered Jack rehearse and adjudicate the problems of island rebellion and the solutions administered by a colonial police state. This study offers a cultural and literary history that weaves together narratives from Britain, Jamaica, and the United States to examine the persistence of stories about this black outlaw who continues to resist classification or absolute judgment. It begins by reaching back to 1655 in its consideration of black resistance to European projects of empire, identifying Jack as the successor to the early, pretreaty maroons, the first freedom fighters in Jamaica, and it identifies the hypermasculine "black badass" in Jamaican and U.S. popular culture as his descendant. For more than two centuries, producers of culture—English, Anglo-Jamaican, Afro-Jamaican, American, and African American—have "thieved" Jack's riveting story, defining themselves through and against their representations of him. *Thieving Three-Fingered Jack* interrogates the appropriation, the *tiefin* (as Jamaican Patois would have it), of Three-Fingered Jack's story.

A Brief History of Representations
of Three-Fingered Jack

The Jamaican *Royal Gazette* published the first-known account of "BRISTOL, alias *Three-Fingered Jack*," an escaped slave from the Rozel estate, warning travelers to avoid the murderous thief and his bloodthirsty gang (vol. 2, no. 67: 458).[2] Subsequent news stories tracked Jack's depredations, issued proclamations for his arrest, and advertised a cash reward for his capture, first for £100, which then increased to £300 and manumission if a slave captured him.[3] After the December 1780 report of the capture of Jack's wife and crew, the paper announced in January 1781 the death of the "daring freebooter" who, armed with two muskets and a cutlass, submitted finally to three bullets and a forty-foot fall before losing his head and hand in the fatal blows (3: 79). With the severed parts held aloft, the victorious Maroon John Reeder and his associates marched to town to claim the hefty cash reward.

Although the *Royal Gazette* identified Three-Fingered Jack as the leader of a large group of rebels, after 1799 accounts consistently described him as a solitary bandit and associated him with obeah (obi), an Afro-Caribbean system of beliefs associated with rebellion on the Jamaican plantation.[4] In his *Treatise on Sugar* (1799), surgeon Benjamin Moseley (who practiced in Jamaica from 1768 to 1784) first introduced English readers to the battle between Jack's black magic and the "white obi" (Christianity) of Reeder; Moseley's allegedly firsthand account informed many of the subsequent English versions. In 1800 William Earle published his sentimental novel, *Obi; or, The History of Three-Fingered Jack*, and William Burdett released his adventure story, *Life and Exploits of Mansong*. Both relied heavily on Moseley, and Burdett borrowed extensively from Mungo Park's *Travels in the Interior of Africa* (1799), from which he took the initial African setting and Jack's surname, Mansong. In 1851 Thomas Frost published *Obi; or, Three-Fingered Jack*, which significantly expanded the prose version, and for the next two decades a handful of short, often anonymous, prose texts circulated in England, following the storylines of Burdett and Earle.

The same year that Burdett and Earle published their prose texts, John Fawcett's *Obi; or, Three-Finger'd Jack: A Serio-Pantomime* opened in London's Haymarket Theatre.[5] Immediately successful, it enjoyed a nine-year run in London, and it played in the repertories in the provinces as well as in the northern United States for another two decades. In New York in 1823, William Brown mounted the first black production of Fawcett's *Obi*. In the late 1820s, Edinburgh theater manager William Murray adapted Fawcett's *Obi* into a melodrama featuring African American actor Ira Aldridge as Jack, also called Karfa, his African name. These nineteenth-century literary and theatrical adaptations use the figure of Jack to consolidate racialized English and American national identities (and masculinities). Later these adaptations asserted an African American identity critical of the new republic's attitudes toward and participation in planation slavery.

The story of Three-Fingered Jack saw far less popularity in Jamaican print culture. An 1804 map by Jamaican surveyor James Robertson located "3 Finger Jack Huts" in Surrey County, closer to the Portland parish than the *Royal Gazette* had placed the hideout, but this site disappeared from maps early in the nineteenth century, as did most mention of the outlaw in Jamaican print or theater culture.

Even Fawcett's *Obi*, so popular in England and the United States, appeared only once on the Jamaican stage.[6] Jamaican fictional reproductions of the story did not reemerge until the 1930s—a very long gap, attributable to the social and economic preoccupations of the colonial elite, likely disinclined to linger on fictional accounts of black rebellion. In 1930, however, Jamaican historian Frank Cundall observed, "few persons connected with Jamaica have been the subject of so many publications as Three-Fingered Jack, the Terror of Jamaica" (9).[7] In the years following Cundall's publication, a handful of Jamaican texts emerged, such as Herbert George de Lisser's *Morgan's Daughter* (1931); Clinton V. Black's *Old Tales of Jamaica* (1958); Philip Sherlock's *Three-Fingered Jack's Treasure* (1961); and a didactic version of the Jack story in a *New Interest Reading Series* published by Collins Sangster Press in Kingston (1970). Emerging during the volatile period of decolonization and independence,

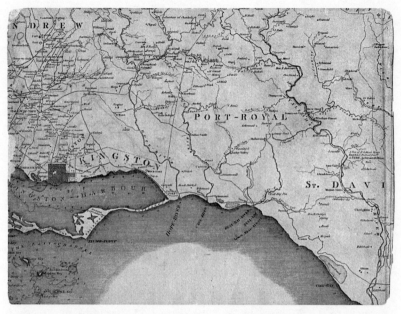

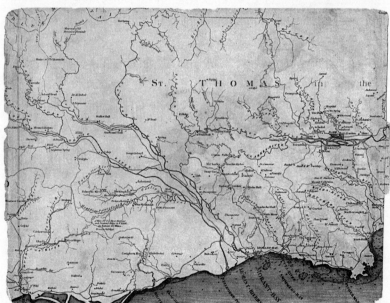

Figure I.1. *Map of the County of Surrey*, by James Robertson, 1804.
Ref. no. 727.4acg, National Library of Jamaica, Kingston.

these renderings call on the figure of Three-Fingered Jack in response to socioeconomic tensions among the white elite, the growing brown middle class, and the masses of working-class and poor black folk. Combining Jamaican folklore and English text source materials, these accounts nonetheless work within the conservative, Anglocentric purview of colonial print culture. Later twentieth-century Jamaican accounts of Jack Mansong, however, claim him as an emblem of black power that can at once articulate and unravel conceptions of a Creole national identity that promoted "Out of Many One People."

In 1973 the British-born Jamaican "environmentalist" geographer Lawrence Alan Eyre extended Cundall's essay in "Jack Mansong: Bloodshed or Brotherhood," an updated review of existing accounts of the life Three-Fingered Jack, including maps and photos. Eyre ponders the historical interest in the "ruthless" but "noble" outlaw, and he concludes that his "little guerilla war . . . was widely seen as a warning that in human, racial, national and international relations there is only one choice: bloodshed or brotherhood" (9, 14). Eyre's geopolitical approach locates the story as both particularly Jamaican and uniquely global. His invocation of "*brother-hood*" and "bloodshed" reflect a historical moment (the early 1970s), when competing rhetorics of peace and violence dominated the political landscape (emphasis mine).

It was not until 1980, however, that an Afro-Jamaican author would overtly politicize the story for Jamaicans, giving the text an Afrocentric twist and transnational register. Taking the folk hero to the stage, Ted Dwyer's *Mansong* opened in the midst of Kingston's "troubles" during the Michael Manley and Edward Seaga general elections, resurrecting Jack as a hero, despite the ongoing street violence that might well have rendered a machete-wielding warrior suspect.[8] Moreover, the play criticized Jamaica's relationship with international organizations such as the International Monetary Fund and its implications for local politics and economics. Some thirty years later, during the 2008 global economic crisis and while local dons still reigned, Aston Cooke worked with the Jamaican Youth

Theatre to direct a nonmusical adaptation of *Mansong*. Performing for the Kingston community and circulating abridged versions to schools around the island, Cooke and his students reproduced and disseminated their highly positive version of Jack's life.[9] For this group Jack represented a freedom fighter and role model for Jamaican youth.

Between the productions of Dwyer and Cooke, Boston University professor Chuck Rzepka produced a play called *Obi: A Play in the Life of Ira Aldridge* (2000), a unique multimedia tribute to Aldridge and Jack. Rzepka first collaborated with African American actor-director Vincent Earnest Siders, performing the play at the Boston Playwrights' Theatre. A few months later he worked with professor Jerry Hogle to mount the play for the North American Society for the Study of Romanticism at its annual conference that year in Tempe, Arizona. These productions, like Srinivas Aravamudan's Broadview edition of Earle's *Obi* (with relevant appendices), attest to the relevance of Jack's story among contemporary English and American literary scholars.

The story of Three-Fingered Jack appears with some regularity in Jamaican popular culture. For example, Hartley Neita's 2008 editorial in the *Gleaner* mentions Jack in a lament for the neglect of Jamaican legends, proposing that they should be celebrated with festivals or celebratory events as well as with monuments, uniting categories that Pierre Nora polarizes, the *lieux* (places) as opposed to the *mileux* (embodied environments) of memory. Neita alludes to the monument of Jack, erected by the Jamaica National Trust Commission (later the Jamaica National Heritage Trust), in the parish of Saint Thomas, near the ostensible site of Jack's hideout. Though largely unvisited, the historical marker appears as a tourist site in the most recent *Rough Guide to Jamaica*. The inscription on the marker reads,

> North of this road, in the hills and valleys beyond this marker, was the territory of the famous Jack Mansong or Three Finger Jack. It is not certain whether he was born in Jamaica or came from Africa, but it is

known that in the years 1780–1781 he fought, often single-handedly, a war of terror against the English soldiers and planters who held the slave colony. Strong, brave, armed with machete and musket, his bold exploits were equaled only by his chivalry. He loved his country and his people. He was said to have never harmed a woman or child. His life became a legend. Books and plays about him were written and performed in London Theatres. He was ambushed and killed near here in 1781.

This laudatory monument, underscoring Jack's strength, chivalry, and popularity, elides the role of the Maroons in Jack's demise, perhaps in the interest of imagined national unity; however, the Jamaica National Heritage Trust erected another stone marker that memorializes Jack at the corner of Emancipation Square in Spanish Town. Its neutral text states, "The head and hand of Three-Finger Jack Mansong were brought here by Maroons in 1781." This marker commemorates also a handful of pirates, including Calico Jack Rackham (gibbeted on a small cay near Port Royal in 1720), but, tucked away in a shady corner of the square, it gets foot traffic almost only from scholars visiting the Jamaica Archives.

Maroon country, too, memorializes Jack, his story etched in the very landscape of the island. The Bowden Pen Farmers Association in Portland maintains the landmark "Three Finger Jack Spring" and posts a sign that marks the spot from which Jack fell while running from Maroons.[10] This site sits on the Cuhna Cuhna Pass, one of many trails that wind through the Blue and John Crow Mountains. These mountains sheltered and sustained the Windward Maroons for centuries, and UNESCO designated the Blue and John Crow Mountains National Park a World Heritage Site in 2015. Eric "Worries" McCurbin, a founding member of the association, explains that the Cuhna Cuhna Pass was used first by Tainos and then by Maroons (as well as escaped slaves and other fugitives) for safe travel to markets or mountain hideouts.[11] The name, Cuhna Cuhna, he elaborates, refers to the treacherous nature of the trail, indicating the point beyond which fugitives "could not, could not" pass. McCurbin opines that Maroons killed Jack because he had defected from their ranks after having fought alongside them during the Maroon wars. In the eyes of this contemporary Maroon, Jack was a traitor, a Maroon gone renegade (interview).

Other Maroons proudly associate Jack with their unique cultural heritage of freedom fighting, despite the view of many Jamaicans that the Maroons betrayed their enslaved counterparts by signing the 1738–1739 treaties with the English, giving them land and money in exchange for returning fugitive slaves and quelling rebellions (see chapter 1). The inextricable relationship between Jack and the Maroons who killed him creates a critical space to think about the different ways to practice marronage, to fight or resist dominant cultures. Maroons today continue to grapple with Jamaican mainstream culture, struggling with issue of land rights, representation, and cultural heritage in a developing country where tourism heralds the new colonialism. Though visitors can visit Three Finger Jack Spring as part of a Maroon ecotour in Portland, they generally flock to the beaches and all-inclusive hotels. Tourism has not quite reached the poor parish of Saint Thomas, a fascinating hotbed of Kumina, obeah, and history. David Wong Ken, however, opened the Three-Fingered Jack Hotel in 2016, naming it after the bandit with hopes of "spring boarding" into ecohistorical tours to stimulate visitors to the area (interview).

Thieving Three-Fingered Jack identifies discrepancies and intersections in these many tales about Jack, piecing together a coherent, if fragmented, narrative. Like Jack's three-fingered hand and decapitated body, the dis- and re-membered narratives tell a brutal history of violence, loss, and retribution. This elusive Jack has functioned as a transatlantic vehicle for stories about slavery, colonialism, and their aftermaths. He has been called Bristol, Karfa, Mansong, *Obi*, and Jack; his story is a cultural product at once of Britain, the United States, and Jamaica, but he is a citizen of nowhere. He exceeds Western systems of categorization, permitting him to occupy several at once: criminal and victim, hero and villain, brutal and brutalized. Though dismembered and dispossessed, he embodies count-less possibilities for signification, eluding colonial efforts to emasculate or erase him. His story persists in classrooms, in conference papers, in critical editions, and in academic journals. He lives on also in physical spaces and in oral histories. This study examines these different kinds of texts to interrogate the significance of this "badass" black rebel in his permuta-tions around the Atlantic. Though he never told his own story (that we know of), different cultural groups tell stories about themselves as they tell stories about Three-Fingered Jack.

The Critical Record

Previous critical studies about Three-Fingered Jack have focused entirely on the nineteenth-century Anglo-European or Anglo-American texts, and these article-length studies have largely opposed categories such as English and African, white and black, and colonizer and colonized.[12] Unlike these accounts, *Thieving Three-Fingered Jack* considers the ways that Jamaican authors, actors, directors, storytellers, and Maroons have adapted the legend, enriching existing conversations in ways that blur and complicate these Eurocentric oppositions.

Intellectual developments in Atlantic and Caribbean studies have paved the way for this kind of research, inventing new categories and vocabularies to move beyond the boundaries of national specificity or geographic borders.[13] Others have welcomed different methods of scholar-ship that take into consideration the stories of the unlettered and unrep-resented.[14] More recently still, several monographs and collections have identified the significance of the West Indies to studies about England and the United States, a relationship that Sean Goudie has usefully identi-fied as a "creole complex" in his discussion of the "paracolonial relation."[15] This transatlantic, relational approach highlights what Elizabeth Dillon, echoing Sylvia Wynter, conceptualizes as the "colonial relation," the ways that colonies become "entwined" with the central site of English political and economic power. "[The colonial relation] names," she elaborates, "the centrality of colonialism to metropolitan modernity and denominates the representational strategies that simultaneously conveyed and masked this fact" (31). *Thieving Three-Fingered Jack* builds on these ideas to propose that the figure of this transatlantic black outlaw emblematizes resistance to such entwinement, the refusal of relation or accommodation by way of antagonism or disunion, despite the ways different groups have come to rely on him for self-definition.

Jenny Sharpe's study of the first national heroine of Jamaica, Nanny of the Maroons, offers fruitful ways to think about Jack Mansong (1). Nanny's story, Sharpe writes, emblematizes slave women's resistance to slavery, and it involves "contending forms of knowledge, written versus oral histories, colonial versus national cultures, institutional versus popular ways of knowing" (2).[16] Sharpe's discussion recalls Sylvia Wynter's approach to the "colonial relation of exile" that characterizes Caribbean writing, urging academics to replace it with one of engagement with folk and popular culture ("We Must Learn" 1: 31, 2: 41). Nanny's history parallels Jack's in its fragmented archival material as well as in its raced and gendered representation.[17] Sharpe links Nanny's significance as a rebel woman to decolonization and the emergence of Jamaica as an independent nation, and she makes a case for "the diasporic experience of slavery that allowed black women to assume an authority they did not have in Africa" (4). Jack Mansong, it is important to note, did not make the cut for Jamaican national hero; however, his story provides the occasion to consider the ways that the experiences of slavery have contributed to conceptualizations of black masculinity in Jamaica and beyond.

More than it does Nanny's, Jack's story parallels that of his earlier counterpart, the Afro-Jamaican slave rebel Tacky: both men represent a distinctly black, non-Christian, and African-identified masculinity associated with obeah. Tacky led an eighteen-month uprising in 1760 that involved at least fifteen hundred slaves, killed more than sixty white people, and destroyed property across the island, taking the joint efforts of Maroons, military, and local militia to restore order. Jack and Tacky represent powerful examples of violent black resistance, enacting Hilary Beckles's description of slavery as a "contest between black and white masculinities" ("Black Masculinity" 229). Anthony Lewis and Robert Carr have proposed that this contest developed into the creation of a problematically masculine body politic (2). Tacky's Rebellion, Lewis and Carr argue, triggered a decisive moment of "creolization or de-Africanization" that shaped and gendered the development of Jamaican cultural nationalism (1–3).[18] Jack and Tacky have been thus excluded from a gendered national narrative, for example, that of the national hero, which promotes models of black middle-class male respectability, reputation, and (colonial) relation.[19] Their currents of black resistance to the Anglo-Jamaican plantocracy have recurred and endured, with avatars that challenged the lighter-skinned, Christian hegemony of the postemancipation period, the subsequent Creole nationalism of independence, and the neoliberalist white heteropatriarchy of the present day.

Jamaican artist Omari S. Ra, also known as "Afrikan," has paired paintings of the heads of Jack and Tacky as part of a series that visually depict these counternarratives.[20] In their features, hair, and dark skin, the disembodied heads evoke the Africanness of these warriors and their shared fate of decapitation. In *Excavation: Head of Jack Mansong*, Jack's face stares directly outward with a stern, thoughtful gaze. Around his neck he wears a choker necklace of barely decipherable words ("white man," "burned," "slavery"); he appears strangled by text, as if to depict the way print has misrepresented him. Ra's representations of these national "unheroes" create a visual counternarrative to those of the seven national heroes. If, as Petrina Dacres argues, the male body of the national hero came to stand as a "metonym" for the body politic, then these decapitated heads might represent that which sits outside of it (or, rests on a pike or in a pail of rum).[21]

Figure I.2. *Excavation: Head of Jack Mansong,* by Omari "Afrikan"
S. Ra, n.d. In artist's possession.

BADASSERY

White hegemony and black badassery in colonial Jamaica were mutually constitutive. The subsequent struggles between Anglo- and Afro-
Jamaicans have shaped contemporary constructions of masculinity in

Jamaica and elsewhere. This contest emerged in Jamaica's early colonial history, in tensions between the vulnerable English and their fierce maroon adversaries. It developed during slavery, as Afro-Jamaican rebels compromised production on the plantation and threatened the lives of Anglo-Jamaicans. It continued into the postemancipation Caribbean (and during the Jim Crow era in the United States), as black men fought against new modes of labor-intensive capitalist oppression that, like the old system of slavery, at once relied on and feared black male bodies.[22] In the twentieth century and beyond, as in slave times, resistance to social and economic strictures has been criminalized, and indeed criminality offers an alternative to the unjust strictures of neoliberalist heteropatriarchy. From these circumstances the problematically violent "hypermasculine" rebel has arisen, associated with a history of marginalization but also with a counterhistory of heroic resistance. Strong, brave, and by most accounts chivalrous, Jack Mansong robbed and killed to survive. His powerful legacy, with its contradictions and moral ambiguity, persists in politics and popular culture in the Atlantic world today, particularly in the figure of the gangster.

In contemporary Jamaica the don or shotta (shooter) figure uses violence to demand freedom, offering an alternative to middle-class respectability for lower-class Afro-Jamaicans who must "negotiate the treacherous spaces between their marginalized lives and the hegemonic images of masculinity" (Hope 119). Jamaican men face new "social imperatives" to be masculine, many that have emerged in response to feminist and postfeminist movements (Beckles, "Constructions" 12).[23] In addition, they contend with stereotypes about male domestic violence and negligence as well as with rampant homophobia.[24] As Deborah Thomas puts it, "black men have become problematic in new ways, their marginality defined in relation to new institutional configurations" (*Exceptional Violence* 85). Jack Mansong has been used to embody, contradict, undermine, and reconceive—sometimes in the very same text—representations of black masculinities.[25]

In its most basic form, the story of Jack Mansong tells the tale of a black man who resisted white authority and died for it, killed by the lackeys of a police state. This story of a racist police state persists today, not only in the Global South, but also in northern and midwestern American cities and around the world. Sometimes the black man is armed, and sometimes he's not; recent statistics show that in the United States, mostly he is not. Sometimes he has committed a crime, and sometimes he has not. Sometimes his crime is being poor, black, and angry, and sometimes he gets incarcerated instead of killed; sometimes he kills the cop. The *scenario* (as Taylor uses the term to describe meaning-making paradigms that structure alternative behaviors) has played out in Ferguson, Kingston, and Baltimore, as well as in Dallas and Baton Rouge.[26] This black avenger has been criminalized and victimized, but he also represents a powerful stance against white oppression.[27] He has inspired voices that rightly insist that Black Lives Matter. And, like Jack Mansong, he raises questions about race, masculinity, and power as well as about stereotypes that have evolved and emerged around these issues.

Thieving Three-Fingered Jack locates in the history of Jack Mansong the unfortunate backstory to these current crises of violence against black men and women as well as the role of the justice system in constructing, perpetuating, and mishandling rather than mitigating them. My diachronic, transnational project looks at this story of resistance to slavery through lenses of race and gender, watching it refract into stories about a black man fighting a powerful police state, foreshadowing contemporary narratives about racial profiling and structural racism.

The Chapters

Chapter 1, "Divide and Conquer: Three-Fingered Jack and the Maroons," approaches the story of Three-Fingered Jack historically, using early Anglo-Jamaican newspaper accounts, the journals of the Assembly of Jamaica, Surgeon General Benjamin Moseley's *Treatise on Sugar*, and

Maroon historiographies to illuminate its implications for later conceptions of black masculinity. These documents reflect the circumstances that drove the English to collaborate with maroon adversaries, pitting self-emancipated Afro-Jamaicans against one another as well as against their enslaved counterparts. These accounts tell stories of white weakness and black strength, stories that compelled the English to resort to familiar methods of divide and conquer. This chapter reveals the complexities of black resistance in Jamaica beyond the plantation structure and into the present day.

Chapter 2, "'Jack Is a MAN': Prose Obis, 1800–1870," compares prose texts by William Earle and William Burdett to argue that these popular representations of colonial Jamaica and their permutations construct a range of possibilities for English audiences to witness, champion, or question their participation in the colonizing projects in Africa and the Caribbean. In their explorations of English identity, these texts put into fatal opposition obeah-protected Jack with his Christian rival, constructing also oppositional Anglo- and Afro-Jamaican masculinities that reify whiteness for English readers.

Chapter 3, "Staging *Obi*: Three-Fingered Jack in London and New York," examines versions of the life and death of Jack staged in the two cities in the first quarter of the nineteenth century. John Fawcett's 1800 blackface pantomime performed the perceived racial and moral superiority of Anglo- over Afro-Jamaicans for white English audiences, celebrating British dominance on the world stage. In 1823 William Brown's all-black "African Company" appropriated Fawcett's *Obi* for inclusion in a production that insisted on representation, legal and dramatic, at a critical moment in a racialized antebellum America. This chapter examines the rebellious black outlaw as a flexible vehicle for the representation of a raced national identity (white English, white American, black American) articulated against its perceived opposite (black Afro-Jamaican, white British, and white American).

Chapter 4, "Being Jack Mansong: Ira Aldridge and Three-Fingered Jack," unites William Murray's 1830 *Obi* melodrama with Chuck Rzepka's

2000 production, *Obi: A Play in the Life of Ira Aldridge, the "Paul Robeson" of the 19th Century* to explore Aldridge's embodiment and performance of the possibilities for challenging racial stereotypes and oppression. The chapter argues that the creative intervention of actors, producers, and directors highlights the ways that the figure of Jack can represent both the victim and predator of a system that criminalizes the black man; it reveals, too, the structural racism of the institutions (theatrical and academic) that participate, however radically or sensitively, in the cultural production of race.

Chapter 5, "After Emancipation: Masquerade and Miscegenation," compares Thomas Frost's *Obi: A Romance* (1851) to Herbert de Lisser's *Morgan's Daughter* (1931) exploring, respectively, the racialized consolidation of English and Jamaican national identity. The figure of Jack Mansong for Frost questions the legitimacy of English imperialism, and for de Lisser it registers colonial ambivalence toward Afro-Jamaicans in the period of decolonization. Novels of sexual encounter and masquerade, they play with possibilities for racial and gender passing at historical moments especially preoccupied with the instability of identity.

My final chapter, "*Mansong*: No Longer 'Nearly Everybody Wite,'" proposes that Ted Dwyer's 1980 Jamaican pantomime dramatizes the struggles of an independent, politically fraught Jamaican nation. It identifies contemporary sociopolitical violence in Jamaica as the inheritance of British colonial rule, revealing ruptures within a Creole national narrative of "Out of Many One People." Transforming Jack into an African-identified hero and radically revising English genre and storyline, *Mansong* conflates the agendas of historical enemies Jack and Quashie into a utopian vision of peace, unity, and black power.

My epilogue explores the legacy of Jack Mansong in mainstream popular culture, press, and politics. Out of the state-installed conflicts among self-emancipated and enslaved black people in colonial Jamaica emerged the garrison politics of contemporary Jamaica. In the twenty-first century, figures such as the don, like Dudus Coke (currently in an American prison), and musical artists such as Vybz Kartel and Buju Banton (also in prison) continue to blur the lines between criminal and freedom fighter. The popularity of the antihero in film and in music has emerged in Jamaica and elsewhere out of social and economic conditions that continue to oppress poor black folk, and it draws from a number of sources, including Rastafari, blaxploitation films, and the "spaghetti Western." The outlaw, especially when racialized, provokes polemical responses, often (but not only) when white men (such as Perry Henzell and Quentin Tarantino) control the cultural production of black masculinity. The epilogue circles back to narratives of contemporary Maroons, descendants of the freedom-fighting warriors who provide a model for Jack's enduring example of radical black resistance in the Atlantic world. Three-Fingered Jack has become an outlaw of mythical status who heralded later black avengers.

Thieving Three-Fingered Jack puts literary texts in relation to corresponding accounts from different periods and nations to reflect the circum-Atlantic trajectory of the narratives it discusses. Spanning over 350 years, it brings together oral histories and archival records; stage productions from London with others from New York and Kingston; literature with popular culture; white academia and black professional theater; and historiographies with contemporary film and folklore.

Note on Methodology

It feels important to position myself in this narrative of appropriation, so I will indulge in a confessional interlude. I am a literary critic. I am not an ethnographer, an anthropologist, or a historian. I was trained as a romanticist, a student of the archives, and immersed in a field dedicated first and foremost to the imagination and subjectivity of the white English (male) author. My interest in Three-Fingered Jack grew out of research on the Anglo-Irish woman writer Maria Edgeworth's moral tale "The Grateful Negro" (1804) in its representation of an obeah-driven slave rebellion in

Jamaica, a creative imagining of Jamaica from the pen of an English-born woman living on her father's estate in Ireland. I made my way from the British Library to the National Library of Ireland to the National Library of Jamaica, where all signs of obeah and rebellion led me to Three-Fingered Jack. Mine was not simply a move from metropole to colony, though indeed this move shifted my perspective; as Paul Youngquist has noted, the West Indies do not merely sit at the edge of Empire: "They are its engine: the economic, material, and cultural condition of British prosperity and dominion during the Romantic era" (Youngquist and Botkin). Mine was a move from British romanticism to transatlantic studies. I did not move merely from archive to archive, either. I moved from archive to field, and I had to learn new ways to conduct research.

Recent contributions to Caribbean studies have prompted methods of research that intervene in and intermix traditional disciplines. Shalini Puri, for example, has carved out a space for "fieldwork in the humanities" that privileges "place over [cultural studies' preoccupation with] space" ("Finding the Field" 59, 64).[28] Deborah Thomas dilates on the creation of counterarchives that would forge new possibilities "for seeing connections previously unexamined and for reordering our ontological taken-for-granteds" ("Caribbean Studies" 27).[29] These methods, like Jenny Sharpe's and Sylvia Wynter's, use a combination of history, social science, cultural studies, and especially fiction to stage "how a lost or forgotten path continues to exert its influence" (Sharpe xii). These scholarly models gave me a way to think about my own growth and transformation as a scholar.

When I first started this project in 2008, I spent many productive hours at the National Library of Jamaica in Kingston and in the Jamaica Archives in Spanish Town, searching for maps, manuscripts, and documents. Housed in the National Library, Ted Dwyer's unpublished play text *Mansong* showed me a way out of the library and into the world. Though Dwyer had recently passed, his collaborator Carmen Tipling graciously granted my request for a meeting. My conversations with Carmen (who, by the way, took me to my first Jamaican pantomime) gave me my first taste of Jamaican hospitality and broadened my scope beyond the archives. Carmen showed me that I needed to talk to people—and listen— if I were going to write about a primarily oral culture. She introduced me to people and places in Kingston, such as architect Evan Williams and his venue, Red Bones Blues Café, a popular spot for live music, spoken-word poetry, and film. Evan in turn introduced me to the late and truly remarkable Col. Frank Lumsden of the Charles Town Maroons. So I left Kingston and traveled to Charles Town and other Maroon communities, and in my travels I found most people happy to talk.

Instead of Jamaica's famed violence, I experienced warmth and welcome just about everywhere I went. Once, just once, a very angry man demanded of me (in language harsher than I describe here), "*What* are *you* doing here?" His question, I think, held merit, even if his hostile approach did not. What *is* a white American academic woman doing in random parts of Jamaica researching a project about a black outlaw of the eighteenth century? This man and I have since discussed this question further under more affable circumstances, because we have become friends; the social space where these clashes happen also creates a space where learning can happen. The answers? Learning about Three-Fingered Jack, certainly. Learning about Jamaica and Jamaicans. Listening to all sorts of people. Learning about my limits as a scholar. Thinking about what to bring back to the classroom. Drinking rum. Listening to music. And, in the language of my discipline, searching for counterarchives—and finding them.

I pursued counterarchives in hopes of contributing to them, advancing a literary theory of marronage, which Michelle Stephens has helpfully dubbed a "subversive, discursive phenomenon," to track the movements of Three-Fingered Jack across different kinds of Atlantic texts (e-mail). As a literary critic working "in the field," I relied on luck, intrepidity, and trial and error. Reading across genres, periods, and nations, I practice a kind of discursive marronage, whereby I mimic, engage with, resist, and depart from different academic methods and disciplines, thus creolizing the institutions that produce them.[30]

Interweaving archival research, literary analysis, folklore, film, and oral histories, I undertake an interdisciplinary approach that navigates the tensions that Diana Taylor identifies between "the archive and the repertoire," between texts and traditions (16–17).[31] I intervene in British literary studies, identifying the amnesias of Anglo-European disciplines (Youngquist and Botkin; Rzepka, "Obi Now"), striving to nudge these traditionalist disciplines into new directions, moving forward in practice, priority, and pedagogy. In its movement around Jamaica, England, and the United States, my project contributes to contemporary studies of Caribbean cultures, because my methods work to reinforce the Caribbean as an always-globalized region. Finally, my emphasis on Jack Mansong's black masculinity contributes to intersecting conversations about gender and national identity in Caribbean studies and British romanticism.

Jack Mansong has changed the way I teach too. I have brought his story into my Baltimore classroom, and it has provoked conversations about Freddie Gray, police brutality, and racism. His story provides a contrast to the self-representations of Equiano and Mary Prince, texts that already expand the parameters of courses such as British Literature from the Romantic Period through the Present; I now conclude this fifteen-week survey with texts by Louise Bennett, Kamau Brathwaite, and Ngũgĩ wa Thiong'o, showing my students how voices from Jamaica, Barbados, and Kenya have shaped British national identity—and how to complicate categories like national identity.[32] I also teach versions of Three-Fingered Jack in courses on Caribbean literature. Jack Mansong fits right in with figures like Earl Lovelace's Aldrick from *The Dragon Can't Dance*, Aimé Césaire's Caliban from *A Tempest*, or Michelle Cliff's Christopher from *Abeng*.[33] In other words, I have creolized my teaching as well as my research.

Gloria Simms, Mama G (Paramount Queen of the Maroons, by some accounts) and founder of the Maroon Indigenous Women Circle, gave me a way to understand how I work. She taught me a Jamaican proverb, "Tunyahan mek fashion" (Turn your hand and make fashion). In other words, improvise (turn your hand) with whatever materials you have, recycle when you can, and conserve your resources, natural and otherwise; Simms advocates a way of life that honors community over capitalism. When applied to research, these methods, improvisational as they might be, make way for counternarratives; they open up new possibilities for the production of knowledge. Stories about Three-Fingered Jack have been recycled for centuries, *tiefed* by people and cultures seeking an ideologically and ethically varied range of agendas. I am not trying to tell the true story of Jack Mansong. I aim to demonstrate what different permutations of this transatlantic story tell us about storytelling in the Atlantic world.

I want to conclude with a story about a sign. As I was traveling with Paul Youngquist, my friend, colleague, and fellow "Gonzo researcher" (as he has put it), we saw a sign on crowded coaster bus that carried us from Halfway Tree in Kingston to the Jamaica Archives in Spanish Town. The sign read, "Nuh Drinking. Nuh Smoking. Nuh Knowing." This message—this apparent epistemological crisis—seemed particularly auspicious that morning, because we were, after all, headed to the archives to find answers, to know things. We were thousands of miles away from the hushed grandeur of the British Library as we walked from the bus stop to the library, on a street that sits under the shadow of the imposing prison structure, surrounded by guns, goats, and ganja. I realized then that to reconsider our discipline, we need to reevaluate what we think we know about knowledge and its production—especially knowledge about slavery and colonialism, and its counter-cultures and aftermaths. More important, we realized that "not knowing" creates both a problem and an opening. So I say, "Tunyahan mek fashion."

CHAPTER 1

Divide and Conquer

THREE-FINGERED JACK
AND THE MAROONS

This study begins with the early maroons of Jamaica because these deadly warriors furnished Three-Fingered Jack (and many others) with models of resistance to slavery and colonialism. The English employed strategies to enflame the spiritual, cultural, and ethnic conflicts that already festered among the island's black population, in efforts to prevent the "infection" of marronage from spreading and to "suppress [the] rebells" (*Calendar* 41: 150.i). Narratives about Three-Fingered Jack provide the occasion to consider counternarratives about colonial methods of divide and conquer beginning as early as the English invasion of Spanish Jamaica in 1655. These narratives likewise shed light on the problematic legacy of black masculinity in the Atlantic world, as the English fostered violence among Afro-Jamaicans, defining themselves against those who worked their land and fought their battles. Stories of English weakness and African strength remind us that in signing treaties in 1738 and 1739 with the "First Time Maroons," the English pitted Afro-Jamaicans against one another to ensure their own security.[1] The treaties criminalized resistance in advance, giving rise to outlaws like Three-Fingered Jack.

Eighteenth-century narratives about Three-Fingered Jack reflect the social dis-ease that compelled the English to collaborate with former adversaries for protection against African rebellion and European invasion. These collaborations in turn prompted divided loyalties among

Afro-Jamaicans. The relationship between Three-Fingered Jack and the Maroons foregrounds the social spaces and relationships at the margins of and beyond the porous boundaries of the plantation and its markets, roads, and mechanisms of control. These interspaces hosted runaway slaves and military men of different ethnicities who lived outside the law, challenging the imagined spiritual and national wholeness that British colonial discourse endeavored to assert.

The accounts of Jack's exploits in the Jamaica *Royal Gazette* (1780–1781) and Benjamin Moseley's *Treatise on Sugar* (1799) reflect the disorder on the island. They climax with the gruesome spectacle of Maroons parading Jack's severed head and hand through the streets of Kingston and Spanish Town, a much-recycled image that underscores the efficiency of the colonial militia and the sure fate of those who rebelled. The image also reveals the violence visited on the black body by a brutal system, and sometimes by other black people as tactics of survival, suggesting the extent to which the British feared, provoked, and relied on racial violence to protect their interests. While subsequent stories about Jack retain the grisly image, they market other fictions about the compassion and strength of the English planter class and the loyalty of the enslaved, generally eliding the role of the Maroons.[2]

Contemporary Maroons still tell stories about Jack, but they celebrate a tradition of freedom fighting, not bounty hunting, in Jamaica. Maroons found in Jack a worthy adversary in conflicts fueled by cultural and spiritual differences. Frank Lumsden, the recently deceased colonel of the Charles Town Maroons, remembers an elder's rendition of the story:

> Bobo Shackleton told me about the capture of Three-Fingered Jack. The Maroon that actually cut off two of his fingers in an earlier dispute was seeking him, and he was told by the very same obeah woman who was protecting Jack Mansong that they had to go through certain steps before they could actually go in search of him. And the first step began with a hawk appearing at noon in the sky, and of course we had to shoot

the hawk. If we didn't, there's no point in going after Three-Fingered Jack. Once having done that, then we were to go to the village where a little dog would then take him to where Jack was hiding. And, then . . . when Quashee found him, Three-Fingered Jack said, "You brave. You come again." And Quashee said, "Yes, but this time me sanctified," meaning he was baptized in a Christian church. So when Quashee said that, it unnerved Jack for a minute, and he broke and ran from hiding, and he was shot. Quashee finished him off and severed his head and collected his reward. . . . But I suspect, in reality, Quashee was really finishing old business more than going after the reward. (Interview).

This anecdote reflects a process that Colonel Lumsden identifies in many aspects of Akan-influenced Maroon culture as "African retention and Caribbean invention" (interview). Col. Lumsden's retelling of Bobo Shackleton's narrative shares elements with written histories about Jack (Quashie's baptism, Jack's obeah, and the government reward, for example) and the departures (the hawk, the dog, "old business"), and opens up the spaces between "the archive and the repertoire," between written and embodied history. It suggests a relationship between Jack and the Maroons that does not hinge only on the proclamations or treaties of the colonial machine but also on other kinds of cultural encounters, reminiscent of those that motivated the early Afro-Jamaicans to fight against or align with one another. The English in Jamaica endeavored to stimulate and profit from the disunities among and between the self-emancipated black people of Jamaica.

After invading Spanish Jamaica in 1655 as part of Lord Protector Oliver Cromwell's famed Western Design, English military forces struggled to settle the colony. Until the English treated with them in 1738 and 1739, the maroons, or "wild negroes" as they were known, harbored fugitives, stole from the plantations, abducted women, and killed soldiers. Their brutal tactics terrified the wretched English, who could not defend themselves or their possessions against the marauders. At times the maroons assisted rather than harassed the English, leaving their enemy constantly vulnerable and confused.

Cromwell's Western Design had aimed to emulate British conquests in Scotland and Ireland, driving the Catholic Spanish out of the Americas in order to control trade and treasure routes in the Spanish mainland. Cromwell's plan foundered pitifully in Hispaniola. Disgraced and ill, Adm. Robert Venables retreated to his fleet, where to the disgust of his men he submitted to the tender care of his unpopular wife. Admirals Venables and William Penn subsequently headed to Jamaica for what they wrongly imagined would be an easy victory that restored their honor. Instead, for the next several years the sick and weary English grappled with a hostile environment and shifty enemies. Most of the Spanish had fled to Cuba, and some of their former slaves defected to the English, while others raided and plundered English settlements well into the eighteenth century. The Spanish maroons took advantage of the chaos, recognizing alternative means of securing their freedom (Campbell 19). The embarrassing failure of the Western Design signified what Carla Gardina Pestana has called a "failure of character, a failure of English manhood" (16).[3] As James Robertson drily puts it, "the only thing worse than an exercise in imperialist aggression is a mishandled exercise in imperialist aggression" (15).

The seventeenth-century criticisms of the English performance against the Spanish in the West Indies emphasized a lack of manly spirit, particularly in comparison to Sir Walter Raleigh and Francis Drake, the Elizabethan "models for vigorous endeavor" (Pestana 11). Army chaplain Hugh Peter, for example, commented that the English were "more effeminate than our Predecessors in Queen Elizabeth's time" (qtd. in Pestana 11). In Hispaniola local forces of Spanish and Afro-Dominicans routed Cromwell's troops, killing six hundred and sending some two hundred running into the woods, inducing accusations of cowardice and sloth. The regular officers tried to blame the white troops who had been raised in Barbados for the defeat, but these former indentured servants, claims

Robertson, were not in fact the deserters (20). Venables too blamed the common soldiers, mostly poor, untrained men from England and servants or runaways from the colonies: "men kept so loose, as not to bee kept under discipline and so cowardly as not to bee made to fight" (qtd. in Pestana 11). Col. Francis Barrington, who survived the disaster of Hispaniola only to be shot to death accidentally by his own sentry, described the army as having "not the common Spirit of Children" (qtd. in Pestana 14). The lack of spirit and mental decline, argues Pestana, made the emasculated soldier unfit for service (14). The motley, cowardly crew wilted in the tropical environment, miserably failing to live up to Drake and Ralegh's heroic example. The soldiers fighting on behalf of England were failing both as English and as men.

The black soldiers particularly terrified the British troops, prompting them to drop their weapons and flee. Robert Sedgwick, who came to Jamaica to take command, wrote about the Dominican disaster: "My heart and soul grievieth when I think of . . . one or two negroes to make 500 Englishmen fling down their arms and run away" (qtd. in Pestana 13). The threat of the "wild negroes" in Jamaica too loomed larger than that of their European counterparts. Sedgwick later wrote, "Concerning the state of the enemy on shore here, the Spaniard is not considerable, but of the Blacks there are many, who are like to prove as thorns and pricks in our sides, living in the mountains and woods" (qtd. in Campbell 19). The untrained and dispirited soldiers fell easy prey to the Afro-Jamaican warriors who used the hostile bush environment to their advantage with tactics of ambush (camouflaging themselves as foliage) and surprise.

By the end of 1655, and for the next six years, the English lost soldiers to sickness, starvation, and desertion.[4] John Thurloe describes them as suffering a "sad" and "deplorable" condition . . . some dead, some sick, and some in indifferent health . . . [and] many of them that were alive walked like ghosts or dead men . . . groaning and crying out (153). A "stream" of English and Irish soldiers attempted to desert to the Spaniards, and the English had to shackle their remaining Afro-Jamaicans to keep them from absconding as well (Robertson 20). Black and white men fled to the woods and mountains, leaving behind a shrinking and vulnerable English stronghold, subject to raids by the maroons.

In their first decade of occupation, Anglo-Jamaicans dealt with at least four groups of maroons living in "palenques," stockaded mountain farms. Juan de Bolas led a group of free black people and agricultural slaves in the mountains in Lluidas Vale. Juan de Serras led the second group, the Karmahaly, hunter-warriors who lived on the northeast of the island and eventually became known as the Windward Maroons.[5] The third group probably lived in the mountains on the borders of Clarendon and Manchester, avoiding contact and conflict with the other residents of the island. Finally, some Spanish maroons allegedly lived in the Blue Mountains with Taino people, "likkle brown men" (Craton, *Testing the Chains* 70). The English and Spanish both relied on and feared these groups, who tactically shifted their loyalties to protect their freedom.

In 1660 English patrols found the maroon settlement of Juan de Bolas, and governor Edward D'Oyley used the discovery to bargain with the "rebel negroes" (Robertson 20; Campbell 20–21). One correspondence to the commissioners of the Admiralty indicates that the English had been somewhat successful in these endeavors: "The enemy in our bowels, to whom our lives have been a prey, and many men have been subjected to their mercy (I mean the negroes) are now become our bloodhounds, and we are daily making depredations on them, and they are in our behalf more violent and fierce against their fellows than we possibly can be" (*Calendar* 9: 345). The English worked to turn the "enemy in [their] bowels" into their "bloodhounds," and in 1663 the Jamaican governor and council issued a charter, an "inchoate treaty," with de Bolas, who had previously helped the Spanish resistance movement (Campbell 21–23).

The charter further divided the Maroons. In a formal proclamation the governor granted de Bolas and his people freedom and thirty acres of land to men over eighteen year of age. The proclamation also gave de Bolas the title of "Colonel of the Black Regiment" in the island's militia and the right with his magistrates to determine all legal proceedings among his people, except those of life and death. Though the British offered Juan de Serras and his group the same terms of freedom and land, they refused, becoming "Outlaws" and Traitors," as the language of the charter referred to those who did not yield (Campbell 24). Juan de Serras allegedly killed de Bolas because of his defection to the English, and from 1663 until the treaties of 1738–1739, this group of Windward Maroons reinforced their numbers with runaway slaves.

Despite the charter, the English continued to struggle with unruly rebels and problematic troops. Dr. John Stewart wrote to Sir Charles Wager in 1730, "We are at present surrounded by strong bodys of rebellious negroes in several parts of the island, but particularly at windward near Port Antonio, who have already beaten two strong partys that have been sent out against them and if they should now beat a third . . . it may prove fatal to this island" (*Calendar* 37: 309). In addition to the crushing losses suffered by their men, the English soldiers had other issues as well, such as drunk and disorderly behavior: "The men to be employ'd in the reduction of the slaves must be of the same sort with those hitherto employ'd, that is to say drunken and disorderly, for rum, the ruin of this island, is easier to come at here than small beer in England (*Calendar* 40: 331). The drunken, sloppy English were no match for the "strong bodys of rebellious negroes."

To enhance the efforts of its militia units and regular British soldiers and sailors, the Jamaica Assembly imported Moskito Indians from Suriname and Hispaniola and tracking dogs from Cuba to supplement the services of their "Black Shots," loyal slaves, and free black people (Campbell 37; Kopytoff, "Maroons of Jamaica"). The maroons, Colonel Lumsden explains, had encountered many of these "black shots," and "some of them they knew by name." The English thus wrought divisions between the plantation slaves and the maroons, sometimes using methods of deception. Colonel Lumsden explains this dynamic: "The British would release a slave to appear as a runaway with the promise that if they could deliver the Maroons or their hiding places, then they would have their work lessened on the plantations. So the Maroons, in the beginning, would pick them up, treating them as runaways, and would expose their secret hiding places to them, only to see that same slave leading the British directly to their hideouts" (interview).

The canny maroons in turn developed methods to protect themselves from infiltration by Afro-Jamaicans who served the government. For example, they would subject fugitives to a blood oath to test their loyalty: "And, so the Maroons . . . when they picked up a slave, he had to either take a blood oath, which Africans understand that if you break a blood oath, then you not only affect yourself, but it affects your future generation and your past generation. And so, if they weren't serious about joining them, then they wouldn't take it. And if they didn't take the blood oath, they were either enslaved—yes, Maroons had slaves—or they were killed or returned to slavery." The refusal of the sacred oath, Colonel Lumsden explains, signified subterfuge or cowardice (or both), punished by death or enslavement. In addition to protecting themselves from discovery with these tactics, the maroons increased their own numbers with strong warriors, vexing English efforts to keep the island residents under control (interview).

The disorder on the island worsened over the next several years, particularly in Saint Thomas and Portland, the same area Three-Fingered Jack would inhabit fifty years later. The English continued to lose slaves to the maroons, and a letter dated February 15, 1734, complains about the desertion of twenty-two Port Antonio plantation slaves defecting to the rebels with an additional number of fierce "Cormantine" joining as well:

We received advice yesterday from Port Antonio of 22 plantation negroes, and some which belonged to the party having deserted and going over to the rebells, and from St. Thomas in the East, we have an account of about 40 able Cormantine negroes having deserted their masters, and it is supposed are likewise gone over to them. This has

occasioned a fresh alarm, and some people are under such apprehen-
sions that it is confidently reported the Governor has thought Martial
Law as the only means of preventing the *infection* from spreading. . . .
The consequence we fear may prove fatall to us if some measures are
not speedily taken to suppress those rebells, who certainly encrease in
strength. (*Calendar* 41: 150.i; emphasis mine)

The "infection" of marronage was spreading faster than the English
could contain it. At the same time, they worried about external threats.
Another letter expresses concern about French and Spanish support for the
maroons: "if either French or Spaniards openly or secretly go on in assist-
ing these rebellious negroes, the said island will soon belong to one or the
other of them (Harris to Popple, qtd. in *Calendar* 41: 171). The spreading
infection, Mr. Harris feared, would be fatal if they could not stop the rebels,
who seemed to grow stronger as the English weakened. The 1738–1739 treaties with the Maroons helped reverse the recent misfortunes of the British,
securing a police force and reifying their program of divide and conquer.

Unlike the "inchoate" charter with de Bolas, the treaties of 1739 and
1739 subjected the Maroons to the imperative of nation, changing the
power dynamic on the island. Outfitted with horses, uniforms, and guns,
the Maroons became a special class of subjects of the Crown, tasked with
returning runaways and fighting invaders. The fourth clause of the treaty
stated, for example, that the Maroons must "suppress and destroy all other
Party and Parties of rebellious Negroes, that now are or shall from Time
to Time gather together or settle in any Part of this Island, and shall bring
in such Negroes as shall from Time to Time run away from their respec-
tive Owners" (qtd. in Krug 246). With the treaties the English attempted
to solve the parallel problems of Maroons attacking their plantations
and inspiring the flight of the slaves; they likewise offered protection
against the invasions of their Catholic European adversaries. The treaties
marked an important moment in the transformation of Afrocentric "rebel
negroes" into the creolized culture of "the Maroons."

In a process that combined written documents and embodied ritual, the British colonel John Guthrie and Maroon captain Cudjoe signed the Leeward treaty with a ceremony that involved drinking blood mixed with rum in a calabash: "the Asante Oath." But as Barbara Kopytoff argues in "Colonial Treaty," the British and Maroons held completely different notions about the treaty. For Maroons the treaty consecrated their sacred oath and honored their "victory" over the English, or as Colonel Lumsden describes it, Jamaica's most "significant achievement. He says, "When you think that perhaps Jamaica's greatest achievement is the fact that the largest, the greatest, power on earth, which was the British Empire, signed . . . a peace treaty with the Maroons, I still consider that the most significant achievement of Jamaica" (interview).[6] C.L.G. Harris, former colonel of Moore Town, considered the treaty not an achievement, but a means through the "ignominious" clause to advance the guerilla tactics that would confuse the English. "Being natural tacticians, then," he wrote, "they [Maroons] did not make an outright attack on the ignominious clause because it represented a perfect facade behind which operations could be carried out for the benefit of their 'brethren' in distress" (Harris).

The British, on the other hand, viewed the treaty as the means to regulate Maroon activity, limit the growth of the communities, and ensure, as the language of the treaty indicated, the "submission" of the captains and the "rebels" under their command (Kopytoff, "Maroons of Jamaica" 119). Present-day Trelawny Maroon Gloria Simms, however, views the treaty as another British manipulation of the Maroons: "The treaty was a trick" (interview). The trick of this nefarious treaty was that it put slaves and Maroons into opposition with one another to enforce British control over them all.

The failure of Cromwell's Western Design eventually led to the economic success of the British plantation system in Jamaica, but only after a difficult eighty-five years, which Orlando Patterson has famously called "one long series of revolts" (289). The decades after the treaties provided some security for the English, who had settled in for the long haul. This period witnessed a growth in the development of plantations on the island, especially in Portland and Saint Thomas (Campbell 46). The Maroons helped protect the island from Spain and later from France, while they also provided security on the roads within. In 1760, however, the island experienced a series of slave rebellions, the first real upset since the treaties. The English deployed the handy method of divide and conquer to quell them, using the Maroons to subdue rebels like Tacky, the leader of the first revolt, and, two decades later, Three-Fingered Jack. With the treaty the English orchestrated a system that brutally crushed those who tried to resist it. And Three-Fingered Jack tried to resist it.

The first accounts of Jack's life emerged in the *Royal Gazette*, an Anglophone island newspaper printed by and for white planters and merchants in Jamaica. A weekly supplement advertised items for sale, postings for runaway slaves and animals, and rewards for those who returned them. This supplement also tracked the news about Jack and published the royal proclamation for his capture. The first news item warned readers about Jack and his gang of fifty-eight Congos, who vexed travel and trade around the island:

> [They] rendered traveling, especially to Mulattoes and Negroes, very dangerous; one of the former they have lately killed, belonging to Mr. Duncan Munro of Montrose, and taken a large quantity of Linen of his from his slaves on the road; they also have robbed many other persons' servants, and stolen some cattle, and great numbers of sheep, goats, hogs, poultry &c. particularly a large herd of hogs from Mr. Rial of Tamarind Tree Pen. They are chiefly Congos, and declare they will kill every Mulatto and Creole Negro they can catch. BRISTOL, alias *Three-Finger'd Jack*, is their Captain, and CAESAR, who belongs to Rozel estate, is their next officer. (Vol. 2, no. 67: 458)[7]

This notice constructs a scenario in which the island's authorized spaces (plantations and roads), its planter class (Mr. Duncan and Mr. Rial), and their possessions (slaves, linen, cattle, hogs, and poultry) are threatened by criminal elements (Jack, Caesar, and the Congo gang). Jack's rogue group targeted those who were absorbed into the colonial structure of the island: the mulattos, who bore the imprint of the planter class on their skins, and the "creole Negroes," who, born on the island, were perceived as more submissive than their counterparts who had endured the Middle Passage, the "salt-water Negroes" (Smallwood 7).[8] This first notice also identifies Jack as "Bristol," his slave name, but it does not link him to a plantation or specific advertiser like his "next officer, Caesar." An outlaw with a faceless gang of Africans, Jack roved the eastern part of the island, stealing and killing.

Jack's alleged bias against mixed-race and island-born slaves and his association with Congos bespeaks tensions among the black population in colonial Jamaica, particularly after the Maroon treaties. In this period most of the Africans on the island were Akan-speaking Coromantees, and the planters associated them with rebellion (Thornton).[9] Jack's ostensibly African-born, Congo crew would have been representative of a small sub-section of runaways on the island who attempted to form African communities in the bush (Campbell 156; Kopytoff, "Maroons of Jamaica" 116–117). R. C. Dallas, for example, wrote of one group that eluded Maroons for years, established "in the mountains, where they raised huts, and made provision grounds, on which some had lived for upwards of twenty years" (27, 101). Mavis Campbell locates this settlement in the Black River area on the southern part of island, suggesting they may have escaped slavery during the disturbances of the 1760s, when the Maroons would have been busy putting down Tacky's Rebellion (159). Another village, "Me-no-sen-you-no-Come," of some twenty Congos appeared around 1812, somewhere in Trelawny (Kopytoff, "Maroons of Jamaica" 128; Campbell 159; Patterson 264). The Akan-identified Maroons routed both of these Congo communities as well as Jack's fledgling group in Saint David's parish, intimating that ethnic conflicts may have contributed to the divides between Maroons and maroons in eighteenth-century Jamaica, disrupting the neat binary of African and Briton.[10]

A mere three weeks after they were deployed (December 16, 1780), the Maroons took into custody Jack's wife and crew "to be dealt with as the law directs" (*Royal Gazette*, vol. 2, no. 87: 747). Maroon oral history, however, insists that Jack's wife escaped, an event marked by the spot called "Three-Finger Woman Tumble." Presumably, then, Jack traveled alone for the next month or so until the gory conclusion of the hunt. In January the *Royal Gazette* reported Jack's death:

> The party came upon him so suddenly, that he had only time to seize the cutlass, with which he desperately defended himself, refusing all submission, till having received three bullets in his body and covered with wounds he threw himself about forty feet down a precipice, and was followed by Reeder, who soon overpowered him, and severed his head and arm from the body which were brought to this town on Thursday last.—Reeder and another Maroon were wounded in the conflict.—The intrepidity of Reeder, in particular, and the behavior of his associates in general, justly entitle them to the reward offered by the public. (Vol. 3, no. 93: 79)

Jack's "refusal of submission" (language that echoes the Maroon treaties) marked him as an outlaw, and the public display of his dismembered head issued a warning to potential rebels. As Vincent Brown explains, "Dead bodies, dismembered and disfigured as they were, would be symbols of the power and dominion of slave masters . . . [and] conveyed a warning to potential rebels and reassurance to supporters of the social order" (136). The Maroons paraded Jack's head and hand through Spanish Town and Kingston while onlookers cheered and blew conch shells (Black 119). The government rewarded the victor handsomely for his intrepidity and paid him an annuity for the rest of his life. Bounty hunting offered ample opportunity for good money, but fugitives continued to run, despite the considerable risks.

The *Royal Gazette* advertisements give a sense of the numbers and varieties of runaways that plagued the island. Jack's second-in-command

Caesar, for example, escaped several times and from several venues over at least two years.[11] Planter Andrew Murdoch reprinted the advertisement for his capture in the weekly supplement regularly during 1780 and 1781:

> RUN AWAY, from ROZELL Estate, St Thomas in the East, CAESAR, a likely, well made fellow, about five feet six, rather high shouldered, has the mark of a cut upon his chin, and a broad mark upon the back of one of his hands, where he was burnt when a child. He was taken up at Aeolus Valley Estate in St. David's on the 20th of December last, but found means to make his escape, about eight days after he was sent home. Any person who will apprehend the above negro, and secure him in goal, or deliver him to the subscriber on the above estate shall receive five pounds reward. And any person who can prove by whom he is harbored, shall be entitled to ten pounds on conviction of the offender. (Vol. 2, no. 51: 236)

Murdoch asks that Caesar be secured in jail, and he offers a larger reward for the person who harbored him than for the runaway himself. This advertisement, one of many that appeared in the *Royal Gazette* during the Jack crisis, demonstrates that despite the best efforts of the colonial machine, enslaved Africans and Creoles escaped into the bush, sometimes for weeks, sometimes for months, and sometimes never to return at all

The *Gazette* advertisements categorized runaways by skin color, language, and religion. David White, a subscriber from the Gingerhall plantation in Saint Thomas in Vale, for example, advertised for a "tall, well-made yellow Woman," who wore a cross, passed as a free woman, and claimed to be headed out of "the Country to the SPANIARDS" (vol. 2, no. 50: 218). An advertisement in the fall of 1780 describes John Baptist, a runaway Creole of Hispaniola, who "speaks French and knows people in Spanish Town" (vol. 2, no. 82: 671). Another posting advertised for a runaway black Creole named "Quashi," who called himself Lawrence, "an artful, cunning chap, [who] passes for a free French Negro, as he can speak a little French" (vol. 2, no. 88: 751). Like the "well-made yellow woman," this man passed for free, suggesting some ways that skin color and linguistic ability helped to both identify and camouflage the fugitives. Though the advertisements used racial, national, and ethnic locators to track runaways, these efforts are contravened by the very fact that the runaways had entered a space—literal and figurative—that blurred legal, linguistic, and social distinctions.

Fugitives of a variety of ethnicities vexed English control of Jamaica, and some men who had once been employed to protect and defend became part of the problem. One advertisement documents the desertion of a group of mixed-race men from the "Corps of the Light Dragoons," allegedly harbored in Kingston onboard a vessel (*Royal Gazette*, vol. 2, no. 84: 684). In the spring of 1780, the supplement to the *Royal Gazette* warned readers of a large group of "deserters" from the "New-raised Corps" of the Royal Batteau—men that included five mariners, aged nineteen to thirty years old, identified as Irish, Welsh, and English. The posting added that whoever harbored these men would be "persecuted to the upmost rigour of the law" (vol. 2, no. 54: 283). The desertion of these soldiers and sailors created additional wartime challenges to British imperial and colonial efforts.

These *Gazette* advertisements constitute a kind of in-between genre that shows parts of the colonial machine breaking down. They describe scenes of disruption that reveal problems, people, and places that the colonial system struggled to contain. Like Marcus Rediker and Peter Linebaugh's vulgar, mobile, racially diverse, "motley" crew, Jamaica's fugitive group was "multitudinous, numerous, and growing. . . . It was . . . onamove" (222–223). Binaries of African and European, black and white, enslaved and free, broke down, throwing the colony into chaos. Despite colonial efforts to categorize, identify, and contain the fugitives, runaway slaves nonetheless found refuge, even among Anglo-Jamaicans. Mr. David White of Gingerhall, for example, "suspected there are white people privy to their being runaway, as well as old, infirm wretches about Mount-Olive

Plantain Walk" (*Royal Gazette*, vol. 2, no. 50: 218). British surgeon
Benjamin Moseley, too, worried about the old, infirm wretches (188) of
the plantain walks in his 1799 *A Treatise on Sugar: With Miscellaneous
Medical Observations*, and he warned his readers of their threat to the
health and security of the colony.[12]

An English physician who practiced in Jamaica from 1768 to 1784,
Benjamin Moseley first links obeah, disease, and resistance to the story
of Three-Fingered Jack, setting the stage for subsequent accounts. Though
he published his treatise two decades after Jack's demise, Moseley lived
on the island during the crisis, and he claimed to have seen the outlaw's
"obi," brought to him by the Maroons who killed him. Moseley published
on tropical disease, military operations, and the production of plantation
crops, three subjects important to English interests in Jamaica. Quite
successful in his early career, Moseley made his fortune treating tropical
diseases in Jamaica. His reputation declined, however, after his return to
England, due to increasingly "unscientific thinking," such as displayed in
his treatise (D. Lee, "Grave Dirt" para. 2). In it, Moseley figures obeah as
an illness, and he discussed the spiritual practice alongside observation on
diseases including yellow fever, the plague, and especially *yaws*, a condition, like obeah, prevalent in West Africa and imported to the West Indies
on the Middle Passage.[13]

Because planters isolated sick slaves to protect themselves and their
other laborers, illness offered ways to escape the confines of the plantation as well as the means to disable its production. Moseley explains that
doctors isolated the yaws patient to prevent the spread of the highly com-
municable bacterial infection, identified by raspberry-shaped lesions on
the skin. Those slaves were exiled to remote infirmaries or to "some lonely
seaside place or some plantain walk where he could act as a watchman
and maintain himself, without any expense to the estate, until he was well;
then he was brought back to the Sugar-Work" (188). However, Moseley
warns, the slaves rarely returned to the plantation but instead retreated to

dark, lizard-filled huts and caves: "in their banishment, their huts often became the receptacles of robbers and fugitive negroes" (191). These huts and caves also sheltered malevolent obeah practitioners:

> Many of their wayward visitors were deeply skilled in magic, and what we call the *black art*, which they brought with them from Africa; and in return for their accommodation, they usually taught their landlord the mysteries of sigils, spells, and *illuminated* him in all the occult science of OBI.
>
> These ugly, loathsome creatures thus became the oracles of the woods, and unfrequented places; and were resorted to secretly, by the wretched in mind and by the malicious for wicked purposes. (192)

African obeah, according to Moseley, was a repository of evil, a practice that permitted wicked "scientists" to take advantage of the "wretched in mind." His contemporaries associated obeah with social and mental disorder, particularly after Tacky's Rebellion in 1760. Jack's exploits, like Tacky's, reinforced the already hostile attitudes toward the African-derived practice, and their resistance carried ethnic and spiritual registers. Both men, allegedly protected by obeah, met their deaths at the hands of Maroons who policed the island for the Anglo-Christian planter class and government.

The most significant revolt in the Caribbean until Saint Domingue, Tacky's involved at least fifteen hundred enslaved people and lasted eighteen months, taking full advantage of England's preoccupation with the Seven Year's War against France and Spain. The rebellion employed guerilla tactics, included at least three uprisings, and required the assistance of a "diversified" colonial response that included the regular military, the local militia, and Maroons (Brown). The rebels killed more than sixty white people and destroyed property across the island, from Saint Mary's through Westmoreland parishes. Associated with obeah, the Coromantee Tacky planned to occupy the island, setting up communities "in the African mode" (Long 2: 416). After the death and deportation of some thousand rebels, Captain Davy, the chief of the Scots Hall Maroons, killed Tacky, cut off his head, and displayed it on a pole at the side of the road to Spanish Town, and some claim that the Maroons roasted and ate his heart (Wilson, "Performance of Freedom" 63; Brown 148). The events surrounding Tacky's revolt intensified the tensions and prompted the criminalization of obeah in Jamaica.[14]

Two decades later, immediately after Jack's death in 1781, a new slave law documented the malevolent but fraudulent effects of obeah. It addressed "the wicked art of Negroes going under the appellation of Obeah men and women, pretending to have communication with the Devil and other evil spirits," and the practitioners, who allegedly used the practice to delude "the weak and superstitious" (qtd. in Bilby and Handler 158). These documents informed important accounts of and attitudes toward obeah, such as those of Bryan Edwards and Edward Long (154–156; Paton, "Witchcraft"). Srinivas Aravamudan rightly notes that the practice "was perceived and defined by colonial discourse, primarily through the criminal cases brought against it" (introd. to *Obi* 25). However, Moseley surely knew, the "oracles of the woods" used their obeah to heal as well as to harm, and many residents of the island (black and white) preferred African herbal remedies to European medical practices (33; D. Lee, "Grave Dirt").

Nonetheless, Moseley insisted in his treatise that obeah contaminated the plantation complex, with dank caves and ramshackle huts serving as sites of infection: "No humanity of the master, nor skill in medicine, can relieve a negro, labouring under the influence of Obi. He will surely die; and of a disease that answers no description in nosology" (194).[15] Obeah, he suggests, eludes classification, a characteristic that renders it particularly pernicious to the colonial machine. Impossible to classify or cure, obeah defied medical and discursive restraint. Moreover, it disabled productivity on the plantation and beyond.

Obeah represents, for Moseley, the evasion of laws and boundaries in Jamaica: "Laws have been made in the West Indies to punish this *obian* practice," he confides, "but they have had no effect. Laws constructed in the West Indies, can never suppress the effect of ideas, the origin of which, is the centre of Africa" (194). Africa represents for him the heart of darkness, the originary source of obeah, a wildness that cannot be contained by Western systems or discourses. In other publications, too, this spirit of resistance—the unreason of African ideas—is figured as a kind of sickness, spreading like yaws. James Stevens's 1802 *Crisis of the Sugar Colonies*, for example, refers to the runaway slave as an "incurable disease."[16] Some of these virulent beliefs, as Moseley writes, traveled from Africa to Jamaica, blighting the population with their effects, effects that were then mediated and carried by Moseley himself to England. Moseley narratively transitions from obeah to Three-Fingered Jack by way of the Salem witch trials in New England and the problems endured by superstitious American settlers. For Moseley the crime in Salem was not witchcraft itself, but the contagious superstitions of the "endemial despondency" of the descendants of the "moody melancholy" English (194).

Moseley likewise views Jack's obeah as causing in slaves a dangerous illness of the mind and spirit. With a saber, two guns, and his obeah—a horn filled with grave dirt, ashes, cat blood, a cat foot, a dried toad, a pig's tail, human fat, and a parchment of kid's skin—Jack "terrified the inhabitants, and set the civil power, and the neighboring militia of that island, at defiance, for nearly two years" (198). Obeah, Moseley proposes, is best mitigated by Christianity and Maroons, and he makes much of the victory of Quashie's "white obi," his Christianity, over Jack's black arts: "He got himself christianed, and changed his name to John Reeder" (199). With the help of a "little boy" and Scots Hall Maroon Sam (the son of Tacky's killer, Captain Davy), Reeder tracked Jack.[17] With his new English name and religion, Reeder fought bravely, "like an English bulldog," as tenacious and strong as the determined namesake canine, though the comparison reveals Moseley's ambivalent (at best) attitudes toward even baptized Maroons (203). Reeder's obeah helped vanquish Jack in the close, bloody three-to-one fight: "Jack was cowed; for, he had prophesied that white obi would get the better of him" (204). Moseley concludes with the celebratory procession of Jack's head and hand: "There they put their trophies into a pail of rum; and, followed by a vast concourse of negroes, now no longer afraid of Jack's *Obi*, blowing their shells and horns, and firing guns in their rude method, they carried them to Kingston, and Spanish Town; and claimed the rewards offered by the King's Proclamation and the House of Assembly" (205). Moseley depicts a sugar colony safe from outlaws, protected by loyal security officers and slaves. Rewarded by the king and praised by the island elite, Reeder and his crew likewise delight the "vast concourse" of Afro-Jamaicans.

Many subsequent versions of Jack's life and death relied on this account, and Moseley used the governor's proclamation and his acquaintance with the Maroons to validate his own. With the exception of William Burdett's 1800 novelette, the fictional accounts omit the Maroon involvement, elisions that reduce the complex social dynamics of colonial Jamaica to one of British soldier and African slave, eliding as well English methods of divide and conquer. Most accounts, however, retain the details of Quashie's christening and name change. Though Moseley wrote several decades before Christian missionaries officially descended on Maroon communities in the early 1900s, his narrative suggests that the creolization of the Maroons began much earlier. As they increasingly intermixed their culture with the English language, customs, and spiritual beliefs, they became, as Jessica Krug puts it, "less Kromanti" and "more Maroon" (540). The story of Jack and Reeder tells also the story of black survival in colonial Jamaica. Reeder's story runs parallel to and sheds light on a much more ominous history, that of the colonial police state in Jamaica.

The Jamaican government paid the price for Jack's execution for thirty-five years, almost a decade after Reeder's own death in 1816. The Assembly of Jamaica resolved to "direct a clause to be inserted in the poll-tax bill, for paying the sum of 200£ to the Maroons of Scott's Hall and Moore-Town, being the additional reward offered by the House for taking the rebellious runaway, called Three-Fingered Jack."[18] At Reeder's death in 1816 and in response to the request by his son, Nathanial Beckford, the assembly paid for the burial and provided an annuity.[19] They also compensated the "little boy" who assisted Reeder in the fight against the outlaw, William Carmichael Cockburn. White superintendent of Charles Town, Robert Gray, also in 1816, petitioned on behalf of the elderly, poor, and infirm Cockburn, "formerly called Little Quaco, who was the boy who accompanied Sam Grant and Reeder when they attacked and killed Three-Fingered Jack" and who "shot that outlaw in the belly while he was engaged with Reeder."[20] The House granted the requests of both Beckford and Cockburn. The rewards for loyalty to the colonial state were gifts that kept on giving.

As literary and stage representations about Jack proliferated in England, Reeder, too, made the news when he died. His death notice appeared in newspapers in Hereford, Chester, and North Wales in November 1816:

> We have already noticed the death, at Jamaica, of John Reeder, so celebrated for his conquest of Three-Fingered Jack, on the 27th of January, 1781. For this exploit, Reeder received the reward of 100£, offered by the proclamation of Major-General John Dalling, then Governor of the island, and afterwards had an annual stipend of 25£ which was increased of late to 30£ and paid under the poll-tax law. Though this subject has been dramatised, and was well known in all its particulars at the time, yet there is so much chivalrous interest in the story, that it will bear repetition even to those of our readers to whom it does not bear the charm of novelty.[21]

Reeder's death notice highlights for British readers the strong economic, military, and administrative presence in Jamaica and the ongoing deployment of the Jack story to celebrate it. The literary and historical accounts support one another in the construction of a secure and profitable colonial endeavor, even as they distinguish between the dramatic and the factual.

On December 1, 1816, *Scots Magazine* posted the death of Reeder (now the captain of Charles Town) in a section titled "Deaths, Stocks, and Markets," suggesting the significant links among death, investment, and trade in Jamaica:

In Hannah's Town, at a very advanced age, John Reeder, a well-known black man, as having been many years Captain of the Charles-Town Maroons. He is the person who, in 1781, after a most severe personal conflict, killed the noted and desperate robber Three Finger'd Jack, who was supposed by the negroes to be possessed of supernatural powers, and deemed invulnerable from all attacks. In consequence of this service, Reeder received an annual stipend from the government of this island—He did not know his exact age, but said, only a few days ago, that he was a stout boy at the first peace with the Maroons, in the year 1739.—Jamaica, October 1.

This clip from the *Scots Magazine* presents Reeder as an elder statesman of the Maroons, a loyal subject of the state, and a military hero with a long and lucrative career that reached back to treaty times. By this account Reeder witnessed the treaty in 1738 and thus would have been well into his fifties at the time of Jack's death in 1781, intimating like the Maroon oral histories that Jack and Quashie had been rivals for half a century. By 1816 Great Britain had triumphed over Napoleonic France and again established itself as a global power. The humiliations of the Western Design long passed, the English in Jamaica had established a system that worked to reduce the problem of runaway slaves in efforts to keep the sugar colony productive.

Contemporary Maroon versions of the conflict refer to Reeder as "Quashee" or "Quashie," rejecting the English honorific in favor of a version of "Kwasi," the "African day name" for a child born on Sunday. However, in the eighteenth century, the English used Quashie as a generic and derogatory name for a black person (*OED*).[22] For present-day Rastafari, a Quashie refers to a servile black Jamaican who complies with "Babylon" (the Rasta term for white Western social, economic, and political systems). Prefiguring the "informer" of twentieth-century Jamaican culture, the "quashie" helps the "shitstem" (system) police its criminal elements (McFarlane 108). This linguistic multivalence of the name Quashie registers the Afro-Jamaican ambivalence surrounding Maroons, regarding them as African warriors on the one hand and informers on the other. The figure of Reeder/Quashie occupies the problematic in-between space of the Maroons, moving between political, cultural, social, and legal boundaries constructed by an uneasy colonial system and complicating binaries such as free and enslaved, lawman and outlaw, Christian and heathen, mimic and masculine.[23] In contrast, Jack lived and died outside the law; his mission was one of destruction, not accommodation.

The relationship between Three-Fingered Jack and the Maroons reveal the troubling dynamics, particularly among men, generated by the colonial machine. The Maroon treaty and lands linked them to the slave colony they at once policed and destabilized, but their reasons for annihilating the rebel exceeded legal and economic rewards. Despite residual ambivalence toward them in Jamaica today, Maroons take pride in the warrior culture that has distinguished them from their non-Maroon counterparts. Their oral histories often tell stories of a struggle between a Maroon and a formidable opponent whose defeat reflects favorably on the victors (Bilby, *True-Born Maroons* 290).[24] "The fighting is what really separated the Maroons from the rest of slavery," Colonel Lumsden relates, "and their preparedness to risk all for freedom" (interview).

Contemporary Maroon elders claim Three-Fingered Jack as an important part of their warrior culture. Colonel Lumsden explains his link to Maroon history: "The fact he was killed by a Maroon and actually got his name from a fight with a Maroon definitely makes him part of Maroon lore, makes [him] linked to Maroon history" (interview). In Jack the Maroons found a formidable enemy. The late colonel C.L.G. Harris of the Moore Town Maroons viewed Jack as an opponent of mythical status, whose demise resulted not from the treaty but from the unfortunate misunderstanding of it: "He must have heard of the offending clauses of the treaty," Harris wrote, and "he became their implacable foe, and thus, as it were, plotted his own destruction." Harris described Jack in supernatural terms: "This man was by no means an ordinary mortal—he had royal blood coursing through his veins and his attributes were phenomenal: He was unusually tall; his physique was superb and his strength was prodigious; his eye was as keen as a hawk's and his aim unerring; he was of superior intelligence and like Houdini appeared to have mastered the secret of immunity from physical hurt." The current colonel of Moore Town, Wallace Sterling, explains the respect Maroons would have had for this "clever man" and "good fighter," because when one defeats someone like that "you know you would have done something" (interview). Colonel Lumsden concurs: "as the Indians say, your stature is shown by the stature of your enemies" (interview).

Jack overstepped his boundaries, however. Colonel Lumsden proposed that Jack disrupted the social order that Maroons privileged and maintained: "The Maroons like order, and Three-Fingered Jack was disrupting that order. He threatened just everyone who had any kind of establishment. So . . . the Maroons would want him dead for more than reasons than just the reward on his head" (interview). As Colonel Sterling put it, "the mistake he made was he tried to prey on the Maroons, you know, that was a no-no" (interview). Comparing Jack to Tacky, Colonel Lumsden likewise identified him as a challenge to Maroon dominance "in terms of who is the baddest man around" and a menace that they needed to "take down."[25]

The compulsion to dominate, Lumsden elaborated, emanated from the conditions of the colonial police state. "Three Finger Jack's motivation for the, let's call it 'the crime spree' that he went on was complicated," he explained, "A lot of times the individuals who were captured were in themselves, in Africa, significant individuals. And so, coming here and freeing themselves, they were attempting to maintain, to recreate, to get back some of that personal glory, the personal satisfaction of being a significant . . . of being once again a great person" (interview). In a contest of brute strength and military prowess provoked by European slavery and colonization, the Maroons and Jack fought for dominance.

Yet some Maroons today consider Jack a common criminal. Colonel Lumsden's brother Keith, for example, insists that Jack was a "renowned criminal, a thug who killed anybody" (interview). Colonel Lumsden does not deny Jack's criminality, but he offers ways to understand it, asking, "During that period, who was a good guy? Henry Morgan was governor of Jamaica; he was a cutthroat brigand, and he was considered a good guy" (interview). Henry Morgan's transformation from pirate to slave-owning politician suggests, as does the story of Jack and the Maroons, that slavery and colonization blurred traditional binaries of right and wrong.

The story of Jack and the Maroons shows the myriad ways that those in pursuit of freedom negotiated the structures that attempted to restrain them. Unable to subdue the black rebels on their own, the English installed a colonial police state that criminalized resistance, giving rise to Three-Fingered Jack and stories that remember him. I conclude with words of Colonel Sterling. As we sat in his yard one hot summer day, I asked him if he views Jack as a hero or criminal. He shook his head and eventually responded,

> You talk about Dons and so on and so forth, and you might want to ask a separate question: Why are people who do so many wrongs villains on one side and on the other they are heroes? Three-Fingered Jack could be viewed in context like that, in some ways. Some people would want him around; others wouldn't want to see him around because . . . of the way he did things. And it is on this premise, it depends on what one wants to extract, the view that one wants to see, in history. If history is told as it should be, in more ways than one, then sometimes we're left pondering, you know.

CHAPTER 2

"Jack Is a MAN"

PROSE OBIS, 1800–1870

Shortly after the publication of Benjamin Moseley's *Treatise on Sugar*, prose fiction about Three-Fingered Jack started to emerge in England. The year 1800 saw the publication of William Burdett's *Life and Exploits of Mansong, Commonly Called Three-Finger'd Jack, the Terror of Jamaica, in the Years 1780 and 1781: With a Particular Account of the Obi; Being the Only True One of That Celebrated and Fascinating Mischief so Prevalent in the West Indies.* That same year William Earle published *Obi; or, The History of Three-Fingered Jack: in a series of letters from a resident in Jamaica to his friend in England.* The more popular of the two, Burdett's adventure story went into ten editions and generated a handful of shorter, often anonymous, adaptations through 1870.[1] Earle's epistolary text has garnered more critical attention of late, its "rights of man rhetoric" and seemingly abolitionist stance appealing to twenty-first century liberal academics (Aravamudan, introd. to *Obi* 50). The trajectory of these texts from Earle's sentimental novel to Burdett's adventure story reflects the shifts in British attitudes toward and conceptions of race—of blackness and whiteness—during the closing decades of the slave trade.

The welter of popular fiction about Three-Fingered Jack throughout the nineteenth century has, as the scant critical attention has observed, focused largely on debates about plantation slavery and modes of resistance.[2] With good reason scholars have emphasized the significance of obeah as an emblem of African culture around which rebels united. Three-Fingered Jack, like the spiritual practice with which he is associated, evokes in the British imagination a figure at once powerful and impotent that aroused British concerns about their own power or impotence on the world stage and at home.

Burdett and Earle use Jack to tell stories about plantation slavery and resistance, but they also tell stories about those who participated in or opposed British interests around the Atlantic. Both texts claim a firsthand connection to colonial Jamaica, further establishing authenticity by citing documents such as the proclamations for Jack's apprehension, Bryan Edwards's account of obeah in *The History, Civil and Commercial, of the British Colonies in the West Indies,* and the story of Jack from Benjamin Moseley's treatise. They also involve an African setting, and Burdett relies on Mungo Park's *Travels in the Interior of Africa* to depict the origin of Jack's treachery and the source of his obeah. Using these sources as a backdrop, Earle's *Obi* imagines reformed Anglo- and Afro-Jamaicans within a rehabilitated plantation system, and Burdett maps the conflicts of African tribal warfare onto the Jamaican landscape, justifying the colonial police state, though lamenting its necessity. These colonial texts adjudicate a compassionate Anglo-Jamaican constructed against that of both the cold-hearted English planter and the savage African rebel, imagining, too, new conceptualizations of white and black masculinities.

WILLIAM EARLE'S *OBI*

In the advertisement to *Obi; or, The History of Three-Fingered Jack,* William Earle claims that the collection of George Stanford's letters to his friend in England "accidentally fell into [his] hands," and with them he proclaims his intention to "commemorate the name of Jack . . . a bold and daring defender of the Rights of Man" (68). The frontispiece cites antislavery verse by Robert Southey and Erasmus Darwin, and the letters include Stanford's own sentimental poetry, a combination that reflects what

Srinivas Aravamudan dubs "sentimentalist abolitionism" (introd. to *Obi* 50).[3] The emotional Stanford engages "daily" in altercations about the slavery and the rights of man with his fellow planters, positioning himself against his apologist counterparts. Earle does not, however, attribute to Stanford a solid, substantial argument against slavery. A sentimental man of feeling Stanford may be, but a convincing defender of the rights of man he is not; his emotions often disrupt his writing: "I more than once laid down my pen, and more than once my tears floated on the page" (95). Stanford bemoans the horrors of the slave trade and plantation slavery and with great feeling lays blame on an outdated colonial system that puts manhood and blackness in opposition to protect its economic interests.

A novel of fifteen letters from Anglo-Jamaican George Stanford to his friend Charles in England, *Obi* gives the background of Jack's parents in Africa and his subsequent vow to avenge them in Jamaica by "extirpating" all Europeans. Stanford relates that Jack's parents, Amri and Makro, rescue a shipwrecked trader, Harrop, who accepts their help, teaches them about Christianity, and then sells them into slavery. Makro dies on the middle passage, and Amri gives birth to Jack three months after arriving in Jamaica. Jack's birth into slavery and the brutal, public incineration of Amri's obeah-practitioner father, Feruarue, fuels her dearest wish that Jack become the "abolisher of the slave trade" (95). Protected but ultimately disappointed by his obeah, Jack terrorizes the island residents (especially Harrop) until his fatal encounter with Quashie, a recently christened slave. Stanford's tale also includes the romance between Harrop's nephew William and the planter's daughter Harriet Mornton, both of whom suffer from Harrop's tyranny. The narrative concludes with Jack's and Harrop's deaths and the couple's happy union.

Stanford's emotional abolitionist sentiments dominate the narrative, but the novel relies also on Anglo-Jamaican sources that document the problems of unruly Afro-Jamaicans and their dangerous practices. For example, Stanford embeds the governor's proclamation and the assembly's resolutions about Jack that appeared in the *Royal Gazette*, documents that reflect the commitment of the colonial administration to expunge the problematic rebel and his gang.[4] Moreover, his direct quotations of Bryan Edwards and Benjamin Moseley on the problems of obeah on the Jamaican plantation further undermine the novel's ostensibly abolitionist stance.[5] Yet, Stanford insists, "Jack is a noble fellow," driven to "desperacy and cruelty" by a corrupt plantocracy and its "hirelings" (157). Falling short of its seemingly abolitionist reach, the novel introduces a new model of plantation slavery, replacing rebellious Africans (Jack, Amri) and degenerate Europeans (Harrop, Mornton) with assimilated slaves (Quashie) and compassionate West Indian planters (William). Stanford describes benevolent white planters and governable black men, creolizing both white and black masculinities.

Amri's unhappy story repeatedly brings Stanford to the tears that hinder his letter-writing process, and he weeps for the wronged Africans and the wrongdoing of his countrymen. Stanford introduces the African portion of his tale with a biblical reference that declares his own blamelessness: "I am innocent of this blood, SEE YE to it" (73).[6] Stanford separates himself from Harrop, on whom he firmly places blame. Stanford believes that Christianity could improve the lives and souls of unfortunate Africans, if not misused by hypocrites like Harrop, who very nearly converts Amri to his own beliefs. "For the moment," Amri relates of Harrop, "he staggered my belief that I was doing right in worshipping, as he said, the servant of the real God." However, as she tells her son, "How wretchedly I was deceived!" (77). Stanford believes that she would have made a fine Christian had not Harrop's cruelty "perverted" her heart, "naturally inclined to virtue," and unleashed her cultural inclination for revenge (71–74).

Stanford sets down Amri's story to "as near as memory can trace" (73), claiming acquaintance with her friend, but he filters it through his colonial lens, lifting his treatment of the vengeful, proud Feloops directly from Mungo Park's *Travels* (1799). Amri tutors the young Jack in their cultural codes of honor and revenge: "Remember the spirit of our [Feloop] nation is, Never to forget an injury, but to ripen in our breasts the seeds of hate for those who betray us" (74).[7] Though Stanford sympathizes with Amri, he laments her "heart rendered callous by the malevolence of fortune" (115). In Amri's tragic story Stanford sees the failure of the imperial and colonial projects, a failure to effectively bring the heathen African into the gentle light of European habits and belief.

Captain Harrop consolidates these global failures, and he represents the worst of European domination at sea, in Africa, and on the West Indian plantation. His father, a London-born gentleman who inherited a Jamaican plantation, "bore the best character in the Island of Jamaica," but the Jamaican-born Harrop inherits none of his father's humanity when he acquired the estate, and he relentlessly, mercilessly pursues financial gain. He takes advantage of the turmoil on the island, profiting from the "Koromantyn" uprising, which he was "chiefly instrumental" in suppressing; subsequently noting the diminished number of slaves, he sells his property to buy two vessels for slave trading (126).[8] He benefits economically as well from his time shipwrecked in Africa "by taking a good cargo, and without hesitation [kidnapping] . . . his compassionate friends [Makro and Amri] (128). Harrop views his free tradism as necessary to the economic and vitality of his English family, his nation, and British interests around the globe: "In Europe we live to assist one another, to share the labors of the day and make life supportable. We barter our commodities . . . extensively . . . and the great exchange is diffusing round the world, like the generating sun, the rays of prosperity and affluence" (81). Harrop's prosperity and affluence comes at the expense of his own affective attachments. He forces his mild-mannered nephew William, for example, to participate in the slave trade by binding him as an apprentice against his wishes. Moreover, he uses deceit and forgery to break up the young man's relationship with his beloved Harriet and forces the young woman to become his own wife.

Harrop's corrupt life takes a toll on his mental and physical health, and he develops a nervous disorder that Stanford attributes to guilt: "Often

times would he . . . leap from the couch, and give a violent scream, while
the big drops of sweat hung upon his brow" (135). In his first encounter
with Jack, Harrop nearly faints: "he trembled . . . his brow was palsied,
and the corrosive drops of terror trickled down his cheeks" (108). When
Jack abducts Harrop later in the novel, the planter screams and faints, in
an unmanly manner: "Had Harrop been a man, Jack had had no need
of fire added to his impetuous soul; but his foe was cowardly and most
pitiful, and Jack could not stab him" (116–117). Unable to participate in
unmanly sportsmanship, Jack spares Harrop's life, instead putting him
in leg irons and forcing him into servitude. Harrop represents the
degenerate, emasculated white West Indian who deteriorates physically
and morally in direct relation to his colonial tyranny and slave-trading
activities. He thus reflects metropolitan, abolitionist depictions of Anglo-
Jamaicans as debased or, as David Lambert puts it, "not English" (1).

Harriet's father, Mr. Mornton, also represents the corrupt, amoral Anglo-
Jamaican patriarch. As a father, he pursues only his own fiscal interests,
forcing his daughter to marry the wealthy Harrop. As a planter, he extends
kindnesses to his slaves out of self-interest rather than out of "charitable disposition" or "tender humanity" to "lighten the load of slavery" (Earle 101).
Of Mornton's alleged humanity, Amri wonders, "If he heals our wounds, for
whose sake is it?" Stanford censures Mornton's falseness, urging Charles to
"blush" for his countrymen who support the slave trade (103).

Stanford contrasts himself to Harrop and Mornton, "disclaiming" the
"cruel, hard-hearted planters." "Those are not my countrymen, whose
inhumanity is the subject of my page," he writes. "They may be Britons
born, but are not Britons at heart, and I disclaim them" (82). This passage
suggests that to be Briton-hearted involves a sensibility ("the feeling tear")
that Stanford must set aside to write his letters. Only when he distances
himself can he find his voice: "ADIEU to the impulse of the moment, to
the feeling tear! I am a West-Indian again, and can proceed" (96). Stanford
struggles to balance the coldness of the sugar-colony resident with the
sensibility of an Englishman.

Stanford's ambivalence situates him in contemporary controversies about abolition that shaped the construction of race in both colony and metropole, drawing distinctions between white Creoles and white Britons.[9] Lambert writes, for example, that the struggle over the abolition of slavery was "bound up with the contested articulation of white colonial identities between colony and metropole" (5). Stanford occupies a category of white West Indian that is at once English and not-English, rooted in Jamaica and able to adopt or reject elements of his birth nation; this creolized status permits him to separate himself from the cruelties perpetrated by those like Captain Harrop. Stanford maintains his self-styled white West Indian humanity, while he reduces Harrop to his Anglo-Jamaican brutality. The white West Indian, then, offers a hybrid category that permits flexibility of identification, complicating categories of whiteness and of Britishness linked to attitudes toward the slave trade and plantation slavery.[10]

Stanford's compassion separates him from the hardness of the Anglo-Jamaican Harrop, but it also links him to a tradition of sentimentalism that is potentially dangerous to the boundaries between self and other. Ildiko Csengei writes, "The tears of the man of feeling always mark ambivalent moments of sympathy," and he adds that "novels of sentiment critically reflect on Enlightenment theories of sympathy, where fellow feeling unsettles the boundaries of the self and blurs the distinction between self and other" (955). A "man of feeling," Stanford configures his unstable selfhood, his white masculinity, in relation to Jack's black masculinity.

Stanford (over)emphasizes Jack's masculinity from his first letter when he counters the other planters' argument that a "Negro" and "slave" cannot be a man. Like Aphra Behn's (female) narrator in *Oroonoko*, Stanford presents the black rebel as a colonial fetish and object of admiration, if not desire. Stanford insists, "Jack is a MAN," who embodies a fierce combination of patriotism and revenge: "He was of the most manly growth, nearly seven feet in height and amazingly robust; bred up to hardihood, his limbs were well-shapen and athletic; he was everything in soul and person requisite for the hero . . . a bold and daring fellow, ready to undertake everything for the good of his country, inspired by a rooted revenge, on the strongest foundation of villainy" (Earle 72–73). Stanford overlays his description of Jack as an African warrior with European standards of male beauty, echoing Behn's description of Oroonoko: "his nose was not like the generality of blacks, squat and flat, but rather aquiline" (72).[11] Stanford describes Jack as "awake to feeling," with love of his country and his mother flowing "warmly" in his heart (118). In Jack's homosocial bond with his countryman Mahali, "entwined within each other's arms while the mingled tears of friendship," Stanford sees heroic "noble hearts" (147). He thus rebukes his countrymen, "Ye sons of Christianity," who deem Jack and Mahali "*unenlightened savages . . .* unworthy of the appellation of men" because "they are black men and slaves" (146). Stanford's excessive feelings for his hero nearly overcome his ability to write: "I must break off. Adieu" (72). Jack's heroic masculine form and occasional "manly tear" throw into relief Stanford's maudlin histrionics, complicating gendered binaries that oppose the black heathen savage to the white Christian gentleman (113).

With (unmanly) tears that "soil" his paper and multiple exclamation points, Stanford faults his counterparts, the bloodthirsty "men of Europe," for Jack's misfortune, and he nearly justifies the rebel's manly rage: "The men of Europe were his foes, and he would hunt the world to revenge himself on the sanguinary sons of the white cliffs. . . . Jack was a Man!! Jack was a Hero!!!" (119). However, the deaths of Amri and Mahali push Jack beyond what Stanford considers a range of acceptable behavior, as he shifts from noble-hearted hero to dangerously aggressive villain. Stanford laments to report that Jack submits to escalated violence, now more savage beast than "MAN." With his anger unleashed, Jack exacts his revenge and "exercised cruelty with all the savage fury of a beast of prey" (149). His manliness seems to Stanford now more dangerous than daring, his "depredations . . . now so great and atrocious that Government was in a manner compelled to publish the . . . Proclamation" (155). Here Stanford turns from his sentimental effusions to the more neutral transcriptions of the governor's proclamation and the assembly's resolution. Sara Salih sees in this narrative shift from sentimental to factual Jack's "demotion" from "the Herculean eroticized hero into the 'thing' he always was, at least according to Jamaican slave law" (82).[12] Indeed, Earle's text comes to definitively associate Jack with his illicit practices, his "malefic obi." This "tremendous evil," Stanford writes in his final letter, "worked upon the hearts of many" (154).

Stanford's view of obeah reflects the complexity of colonial attitudes toward the practice. His unflattering description of Bashra, the obeah man, recalls Moseley's "wrinkled and deformed" obeah men who alleg-edly harbored fugitives and nurtured their delusions: "It was here [Bashra's cave] that fugitive negroes ran, to revenge themselves on those that did them any injury; and here came the self-deluded Amri with her aspiring son—to this horrible cell of iniquity" (188, 104). At the same time, the text renders with relative sympathy Amri's father, Feruarue, who took up the study of obeah after his abduction to Jamaica. Tortured and burned alive, the brave and noble Feloop defends his rebellion and refuses to reveal to Mornton the secrets of his "hidden means." Stanford deems Feruarue's obeah as "weak and "impotent," even as he acknowledges its power to "spirit the negroes up to a rebellion" (99). Jack comes to distrust the efficacy of his own obeah during his episode of imprisonment and subsequent sentence of torture and incineration. In this circumstance Jack "placed but little confidence in the virtue of his obi" (114). Nonetheless, after his escape and in the early days of his "enlargement," Jack seeks out Bashra for company and supplies, and in Bashra's cave he reunites with Mahali, intimating the cultural if not spiritual power of obeah to bond Afro-Jamaicans (121).

Earle's title *Obi; or, The History of Three-Fingered Jack* equates the practice with the character, using for reference early Anglo-Jamaican conceptual-izations of the African system of beliefs. Footnotes citing Bryan Edwards accompany Stanford's descriptions of obeah, and he includes verbatim passages from Benjamin Moseley's *Treatise*. These chronicles of obeah contribute to its disturbing multivalence, to an epistemological flexibility that permits it to both forge and disrupt relationships on the island.[13] Like Three-Fingered Jack, the significance of obeah shifts and permutes in the hands of its author.

The capitulation of Jack's black magic to Quashie's "white obi" signifies the dominance of the white Christian plantocracy over its Afro-Jamaican rebels, but the term "white obi" intimates the hybridization of European and African belief systems inherent to colonial encounters. Obeah and Christianity are mutually constitutive and, as Diana Paton has observed, they become "interchangeable" ("Afterlives" 59). Jack's obeah terrorized Anglo- and Afro-Jamaicans alike, but Reeder's hastily acquired Christianity "cows" him:

> Reeder told him that his Obi had no power over him, for that he was christened, and no longer Quashee, but James Reeder.
>
> Jack started back in dismay; he was cowed for he had prophesied that White Obi should overcome him. (Earle 156)

By embracing Christianity and adopting the English name Reeder, Quashie signals his affiliation with the English plantocracy.[14] Earle's Afro-Jamaican characters either align themselves with England (Reeder, Sam, "the boy") or with Africa (Jack, Mahali, Amri, Bashra, Feruarue, and Makro). The African-identified characters live outside the law and clash with it, and each of them dies at its order. Quashie's adaptation to and of the law permits him to thrive. In his shift from "Quashee, the slave" to "Reeder, the free black man," he moves beyond the stereotype of the submissive male slave into a new category that works for and protects the colonial government against his rebellious black counterpart.[15]

Stanford describes the conflict between Jack and Quashie as "fierce and long contested" (Earle 158). Though Jack initially "shrunk back in fear" from Quashie's white obeah, he rallies and "grasps his cutlass with resolution," despite the blood dripping from his gunshot wounds (157, 158). He fights on, with "his right hand almost cut off . . . streaming with gore and gashes," but only when he is "*enfeebled* by the stouter arm of death" do his three opponents slay him by beating "his brains out with stones" (158; emphasis mine). Quashie, Sam, and the little boy win the battle and carry Jack's head and dismembered hand through Morant Bay, Kingston, and Spanish Town. Unmanned and "thingified," Jack loses not to white obeah, but to the stones, bullets, and cutlass of his black counterparts.

Though Stanford finds Jack deserving of death for his crimes, he persists in blaming the government and its "hirelings." "No doubt," he writes, "in the end Jack died deservedly—had he died like a man. But who worked his passion to the pitch? Who drove him to the deeds of desperacy and cruelty? Oh fie! Fie!!" Stanford implies that the government drove Jack to desperation and compromised his manhood ("had he died like a man") by deploying its loyal slaves to vanquish the "fierce, wild, and terrible" Jack. Yet, Stanford writes, "Thus died as great a man as ever graced the annals of history, basely murdered by the hirelings of the Government" (157). Stanford blames not Jack but the corrupt system, and in his final words he returns to the stories of his white countrymen, relating the death of Harrop, who "starved to death in Jack's cave," and the resurgence of his compassionate successor, William Sebold.

William occupies the liminal category of the West Indian white man, an example of "going native" and surviving by marronage, and he offers an alternative to both Stanford's histrionics and Harrop's grim story. Because of his uncle's treachery, William absconds from the plantation for sixteen years, and he inhabits the woods and mountains, melancholy and "senseless" (151). Transformed over time to a "wild man" of great strength, William proves to be Jack's most powerful adversary when he intercepts the outlaw's attack of a group of black men carrying rum. Quite unlike the three-to-one fight between Jack and his former peers, Jack and William throw down their weapons and fight, like "men," with their strong hands: "This was a severe contest; thrice the earth received them entwined in each other's grasp; and the starting blood strained from the veins; mingled with their sweat, and poured in rivulets down their bodies; but see, the wild man grasps him with fury round the waist, and Jack is thrown with violence some yards back. . . . Never before did Jack meet such a powerful adversary" (115). Powerful opponents, Jack and William fight fairly. Though Jack cannot be assimilated to the plantation system, William can become rehabilitated, a new model of white Jamaican resident. He protects and defends those weaker than him, and his surprising strength and courage suggests that colonial life enfeebles the white man unless he can transform it. Though Jack wins their fight, the event puts William in the path of Harriet, who had likewise fled to the bush to escape her father's tyranny, and together they rejoin the plantation complex. As Captain Harrop's heir, William added to Harriet's already substantial wealth. William has rejected Harrop's legacy of slave trading, and though he inherits the plantation, he runs it without the brutality of his former guardian. Fulfilling the heteronormative arc of a sentimental novel, the union of the young couple provides the final words of the story: "William Sebald and Harriet were at length united, and have for many years enjoyed the sweets of a happy union. Adieu!" (158). Strong, brave, and violently opposed to the slave trade, William embodies a new kind of white West Indian man.

Earle's *Obi* also imagines the reformation of black men on the island. Quashie/Reeder represents an assimilated black man with strength to protect the island from its enemies and loyalty to protect the plantocracy. Stanford describes Quashie as "possessed of an heroic boldness, well-suited to the nature of the enterprise," the colonial enterprise of policing the island (157). Newly Christian, recently manumitted, and possessed of a substantial cash reward, Reeder represents the potential for submissive slaves to gradually become loyal subjects of the Crown. Though Quashie has been renamed "Reeder," Stanford continues to refer to him by his African slave name, a narrative reminder of his creolized status as a West Indian black defender of England's interests in African and Jamaica. The sentimental Stanford, then, imagines a controlled and controllable black masculinity that vulnerable Anglo-Jamaicans can harness for a peaceful and safe Jamaica.

The same year that Earle published *Obi*, William Burdett released his adventure story, *Life and Exploits of Mansong*. He relies on many of the same sources as Earle, but Burdett's slim volume justifies rather than laments circumstances that pit Afro-Jamaicans against one another. He identifies Africa as the source of the violence among black men, assuring English readers that the British intervention will subdue the bloodshed that would otherwise prevail in the West Indies.

WILLIAM BURDETT AND MUNGO PARK

William Burdett's 1800 novelette, *The Life and Exploits of Mansong*, went into ten editions and numerous anonymous adaptations over the course of seventy years, indicating its continued popularity with English readers. Announcing in the frontispiece that he was "Many Years Overseer of a Plantation in Jamaica," Burdett cultivates credibility by lifting historical information about Jamaica from Benjamin Moseley's *Treatise on Sugar* and Bryan Edwards's apologist *History, Civil and Commercial, of the British Colonies in the West Indies*. True or not, in claiming Jamaican colonial experience, Burdett links himself to the interests of the Anglo-Jamaican planter class, many who were defenders of slavery.

Burdett's earlier editions include a four-page description of John Fawcett's popular pantomime, which had opened earlier that year, prompting the public's "general curiosity" about the figure of Jack Mansong (*Life and Exploits*). He also regales his audience with stories of ethnic warfare taken from Mungo Park's popular *Travels in the Interior of Africa*, from whence he derives the manly-sounding eponymous surname, Mansong. Burdett pieced together a text that reads as part adventure narrative, part ethnography, and part romance—a mélange of materials aimed toward an audience curious about the intrepid English experience of Africa and Jamaica. Burdett's *Life and Exploits* maps an imagined African warrior culture onto the Jamaican landscape, simultaneously justifying and displacing the English imperative for a police state to control outlaws like Jack Mansong.

Burdett's *Life* firmly locates the source of the slave trade and its per-
petuation in Africa, deflecting British responsibility for it. The first third
of the text, set in Africa, uses Mungo Park's narrative to paint a picture
of tribal and ethnic wars, the spoils of which are slaves sold by African
kings to European traders, through slatees ("Slave merchants" [12]),
and transported to the colonies. The middle section, relying mostly on
Anglo-Jamaican sources, focuses on the British containment of obeah in
Jamaica, emphasizing the African origins of the practice and linking it
to slave rebellions with a distinctly ethnic register. The final third of the
novel introduces humane English characters, their loyal slaves, and Afro-
Jamaicans who police the colony. In its inclusion of Maroons, Burdett's
edition, unlike Earle's, reveals the layers of a colonial police state. Also
unlike Earle, Burdett fleshes out the contours of African society, highlighting the ethnic and tribal wars that fostered and were fostered by the slave
trade. His depictions of both Jamaica and Africa emphasize the English
compulsion to at once contain and promote violence, using methods of
divide and conquer to protect the colonial and imperial agendas.

Burdett's novelette opens with a description of events in Africa that,
like Mungo Park's narrative, condemns the Moors for much of the unrest
in the region.[16] Mansong loses his father to invading Moors, and the young
warrior vows revenge. Initially, his peaceful countrymen, "unenlightened"
Muslims, refuse to fight, but Mansong eventually convinces them to
join the king of nearby Kaarta in war against the "perfidious" king of
Bambarra, a conflict fueled by "Moorish robbers."[17] With Mansong's help,
the good King Daisy overthrows the wicked King Lubeg, whose betrayal
by the Moors hastens his defeat. Burdett describes Mansong as a strong,
fierce leader of African men, a "tyger" whose "valour inspired his own
men with courage" but a victim of the treachery of African warfare (9).
Though he fights valiantly, Mansong becomes collateral damage in the
wars between Kaarta, Bambarra, and neighboring Moorish kingdoms.
During the peace negotiations, Lubeg kidnaps Mansong and sells him into
slavery, sending him from the banks of Gambia to Jamaica. This series of

events censures African tribal war and savagery, blaming the slave trade on the "Dark Continent" rather than on the enlightened Europeans.

Burdett relies on Mungo Park's popular narrative to create his warmongering, slave-trading Africa. Park outlines the divisions among the "petty" and "jealous" African states (including Bambarra and Kaarta), declaring that prisoners of the tribal wars "are the most productive source and was probably the origin of slavery" (240–241).[18] Though Park was somewhat sympathetic to non-Moorish Africans and likely against slavery in principal, his connection and commitment to the African Association and to the known apologist Bryan Edwards compelled him to adopt a relatively neutral tone.[19] Echoing contemporary proslavery arguments, Park proposes that even if Europe stopped participating in the slave trade, the wars and subsequent traffic in Africa would surely continue. Slavery in Africa, he argues, long preceded the European institution and would continue long after. Moreover, he maintains that abolition would not reverse the problem, despite the fond hopes of "wise and worthy" European antislavery organizations (247).[20]

Park depicts a continent of "unenlightened" natives, strong in stature but weak in intellect, but he makes an important distinction between the "unlettered Negroes" and the literate, lighter-skinned Moors.[21] He positions the Moors as ethnically and culturally different from their African counterparts. Park's unfortunate real-life experience as a captive of the Moors undoubtedly influenced his harsh description of them as treacherous and malevolent: "I have observed that the Moors, in their complexion, resemble the Mulattoes of the West Indies. . . . The enterprising boldness of the Moors, their knowledge of the country, and above all, the superior fleetness of their horses, make them such formidable enemies, that the petty Negro states . . . are in continual terror" (132).

Park's narrative depicts a west-central Africa (Senegal, Mali, and Mauritania) divided by ethnicity and culture, riddled with border conflicts, and corrupted by slavery. The Moors, he complains, combine "the blind superstition of the negro with the savage cruelty of the Arab" (133).

Light-skinned but superstitious, literate but uncivilized, the Moors amal-gamate for Park the Western and non-Western worlds. In addition, they resemble the Jamaican Maroons—armed, fierce, and mobile.

Park's description of the Moors as bold warriors with geographic savvy and fast horses link them to the Maroons of the Americas, who likewise inhabit an interstitial sociopolitical space and divided loyalties. Although planters such as Bryan Edwards viewed literate African Muslims, "Mandingoes," as model slaves, superior to their counterparts, they are in fact inextricably linked to a long history of rebellion and resistance, especially in Jamaica and Saint Domingue (Gomez 59; Diouf 145; Sultana 163).[22] Park also compares the Moors to "Mulattoes of the West Indies" (92) worrying that any kind of creolizing—ethnic, racial, or political—can potentially result in treachery and duplicity, deadly enemies and danger-ous allies all around.

Because the African Moors inhabit this threshold space, Park explains, they were as likely to work with Europeans as with black people, selling slaves to the former and charms to the latter. Park writes that literate Mohammedan priests sell sheep horns filled with charms or amulets to "simple" natives, and often these charms are sentences from the Koran (31).[23] The "simple natives" use the amulets much like obeah to ward off disease, to protect them from harm during war, and to guard them from snake or alligator bites. He notes, however, that even the literate Muslims fall prey to childish superstitions in their purchase of "*saphies*" (charms): "In this case it is impossible not to admire the wonderful contagion or superstition; for, not withstanding that the majority of the Negroes are Pagans, and absolutely reject the doctrines of Mohamet, I did not meet with a man, whether a Busreen [Muslim] or Kafir [infidel] who are not fully persuaded of these amulets" (32).[24] The contagion of superstition, Park warns, cuts across African faiths and classes (Salih 82).

In a passage that echoes Park (and Moseley), Burdett accuses obeah practitioners in the West Indies of preying on the weakness of the credulous negroes "whether Africans or Creoles." In both texts these distinctions of identity are grounded in the spiritual beliefs of those subject to market forces they cannot control. The "treacherous" Moors (Park 93) and the "miscreant" obeah practitioner capitalize on the "ignorant negroes" (Burdett 15). Burdett writes, "The trade which those imposters carry on is extremely lucrative; they manufacture and sell their obies, adapted to different cases and at different prices" (15). For Burdett (like Park), the unlettered, "deluded negroes" live in thrall to the "imposters" who financially and spiritually exploit them (Burdett 15).

Burdett cites Park almost verbatim, borrowing the name "Mansong" from the king of Bambarra, but he demotes his fictional hero from Park's king to an exceptional, but fallen, warrior.[25] Burdett thus simultaneously disempowers both the sovereign leader and Mansong. Though Burdett's Africa lacks the specificity of Park's account, it maintains the tensions of ethnic warfare. Burdett conflates Park's African warrior with Moseley's Jack (and Behn's Oroonoko) to create an Afro-Jamaican Jack Mansong for his English audience. "This daring marauder," Burdett begins, "was of a bold and martial appearance; he was above common stature, and his limbs well shapen and athletic." Like Earle's Jack, he boasts an "aquiline" nose and "clear skin" (5). Burdett's Mansong, echoing Earle, echoing Behn, embodies a rebel that unites the African warrior with European standards of beauty, imagining through a colonial lens an idealized and thus unsustainable black masculinity. Once in Jamaica Mansong is stripped of his name, his power, and his voice—his *Mansong*. He thus plots his revenge: "Eighteen long months had now elapsed since he was dragged from his native country . . . and JACK (for he was so named after his arrival in Jamaica, and by which we shall in future call him), devised how to lash his persecutors with a rod of iron" (13). Jack's transformation from proud warrior (Mansong) to vengeful and violent outlaw (Jack) grafts Park's Africa onto Burdett's Jamaica.

Burdett's second section relies heavily on Bryan Edwards, Edward Long, and Benjamin Moseley to emphasize the practice of African-derived obeah and the efforts of the colonial government to contain it.

Immediately after introducing the yaws-riddled obeah man, Amalkir, Burdett dedicates several pages to obeah, a practice "prevalent in the British West Indies, corroborated by the authorities of Mr. Bryan Edwards, author of the '*History of the West Indies*,' Doctor Mosley, &c. &c." (14). Burdett links obeah to Africa: "the professors of Obi are, and always were, natives of Africa, and none other; and they have brought the science with them from thence to Jamaica; where it is so universally practiced that there are few of the large estates, possessing native Africans, which have not one or more of them" (14). Amalkir's name, with its Quarnic sound, intimates that the obeah practitioner like Jack blends African belief systems into a new world practice.[26]

Burdett conveys the inherent difficulty in restraining such intangible practices, even with the traction of an armed police force such as the Maroons: "The secret and insidious manner in which the crime is generally perpetuated, makes the legal proof extremely difficult; suspicions, therefore, have been frequent, but detections rare" (17). Burdett uses the example of Tacky's Rebellion to demonstrate the victory of tangible law over shadowy superstition, particularly in the descriptions of the treatment of obeah men: "At the place of execution, he [Tacky's obeah man] bid defiance to the executioner; telling him that it was not in the power of the white people to kill him; and the Negro spectators were greatly perplexed when they saw him expire. Upon other Obeah men, who were apprehended at that time, various experiments were made with electrical machines and magic lanterns; but with very little effect, except on one, who after receiving some very severe shocks, acknowledged that his master's Obi exceeded his own" (20–22).[27] In language that echoes Moseley ("he had prophesied that white obi would get the better of him" (204) this quotation shows the colonial machine triumphing over the "imaginary charm" and its "mischievous tendency" (22).[28] Burdett uses these sources, as he explains in his preface, to corroborate the "veracity" of his tale, and he thus participates in the construction of the colonial discourse about obeah, which, as Paton writes, is a "creation of colonialism as much as it is a construction of Africans in the Caribbean" ("Obeah Acts" 16). These sources support, in Jack's story, the foregone conclusion that white obeah trumps black obeah, that European force trumps African sorcery. Moreover, the very idea of "white obeah," as Tim Watson has argued, exemplifies the ways borders between "European rationality" and "savage African superstition" were persistently and creatively crossed in both directions" ("Mobile Obeah" 245). Reeder's "white obi," then, signals the mutual creolization of European and African belief systems. In Burdett's *Life and Exploits*, those in possession of white obeah had black soldiers at their disposal, and with them the Anglo-Jamaicans harnessed and policed the African warrior culture on the island.

In furnishing the Maroon warriors with guns to supplement their guerilla tactics, the colonial government simultaneously Africanized and Anglicized its police force. Jack's army at first prevailed, but the Maroons take the final round: "The Governor sent five hundred choice Maroons in pursuit of these rebels. They met, and fought.—The negroes, as before rushed upon their guns; but the Maroons firing as they retreated, kept them at bay, and made great slaughter. Jack, in vain, encouraged his men; he could not rouse them to renew the combat; and they fled in every direction" (24). Burdett's brief but bloody inclusion of the Maroons reveals divisions amongst Afro-Jamaicans.[29] As Jamaican history had shown, methods of divide and conquer worked well for the colonial government.

Burdett makes much of Jack's isolation from other Afro-Jamaicans after the debacle of the insurrection: "He scorned assistance; he robbed alone; fought all his own battles and always killed his pursuers" (26). In the escalation of his violence, Jack turns against the enslaved people, even former friends. For example, he attacks and robs Quashie, who "had been an intimate of our hero's in his days of slavery." A particularly violent struggle ensues: "Jack drew his cutlass; upon which Quashee pulled a pistol from his girdle, and shot off two of his antagonist's fingers. This enraged JACK who now used his sword with savage fury" (25). This incident sets the stage for the later battle between the two men, and it tells stories of betrayal and shifting loyalties. Burdett thus imagines a violent contact zone outside the plantation complex, a veritable Wild West Indies, and it attests to the imperative for and success of the "stiffening of imperial resolve," as Michael Craton puts it, that followed the putdown of Tacky's Rebellion and provided the model for handling outlaws like Jack (*Testing the Chains* 138). The violence of the black rebels provides the justification for counterinsurgency, and Burdett's text opposes the compassion of the white characters to the savagery of Jack.

The final section of Burdett's *Life* depicts Jack's terrible threat to decent white men, justifying their severe measures against him. Burdett borrows from Moseley's treatise and Fawcett's pantomime, using characters and dynamics familiar to his audience: the kindly planter Chapman, his feisty daughter Rosa, and her hapless fiancé, Captain Orford. A "young Englishman of good birth" (26), Orford represents a weakened English military in Jamaica, and he (rather stupidly) falls twice prey to Jack's depredations, first robbed, then shot and abducted. Orford's injuries and defenselessness call into question his military abilities, and he requires rescue first by a black boy and then by a white woman in men's clothing (Rosa). As Orford falls "senseless" (27), Chapman endures a "long illness" with anxiety (30). The white men of the text struggle to maintain their health and wealth against the threat of Jack Mansong. Only Chapman's ostensible humanity toward his slaves saves him, because he has nurtured their loyalty.

Reeder and Sam annihilate Jack in a "horrid spectacle," and their success gives them access to the ranks of free black men who serve the colonial machine (35). Burdett thus imagines a gradual emancipation, managed carefully by a reformed ruling class. The "humane example" of Chapman earns his reward in the form of increased "private wealth" and the larger "good of this country at large" (29). Burdett's Jamaica offers a humane plantocracy that necessarily secures and deploys the loyalty of its black population. Orford follows the example of Chapman, and he sells his commission, buys an estate, and inherits the considerable fortune of his father-in-law. Unable to protect the island, he instead invests in it and enjoys with Rosa "an uninterrupted series of happiness for many years" as one of the "richest men on the island" (37–38). Jack's crimes have justified the government's harsh measures, and the exemplary white elite enjoys an island restored to its peace and prosperity.

Burdett's narrator blames Jack's criminality on the treachery of African tribal war, deflecting responsibility away from the colonial government and plantocracy: "THREE-FINGER'D JACK; a man, perhaps, of as genuine courage as ever existed; and who in all probability, had he not been consigned to slavery by the bale treachery of the King of Bambarra, would have been an ornament to his country" (38). Burdett's apologist text stops short of censuring the slave trade, though some anonymous adaptations condemn it as "the worst of all traffics." Instead, he promotes an island composed of benevolent Anglo-Jamaicans, christened slaves, and a loyal Afro-Jamaican police force, a sure defense against the imported danger of African rebels and their obeah charms.

Versions of Burdett's *Life* and Earle's *Obi* remained popular for more than fifty years, attesting to the ongoing popularity of the obeah-wielding outlaw. In Jack's demise this "bold and daring defender of the rights of man" (Earle 68), a man of "as genuine courage as ever existed" (Burdett 38), shaped English attitudes toward race and empire. These prose renderings of Jack's tragic but necessary execution interrogated and justified British intervention in Jamaica and Africa, using the exploits of the outlaw to configure new models of black and white men, figures of creolized masculinity. These figures of the compassionate Anglo-Jamaicans, assimilated Afro-Jamaicans, and the dead rebel reassured English readers of the good character and judgment of their representatives around the Atlantic world. The same year these prose adaptations emerged, Fawcett's pantomime *Obi* brought the figure of the rebel to the stage in England and, soon after, to the United States.

CHAPTER 3

Staging *Obi*

THREE-FINGERED JACK IN
LONDON AND NEW YORK

Shortly after John Fawcett's *Obi; or, Three-Fingered Jack* opened at London's Haymarket Theatre in 1800, reviewer Thomas Dutton remarked that the pantomime had "gained a fast hold on the favour and partiality" of London (18).[1] Although his review was largely acrimonious, not even he could deny the success of Fawcett's drama.[2] The *Morning Herald* predicted great success for "The Black Hecate of Jamaica," anticipating that it would "throw [its] spells over all the town" (qtd. in Reed "Staging Circum-Atlantic Revolt" 254). Fawcett's *Obi*, it turns out, cast its spell around the country and across the Atlantic too.

Immediately popular, *Obi* played for thirty-nine performances in its first season, and a year later traveled to New York, Philadelphia, and Boston. For the next two decades at least, it circulated in the provinces in England and played almost annually in the United States. Though it never had quite the popularity in the United States as it did in England, *Obi* enjoyed a New York revival in 1823, first at the prominent Park Theatre and shortly thereafter at William Brown's so-called African Theatre, the first all-black theater company in the United States. Fawcett's pantomime has clearly provided a flexible means of representing the exploits of the black bandit.

Scholarly discussions of Fawcett's *Obi* have repeatedly invoked vocabularies of lack, loss, and recovery. Michael Warner and colleagues, for

Figure 3.1. *Three Finger'd Jack*, c. 1840. Ref. no. Mas.1046(19),
National Library of Scotland, Edinburgh.

example, note that the "surviving texts of *Obi* are rather sketchy, in a way that suggests that they were routinely completed by the performers" (7–8). Jeffrey Cox proposes that the "lack" of dialogue permits "a response to certain scenes not restricted by authorial pronouncements" (para. 8). Srinivas Aravamudan considers the historiographical gaps to argue that "the story of Jack's individualism and failure is founded on the suppression of a more complex story, of collective rebellion by many participants" (introd. to *Obi* 14). Chuck Rzepka takes a productive approach to these fissures, suggesting that the *Obi* plays offer romantic period scholars a means to address "our own cultural amnesia" ("Obi Now" para. 6).

The gaps opened up by the sketchiness of Fawcett's *Obi*, this chapter proposes, furnish a point of departure for radical revisions, creating the space for producers of culture like William Brown to advance radically different interpretations of the black outlaw. As it moved across the Atlantic, Fawcett's *Obi* permutated and transformed from a silent blackface spectacle to a liberatory bid for racial equality and legal representation.

OBI IN LONDON

At the time John Fawcett's *Obi* debuted in London (1800), debates about slavery and abolition raged in England, especially with the ongoing rebellion in Saint Domingue, the relatively recent American Revolution, and late eighteenth-century slave uprisings in Jamaica, Saint Vincent, and Suriname. But England was feeling pretty confident in 1800. Even if Fawcett's Jack evoked the heroic François-Dominique Toussaint-Louverture, as Jenna Gibbs has argued, the Black Jacobin would also have represented French failure to suppress its rebellions, throwing into relief the superior strength of Britain's imperial hold. Unlike France, England had thus far managed to quell its recent insurgencies. Fawcett's *Obi* celebrated British power and tempered potentially volatile issues by offering English audiences an idealized representation of Jamaican plantation and English colonial life: compassionate planters, contented slaves, and justly punished rebels.

Performed in blackface to Samuel Arnold's score, *Obi* used signboards and songs, accompanied by a printed wordbook that liberally cited Benjamin Moseley, "The learned Author of the Work we have profited by" (Fawcett 4). Following Moseley's basic story, Fawcett's Jack terrorizes the Jamaican plantation, protected by obeah, but he adds to Moseley's account the fictional love story of the planter's daughter, Rosa, and her fiancé, Captain Orford, whom Jack abducts, then later kidnaps, much to the concern of the black plantation residents. Jack also captures Rosa when she tracks Orford to his cave, but she devises their escape. As in Moseley's account, the recently christened slave Quashie and his associates pursue Jack in response to the "Proclamation of the Reward, by the Officers of the Government" (8). "Publick Rejoicings" celebrate Jack's grisly death.

Critics have generally agreed on the ambivalence of Fawcett's *Obi*, observing subversive undercurrents within its essentially conservative frame.[3] As Jeffrey Cox has shown, Fawcett's decision to stage *Obi* as a pantomime with its use of "illegitimate forms of stagecraft," permitted the inclusion of some "potentially radical material" (para. 1).[4] Characterized by silent stock characters, spectacular stage effects, music, and kinetic bodies, the pantomime offered a variety of ways to explore or complicate representations of race in relation to national identity.[5] Fawcett introduces his rebellious hero, the grotesque obeah woman, and a gang of robbers as threats to the colonial order only to contain and defeat these blackface spectacles. Despite its moments of potentially subversive intervention, *Obi* reinforces European claims to cultural, moral, and spiritual superiority over the enslaved Afro-Jamaicans. And English audiences approved.

The initial success of Fawcett's *Obi* was due at least in part to the casting of leading man Charles Kemble as Jack, who may have invited audience support and sympathy, even as the character registered contradictory valences (Cox para. 8).[6] The *Monthly Mirror* described him as "a heroic personage with the serene dignity of a Greek sculpture" (qtd. in Hoskins, introd. to *Obi* xxvi). Alternately, Dutton comments on Jack's buffoonery in his review, noting that he "acts the part of a downright simpleton and idiot. He no sooner brings a prisoner in his cave, in the recess of which lies another in a state of convalescence, then he gets drunk and takes a nap" (26). He concludes, "It was evidently the author's intention to depict Jack as a savage, ferocious monster; instead of which, he is the best fellow in the whole groupe" (28). These contradictory observations focus on the scene of Rosa's capture, potentially a scene of raced sexual aggression, but instead conveying, in Robert Hoskins's view, a moment of "transracial desire" ("Savage Boundaries" para. 10). It is possible, then, to view Jack as a "downright simpleton," a "dignified personage," an object of desire, or "the best fellow in the whole groupe."

This moment of "transracial desire" was used as publicity for *Obi*, by way of Edward Orne's engraving of Sylvester Harrison's watercolor, *Miss de Campe and Mr. Kemble in the Characters of Rosa and Three-Fingered Jack*. This image shows Rosa singing to Jack and playing a lyre; dressed as a sailor boy, she wears loose white trousers and a low-cut blouse to emphasize her femininity. Kemble-as-Jack lounges with one muscled arm resting on a table, the other thrown seductively over his head, and his legs stretched out in front of him. He wears a Grecian-style dress, invoking, as Gibbs notes, the "classical heroism" associated with Kemble as a Shakespearean actor (636). But reptile skeletons decorate Jack's cave, and he prominently displays his obeah horn, highlighting his gruesome African practices. Kemble's Jack registers conflicting signs: erotized Greek hero and African savage.

Jack's muteness further ambiguates his character. In Arnold's published score Jack speaks only to chant a pseudo-African utterance: "Bang lara banga bossi Bange lara bana bossi (Hoskins, introd. to *Obi* 77). The speechless figure of Jack, motives unexplained, opens up manifold possibilities for interpretation.[7] Kemble performed Jack, as the engraving suggests, as a simultaneously familiar and exotic figure. In blackface, the skilled Kemble could at once contain and commodify Jack's rebellious blackness. The printed wordbook, citing Moseley, likewise registers Jack's contradictions. "He would sooner have made a *Medean* cauldron for the whole island," the extract relates, "than disturb one lady's happiness." Nonetheless, it continues, "even Jack himself was born to die" (qtd. in Fawcett 4). The restoration of order on the plantation, in fact, hinges on Jack's death.

The first act introduces the harmonious, cheerful atmosphere of the "extensive plantation" with happy slaves and kindly Anglo-Jamaicans. The musical accompaniment creates, Hoskins writes, an "Edenic" and "carefree" environment ("Savage Boundaries" para. 5). An early song praises the planter for his benevolence, expressing the slaves' gratitude for his sustenance and protection:

> We love massa; he be good;
> No lay stick on Negro's back;
> Much Kous-kous he give for food,
> And save us from Three Finger'd Jack." (13)

The slaves view Jack as an obstacle to their safety and happiness as well as a danger to the good white people protecting them. They panic when Jack abducts the captain, soothed only by the "superior courage" of Quashie and Sam. Confident in Quashie's power over the charms in Jack's obeah bag ("Tom-cat foot, pig-tail, and duck beak"), they predict that he will "tear the charm to rag" and "make Three-Finger Jack to squeak." Unlike Jack, the slaves conform to and confirm English spiritual and moral values. Quashie represents the most assimilated to the Christian plantocracy, a credit to a colonial system that rewards its acolytes and punishes its rebels. Though Jack never speaks out or fights for his freedom, Quashie claims his own through hard work, Christian love, and brave acts. The planter rewards such loyalty with treats "for poor Negro" such as the "grand ball and Jonkonnu" that concludes the first act (Fawcett 17).

The *Dramatic Censor* describes the Jonkonnu in an explanatory footnote as "a grotesque character, equipped with a ludicrous and enormously large false head, and presides at the negro balls in Jamaica, in the capacity of master of the ceremonies" (Dutton 20). The merry master of festivities,

Jonkonnu, oversees the celebration: "One funny big man be master of all. 'Tis merry Jonkanoo" (17). Also the name for the masked dancing bands that frolic in the Jamaican streets during the Christmas holidays, Jonkonnu fuses African and European cultural elements, an example of ludic liberation inevitably restored to order. As Peter Reed argues, early performance records reveal "Jonkonnu as an always-already-hybridized act," a dynamically transmitted performance with roots that "lead back to an Africa that participated actively in the commercialized Anglo-Atlantic" ("There Was No Resisting" 70). Despite the potential for Jonkonnu as liberatory or subversive, Fawcett reduces the character to a harmless spectacle reminiscent of the traditional pantomime's stock clown character (a "big funny man" (17).[8] Fawcett's "merry Jonkanoo" functions as "master of all," only at the pleasure of "Good Massa," who provides and polices the festivities.

Unlike the jolly Jonkonnu, the grotesque obeah woman cannot be comfortably assimilated into these staged representations of Jamaican plantation life. The "ugly loathsome creature" lives on the margins of the plantation, occupying a space outside of the purview of the planter or overseer, her cave the receptacle[s] of robbers and fugitive negroes" (Moseley, qtd. in Fawcett 4). The wordbook narrates the retreat of the "Negroe Robbers" to her lair, where they pay her "homage" in exchange for obeah (Fawcett 4, 7). Also in her cave and with her help, Jack performs "ceremonies to prevent the Negroes betraying him" (8).

The musical score highlights these subversive moments. The robbers have their own musical interlude, set to the "Surprise" movement of Joseph Haydn's "Symphony No. 94," using, as Hoskins shows, variations that are "consonant with the slouch and lunge of the raid," providing a sense of "displacement meant to emphasize moral inversion and collapse" ("Savage Boundaries" para. 7). The obeah woman dominates, creating, as Hoskins puts it, a "unique musical aura" with the "reptilian chromaticism of Mozart's D minor String Quartet finale . . . and the strange end-phrase repeated notes sound incantatory as she calls up the maroons to do the devil's work" (para. 7). The production, however, introduces these delightfully spooky spectacles only to subvert them.

Dutton's review gives an example of the comical way the obeah practitioner and robbers may have played out onstage, narrating the remarks of an Irish gentleman on his left and an elderly woman with two children behind him. In response to Jack's appearance in the cave, the robbers "dance" and "carouse," described by Dutton as "warlike exercises" and prompting in his neighbor eager support: "'Arrah! By Jasus!'—exclaims my Irish neighbor—'we shall have bloody work of it now! To it! My brave boys!'" (23). But instead of making "bloody work of it," the robbers, Dutton reports, "throw themselves on their faces." Shifting gears, the Irishman (Dutton continues) consequently admonishes them for their cowardice, calling them "a parcel of chicken-hearted poltroons!" (23). Dutton mocks the antics of both the Irishman and the black robbers, relegating them to comic, stock representations. In this review Dutton makes visible both Irish and West Indian coloniality at the site of theatrical production and consumption. In addition, the older woman renders ridiculous the obeah woman's menace, describing her as a "nasty hag" beating the bad robbers: "The *Obi-woman* now advances, and with a bunch of feathers, tied to the end of a long pole, gently touches the *posteriors* of the prostrate group.— 'La! Mamma, (cries the little boy behind) is that nasty woman going to give them a whipping?'—'By Jasus! and serve them right, too, (interrupted my Irish companion) give it them sweetly, my good old dame—down with their brogues, and lay it on them properly.'—'Why sure, Mamma, (quoth the young lady) she won't make them strip in public.' Mama significantly shook her head, and the piece proceeded" (22–23).

Dutton's anecdote suggests the erosion of the obeah woman's power and the robbers' ferocity; his disruptive neighbors interpret the obeah woman's rituals as spanking rather than ceremony, overlaying the dispensation of magic with scenes of flogging. In the penultimate scene, soldiers enter the cave, capture the obeah woman and robbers, and deliver them to their sure punishment, a flogging, or worse.

The obeah woman and robber group contrast sharply with the slaves' loyalty to colonial order, and Quashie and his crew work with the authorities to rout these criminal elements. The Larpent manuscript provides details for the staging of a "desperate fight" between Jack and his opponents, the literal excision of the outlaw: "His body is dragged off; all [Quashie, Sam, and Tuckey] re-enter carrying his head and the hand with the three fingers" (qtd. in Hoskins, introd. to *Obi* xix). In this scene, then, the body of Jack, however heroically rendered by Kemble, is removed from the stage. His powerful frame reduced to body parts and his power undone, he is no longer an identifiable human being but remnants of an outlaw.[9]

In the nationalistic finale, punctuated by "God save the King," the chorus celebrates victory over the fallen traitor. The overseer sings, "may all Traitors fall / By British Proclamation." The chorus responds, "Then let us sing / God save the King, &c.&c." (19–20). The extracts from Benjamin Moseley in the wordbook elaborate on the patriotic conclusion to the play, describing the victors' procession toward their just rewards: "There they put their trophies into a pail of rum; and followed by a vast concourse of Negroes, now no longer afraid of Jack's OBI, blowing their shells and horns, and firing guns in their rude method, they carried them to Kingston, and Spanish Town; and claimed the rewards offered by the King's Proclamation, and the House of Assembly" (6). Fawcett's *Obi* thus establishes English order on the sugar plantation, performing the successful management of British imperial and colonial interests and the devotion of the wildly rejoicing "vast concourse of Negroes."

Early nineteenth-century English obeah audiences came to know (and perform) themselves through and define themselves against the staged performance of their Anglo- and Afro-Caribbean colonial counterparts. "For London to understand itself as the metropolitan center of an expanding empire," Elizabeth Dillon writes, "required that Atlantic colonial goods and bodies appear within its collective view, inhabiting time and space together with the English audience itself" (53). Figures like Quashie,

Tuckey, and Jack reflected the success of and necessity for spiritual and military policing in the British West Indies. If English colonials could take down a ferocious Toussaint-like figure and inspire the loyalty of an island of black slaves, the audience might have reasoned, then Britain dominated center stage in the Atlantic theater, at home and abroad.

Fawcett's silent blackface rebel continued to delight English audiences for another some twenty-five years. But as the figure of Jack moved across the Atlantic, he reminded the new republic of its contradictions and anxieties, particularly surrounding slavery, and Anglo-American audiences could not quite enjoy the spectacle of rebellion with the confidence of its former monarchists. Two decades after its unremarkable entry in the United States, William Brown used the "sketchiness" of Fawcett's pantomime and its ambiguous rebel as a vehicle through which to insist on the rights and representation of African Americans in a racially divided and politically fraught nation.

OBI IN THE UNITED STATES

On May 21, 1801, the Park Theatre in New York staged the first American performance of John Fawcett's *Obi* to little acclaim, though audiences purportedly enjoyed Lewis Hallam Jr. as Orford and John Hodgkinson as Jack (Buckely para. 1). A venue that imported English shows to attract American audiences, the Park Theatre occupied, as Peter Buckely puts it, "the furthest orbit in Britain's constellation of theatres" (para. 2). A review of the New York performances in 1801 spoke of the story as "well told in action," reporting that Jack's "desperate conflict with his pursuers, was sustained with such truth and nature, that it almost excited sensations of horror in the spectator" (qtd. in Reed, *Rogue Performances* 104). In Philadelphia later that year, the New Theatre offered *Obi* as part of its merry Christmas entertainment.[10] A Philadelphia review echoed the sentiment of the New York review that the performance was "well told in action," adding that entertainments of "this class are calculated for the meridian of the holiday frequenters of the theatre only" (qtd. in Gibbs 652). Reed and Gibbs have argued that the reviews "avoid" the political valence of the play in efforts to "mitigate" conversations about slavery or rebellion (Reed, *Rogue Performances* 104; Gibbs 652). Theater managers in Philadelphia, Gibbs proposes, would likely have downplayed the antislavery sentiments of the play, though the racially and economically mixed audience would have at least felt the political charge (652).

Certainly, 1801 was not a great time for staging dramas about slave revolt in the United States. This was particularly true in cities like Philadelphia, so close to the site of the recent Gabriel Prosser uprising in Richmond, Virginia, an aborted attempt that had drawn inspiration from the French, Haitian, and American Revolutions (Gibbs 628).[11] That Philadelphia and other northern cities provided refuge for Saint Dominguan refugees heightened American anxiety about rebellion.[12] In the United States in 1801, these reminders of northward-moving rebellions brought to the fore the conflict between American republican ideology and practices of plantation slavery; northern and mid-Atlantic cities in free states like New York and Philadelphia struggled to assert a distinctly American identity separate from that of the slave-holding South and the British West Indies.[13] Though the early American productions of *Obi* have left scant trace of their reception and even less of their production, they provide a neat link to the 1823 revival in New York City, as the controversies surrounding slavery, race, and representation came to a head.

OBI IN NEW YORK

On January 1, 1823, the Park Theatre revived *Obi* on the day the African American community celebrated the abolition of the slave trade. The renewed interest in Fawcett's *Obi* coincided with a revival of interest in African drama, stimulated in part by conversations that attended the end of legal slavery in New York and discussions about the black elective franchise. That June, William Brown and his "African Company" mounted his version of *Obi* to conclude an evening of provocative and racially charged material. A free black West Indian who worked as a steward on a Liverpool ship and then settled in New York, Brown offered his racially mixed audience a version of the Jack story at a critical moment in a racialized antebellum America. His production echoed histories of resistance in port cities around the Atlantic, and his increasingly integrated theater would change the profile of U.S. performance culture.

In three years and four locations (1821–1823) Brown's venue transformed from a black "pleasure garden" to an integrationist theater. Marked by a history of police closings, audience disruptions, forced relocations, and a major riot, Brown's businesses increasingly provoked hostile responses from white critics, in part because they defied hegemonic expectations of the roles and rights of black people in New York. In so doing, Brown also undermined conceptualizations of whiteness that underpinned racial assumptions about early American identity. This American identity, as Toni Morrison has famously noted, shares with its literature the "championed characteristics of "individualism, masculinity, [and] social engagement" that are responses to a "dark, abiding, signing African presence" (6). In addition to bringing from the shadows this dark presence, Brown and his company engaged in what Marvin McAllister identifies as "whiteface minstrelsy," a "mimetic but implicitly political form that not only masters but critiques constructed versions of whiteness (15). Brown thus appropriated performances of whiteness to articulate a powerful diasporic blackness that redefined American identity and theater.

Brown never referred to his theater as the "African Theatre," though Euro–New Yorkers persisted in doing so.[14] He did, however post a June 7, 1823, playbill for *Obi* that advertised his "African company" to perform at the "Theatre, in Mercer Street. Through its short history, Brown called his venues the "African Grove Pleasure Garden," "the Minor Theatre," "Theatre, in Mercer Street," and the "American Theatre." These changes and inconsistences in its name reflect the problems Brown faced in carving out a distinctly African American theatrical space.

Brown opened his African Grove Pleasure Garden to expand the limited entertainment options for the elite class of Afro–New Yorkers, many of whom had once, like him, been ship stewards or other types of free-black wage laborers.[15] In the *National Advocate* newspaper from August 3, 1821, editor Mordecai M. Noah identified the venue as a place for New York's "black dandys and dandizettes" to flaunt their "numbers" and "consequence" that increased "partly from high wages, high living, and the elective franchise" (2).[16] The theater smacked of the progress it flaunted, located as it was in the heart of white, affluent New York and as it welcomed citizens from other classes and ethnicities. Noah reported the closing of the pleasure garden by police in early September only weeks after it opened:

> It appears that some of the neighbors . . . actually complained to the Police, and the Avenues of African Grove were closed by authority; and thus were many of our ebony friends excluded from a participation in those innocent recreations to which they are entitled, by virtue of the great charter that declares "all men are equal." These imitative inmates of the kitchens and pantries, not relishing the strong arm of the law thus rudely exercised, were determined to have some kind of amusement; and after several nightly caucuses, they resolved to get up a play, and the upper apartments of the neglected African Grove were pitched upon for that purpose. (2)[17]

Noah's condescending language ("imitative inmates") both undermined and validated the social and political potential ("legal entitlement") of Brown's garden, and he reassured his readers that the black patrons "fear no Missouri plot; care for no political rights; happy in being permitted to dress fashionable, walk the streets, visit African Grove and talk scandal" (2). His comments underscore the connection between theatrical and legal representation.

As Euro–New York papers criticized Brown and police shut down his venue, the 1821 New York State constitutional convention in Albany leveled a political assault at the black franchise. Shortly after the convention opened, the suffrage committee presented its draft for franchise qualifications. For the first time, the word "white" was used in that context in response to a petition by the black New Yorkers who asked for "protection against legislative interference with their rights, and especially with the rights of suffrage" (Warner et al. 17). Following heated debate that October the convention voted to strike the word "white" from the draft (16–19). At the same time, the suffrage clause increased the black property requirement to $250, while eliminating it for white men. As Warner and his colleagues note, the Afro–New Yorkers who attended Brown's theater would have been the black elite who petitioned the convention; Noah's language in the *Advocate* "dramatizes that connection" (19). Despite Noah's evident concerns about African American progress, his close coverage of the events created publicity for the venue, drawing intrigued white patrons.

Other publications likewise situated Brown's production in contemporary conversations about race and representation. For example, the new literary periodical *St. Tammany's Magazine* anonymously published on December 4, 1821, the anonymous "Soliloquy of a Maroon Chief in Jamaica," its headnote adding "Lately Spoken at the African Theatre" (Warner et al. 1). Michael Warner and his colleagues propose Brown or leading actor James Hewlett as the most likely author of this speech during a production of *Obi*.[18] The white readership would surely have linked the figure of the Maroon chief to the familiar figure of Three-Fingered Jack, particularly because the monologue was published with two other "Negro Melodies": "Song of an Obeah Priestess" and "Setting Obi." The speaker echoes abolitionist sentiments but also threatens revenge on the white race:

> Come on! And let us reason. *We are men,*
> As I said first, and as I say agen,
> Men like yourselves. I'll prove it by my word,
> And just Gods! Avouch it by my sword
>   (qtd. in Warner et al. 2; emphasis mine).[19]

This speech asserts the rights and masculinity of a proud black man as well as his willingness to resort to violence. Whether or not Brown (or Hewlett) performed this speech at a production of *Obi*, "Soliloquy of a Maroon Chief in Jamaica: Lately Spoken at the African Theatre" clearly links Brown's theater to Jamaican slave rebellions, abolitionist rhetoric, and the rights of African Americans. It also provides a connection to political readings of Brown's *Obi* two years later.

The interest of white patrons in Brown's theater spiked when he moved to Park Row in January 1822, but his residence at this location was brief and troubled. Brown's Minor Theatre directly competed with Stephen Price's mainstream Park Theatre, drawing away from the latter white patrons who particularly wished to see the spectacle of Brown's all-black Shakespeare plays. However, "carousing white voyeurs" made for some difficult evenings for the cast, as the patrons became increasingly disruptive, throwing food and making jokes (McAllister 46). That same January, very likely with Price's directive, police stormed the stage and arrested the company for "civil discord"; the company was released only after promising to stop performing Shakespeare. Brown posted a Minor Theatre playbill that directly accused "his *brother* Managers" for wielding their influence on the police to "quell his rivalry" (qtd. in McAllister 170; emphasis mine). In calling the theater managers his "brothers," Brown alludes to the motto "Am I not a Man and a Brother," first produced for the British Committee for the Abolition of the Slave Trade and later adopted by the American abolition movement as well. In his evocation of this brotherhood of man, Brown called on his rights as an African American man.

Brown's star actor James Hewlett also demanded his rights as a black American man, reprimanding the ungenerous treatment of his "brother actors." In a letter (published by Noah) addressed to English comedian Charles Mathews, Hewlett insisted on his right to perform Shakespeare, as his "proud representative," calling attention to the new nation's relationship to and separation from England (qtd. in McAllister 173). Mathews had poked fun at his black colleagues for having, in performing Shakespeare, "mimicked" their styles, "imitated [their] dialects . . . and lampooned, O shame, even our complexions": "Why these reflections on our color, my dear Mathews, so unworthy your genius and humanity, your justice and generosity? Our immortal bard says (and he is *our* bard as well as yours, for we are all descendants of the Plantagenets, the white and red rose;) our bard Shakespeare makes sweet Desdemona say, 'I saw Othello's visage in my mind'" (173). Hewlett asserts his rights as a free black American to perform the plays of "his" bard, both claiming and disclaiming America's English roots. His words suggest an early American identification with and movement away from English influence toward the creation of a racially mixed America. When the "Shakespeare closings" forced Brown and Hewlett to move back to the Village in July 1822, Brown referred to his new space as the "American Theatre," suggesting that American theater should and would include African-descended people who had, as Americans, every right to perform whatever they wished.

With his American Theatre, Brown openly contradicted the features of early national theater in New York, introducing a new version of a raced, classed America, even as Euro–New Yorkers continued to refer it as the African Theatre (McAllister 69). Brown used the venue to stage European, African, and Native American identities for Euro– and Afro–New Yorkers, including his own drama, *King Shotaway*, which dramatized the insurrection of the Black Caribs in Saint Vincent, a group descended of Caribs and African Maroons.[20] Brown used innovative seating as well, installing a tripartite configuration that separated the classes but integrated races in the audience and in the orchestra. In the large communal box for the upper classes, black and white patrons quietly intermixed, but from the gallery and pit, chaos emerged as patrons threw objects and yelled comments. Though Brown avoided Shakespeare with the exception of "an aborted *Othello* production in the summer of 1822," his white patrons grew rowdier and more dangerous, culminating in physical violence that same August (76, 142).

Consequently, Brown was forced to temporarily close down after white rioters associated with Stephen Price destroyed the structure, stripped the performers of their costumes, and physically assaulted him and others.[21] The significance of this riot, Dillon convincingly argues, moves beyond financial competition among theater managers and "visibly engaged questions concerning the nature of the U.S. commons and the cultural and racial foundations of nationalism itself (224). Brown's theater insisted on understanding "American" as a racially mixed identity, eliciting in response attacks on both himself and his theater as its embodiment. This crisis of racial and theatrical representation in New York City corresponded with the ongoing national debate about slavery that divided the northern and southern states. Moreover, this 1822 riot erupted in the middle of the July–September news coverage of the failed Denmark Vesey plot in Charleston, coinciding also with the worst yellow-fever outbreak in New York history.

The African Theatre riot punctuated an anxious summer during which Euro–New Yorkers worried about the double threat of insurrection and infection, both thought to emanate, like Brown himself, from the West Indies. Also Caribbean born, Denmark Vesey had likewise served as a ship's steward; both men represented Afro-Caribbean threats to white American privilege, making claims for freedom that highlighted the conflict between American liberatory ideology and racial practice. That hot, fetid summer the New York press avidly followed the story of Vesey and his conspiracy to kill South Carolina slaveholders, liberate the slaves, and sail to Haiti. The *Spectator* published the court reports with details that McAllister likens to a "drama" that fueled racial tensions that culminated in the August riot at Brown's theater (127).

The Vesey "drama" featured another West Indian character that shared a name and a mission with Three-Fingered Jack, Jack Pritchard or "Gullah Jack." One of Vesey's conspirators, this Angolan sorcerer allegedly used and distributed amulets for invincibility in battle, and he thus echoed black magic–practicing rebels like Haiti's Makandal and Jamaican-born Boukman as well as Three-Fingered Jack.[22] Gullah Jack was hanged with thirty-four other conspirators, and though the plot failed, rumors surrounding it continued to circulate even in the northern states. White New Yorkers feared that black insurrection would spread from the South, and alarmist newspaper reports fed growing perceptions of black men as violent aggressors.[23] Gullah Jack and Denmark Vesey would have featured prominently in Brown's reading that summer, and the following June he followed up Gullah Jack with Three-Fingered Jack, bringing to the New York stage another African sorcerer who incited rebellion.

Soon after reopening his theater in 1823, Brown mounted his adaptation of *Obi* on June 7, casting black actors in a production that had long been the cultural and representational domain of white institutions and actors. Brown's production at once responded to the current craze for "stage Africans" and enacted the histories of resistance that so troubled Americans. It was for this production that Brown advertised in his playbill that his "African Company" would be performing William Moncrieff's "musical extravaganza" *Tom and Jerry; or, Life in London* with *Obi; or, Three-Fingered Jack* at the "Theatre, in Mercer Street." As McAllister points out, Brown's "neutral" nomenclature "Theatre, in Mercer Street" does not include "African" in its title (116). The production introduced an expanded company as well as a new scene set, *Life in Limbo, Life in Love: Vango Range in Charleston on the Slave Market.* These three pieces (*Tom and Jerry*, *Life in Limbo*, and *Obi*) bodied forth on the stage transatlantic black characters in different modes of unsettling behavior: dancing in London, suffering on the South Carolina auction block, and rebelling on the Jamaican plantation. Punctuating the evening with *Obi; or, Three-Fingered Jack*, Brown underscored the links between the West Indian and South Carolinian plantations, reminding American audiences of its uncomfortable history with and relation to the former metropole as well as censuring English colonialism in the West Indies and the plantation culture of the South.

From what little we know, Brown's *Obi* bears scant resemblance to the original pantomime. The playbill documents only three characters: the planter, his wife, and the Jack character, "Obi," played by the "terrible big ugly" Mr. Bates (G. Thompson 30).[24] However, with African American actors playing both the Afro- and Anglo-Jamaican characters, Brown's *Obi* dislocated boundaries of race and national identity, black actors performing in whiteface, erasing the white body and privileging blackness. In addition, this scene concluded an evening that had already introduced racially and politically charged material.

Brown's evening opened with *Tom and Jerry; or, Life in London*, and as with *Obi* he took liberties with characters, most notably in casting black American actors as the prostitute "African Sal" and the Afro-Brit coal whipper "Dusty Bob."[25] In London and at the Park Theatre, of course, white actors played these roles; however, Brown cast African American actors for the popular "African" material, mimicking and reversing the politics of minstrelsy. Brown complicated gender as well by casting a man in the role of the prostitute, Sal, leading to some negative reviews: "Dusty Bob and the Negro wench, in their characteristic dance, gave existence to a sensation in many bosoms for which there is no name but disgust" (*New York Mirror*, qtd. in McAllister 118). In addition, Bob and Sal performed a comic pas de deux, a suggestive stage dance reminiscent of the Pinkster festival's Afro-Dutch Totau street dance, anticipating and undercutting the increasing racism of blackface minstrelsy.[26] Like the Pinkster festival, Brown's transgressive representational authority simultaneously entertained and censured white New Yorkers.

In another subversive act, Brown cast the company's single white actor, Mr. Smith, as the watchman who beats Bob. Using a white man in this role both highlighted and lampooned the related institutions of racism and law enforcement. The same actor performed the white auctioneer in the subsequent Charleston scene, bringing into sharp relief the central role of the white man to scenes of violence against black people in the Atlantic world. Using black American men to play white Britons, Anglo-Americans, and African women, the production seized white privilege to interrogate and challenge American and British attitudes toward race and gender.

Brown's slave-market scene *Life in Limbo, Life in Love: Vango Range in Charleston on the Slave Market* heightened the evening's tensions.

The slave-market scene, new to the dyad of *Obi* and *Tom and Jerry*, marked the midpoint of the production, targeting directly the ongoing atrocity of slave trading in the American South. This new piece clearly alluded to Vendue Range, the Charleston market that sold among other items human flesh; though the slave trade had been outlawed federally by 1823, many port cities (including New York City and Charleston) continued to participate illegally. Moreover, this scene overtly recalls the Vesey plot in Charleston. Brown placed the entire black cast on stage in shackles with the white Mr. Smith as auctioneer, reenacting for the mixed-race audience the brutal spectacle of the Atlantic slave trade as well as the love and lives lost to it.[27] The scene places characters on an auction block, aptly representative of limbo, a site of transformation and uncertainty, much like the tenuous and slippery position of African Americans in the young nation.

Brown placed *Life in Limbo* between scenes set in London and Montego Bay, port cities he would likely have visited during his travels as a ship steward. The scenes likewise featured black figures with which he would have been familiar: "free" black (sex and coal) workers, black slaves on the auction block, and black Caribbean rebels. Brown's production—in part a product of his own transatlantic history—can be seen as countering what Sean Goudie calls the "paracolonial discourse" that "negates" the formative presence of the West Indies in the young republic's national character (36).[28] The three pieces together document a range of critical issues surrounding the roles and rights of slaves and free black people during a troubled time in the early national period of United States. That year marked the end of Brown's three-season "African Theatre." New York was not, it appeared, quite ready for black progress. Brown closed his theater at the end of that season due to financial difficulties and lack of support from both white and black patrons.

When the theater closed, Brown's protégé Ira Aldridge moved onto England, where he would continue to complicate boundaries of race and national identity, becoming famous in part for his representation of Three-Fingered Jack. In the hands of black producers of culture like William Brown and Ira Aldridge, John Fawcett's *Obi* acquired a distinctly political register, showing the potential for the figure of Jack to challenge and transform conventions and imperatives of nation and race. Brown and Aldridge generate the spectacular force of black bodies revolutionizing the roles and expectations of Anglo-European writers, actors, and directors.

CHAPTER 4

Being Jack Mansong

IRA ALDRIDGE AND
THREE-FINGERED JACK

In the late 1820s Edinburgh theater manager William Murray adapted John Fawcett's successful pantomime as a melodrama to feature the renowned African American tragedian Ira Aldridge in the title role. Murray's *Obi; or, Three-Finger'd Jack. A Popular Melodrama in Two Acts* opened at the Bristol Theatre Royal in 1830, and, with the charismatic Aldridge giving voice to Jack for the first time, it marks a critical juncture in the history of *Obi* plays (Marshall and Stock 89).[1] Aldridge transformed Jack from a silent villain to a complex vehicle for exposing the problems and repercussions of the slave trade. In 2000 professor Chuck Rzepka produced *Obi: A Play in the Life of Ira Aldridge, the "Paul Robeson" of the 19th Century.*[2] A unique tribute to both Aldridge and Jack, Rzepka's multimedia production challenged traditional forms and representational norms, taking its cues from the renowned actor and the character he famously portrayed. The creative intervention of actors, producers, and directors highlight the ways that the figure of Jack can at once reflect and disrupt the structural racism of institutions (nineteenth-century British theater and twenty-first-century academia) that participate in the cultural production of race.

WILLIAM MURRAY AND THE *OBI* MELODRAMA

Ira Aldridge undoubtedly revolutionized the character of Jack, but he could not decisively shift the tenor of the narrative, even as his representation called into question its evident conservatism. Recent scholarship has made much of Aldridge's contribution to the political valence of Murray's melodrama, and Debbie Lee has intriguingly argued that "the fascinating power of the obi bag . . . emerged complete in the character of Jack as played by Aldridge" ("Grave Dirt" para. 16).[3] Rather than emerging "complete," however, Aldridge fashioned himself into a figure as fragmented and ambiguous as the notorious bandit. In so doing, he suggested the ways that tactical identity shifts can dislocate existing perceptions of black bodies on the stage and in British culture.

Murray's melodrama bears some significant differences from its pantomime predecessors, including an antihero voicing sentiments both more vicious and more sympathetic. In this adaptation Jack kidnaps and threatens to kill Rosa, and he had already murdered her mother, providing a clear reason for ongoing anxiety of the planter (renamed Ormond). At the same time, the script offers Jack's tragic African backstory, creating the motive that had been lacking in the pantomime versions. Though Murray's *Obi* (like the pantomime) concludes with Quashie, Sam, and Tuckey vanquishing Jack, he writes out Quashie's conversion to Christianity and the capture of the obeah woman. Much closer temporally and ideologically in 1830 to emancipation than its pantomime predecessor, Murray's drama introduces an antihero who expressively denounces slavery and racism, giving him voice through Ira Aldridge, who spent much of his career doing the same.

A black actor of ambiguous origin who played a variety of roles—black and white, comedic and tragic—Aldridge embodies the possibilities for challenging racial stereotypes and expectations. Born free and educated at one of two African Free Schools in New York, Aldridge participated in a black intelligentsia that later took a leadership role in the abolitionist movement (Marshall and Stock 27). With his acting career, he traveled across the Atlantic, first to Britain and then throughout Europe. In 1827 the Republic of Haiti gave Aldridge its first state honor, putting this England-residing black American actor on a roster with François-Dominique

Toussaint-Louverture, Jean-Jacques Dessalines, Dutty Boukman, and François Makandal.[4] Like Olaudah Equiano and his manifold identities as described by Paul Youngquist, Ira Aldridge "turns identity diasporic, producing new possibilities for mobility and agency among subjected populations scattered throughout the Black Atlantic by the winds of the Imperial trade ("Afro-Futurism" 185). Aldridge seized and reconceived representation of black identity in the Atlantic world and on the stage.

Aldridge consciously contested white perceptions of black people through the roles he chose and the ways he played them. To nineteenth-century English audiences accustomed to "caricatures of black people," Bernth Lindfors argues, "Aldridge's grace, dignity, versatility—in short his theatrical competence came as a complete surprise, forcing them to reconsider notions they had previously held of Africans, West Indians, African Americans, and indigenous British blacks" (*Ira Aldridge* 92). Contemporary actors, too, admired his work. For example, an article in the *Dublin University Magazine* noted that actor Edmund Kean "complimented [Aldridge] highly" and wrote that he had "considerable talent: and spoke better English than many "native" born (qtd. in Marshall and Stock 103). Taking up new roles, Aldridge switched from black to white to Jew to Moor, demonstrating the performativity of identity and his skill at such performances. He can be understood to have experimented with what Daphne Brooks has insightfully called black actors "'doing' their bodies differently" to defamiliarize the spectacle of blackness and to disrupt traditional constructions of race: "We can think of their acts as opaque, as dark points of possibility that create figurative sites for the reconfiguration of black . . . bodies on display. A kind of shrouding, this trope of darkness paradoxically allows for corporeal unveiling to yoke with the (re)covering and rehistoricizing of the flesh. Dense and spectacular, the opaque per-formances of marginalized cultural figures call attention to the skill of the performer who . . . is able to confound and disrupt conventional construc-tions of the racialized . . . body" (8). In playing characters as different from one another as, for example, Othello and Shylock or Three-Fingered Jack and Mungo (even on the same night) Aldridge appropriated and complicated the racialized and often oppositional roles he performed. "Doing his body differently," Aldridge transformed transatlantic performance culture, honing his skills as a performer and as an arbiter of social change.

Aldridge's career followed a transatlantic route based in part on the kinds of roles available to him as a black actor. He worked with New York's African Grove Theater until it was shut down in 1824, and then he moved to England. In his first season he played five major black roles and earned acclaim for his depiction of Othello. In addition to playing Othello, he took roles set in the Americas that appealed to antislavery sentiments, including Oroonoko in *Revolt of Surinam: The Slave's Revenge* (based on Aphra Behn's novel) and Christophe in J. H. Amherst's *The Death of Christophe, King of Hayti*. He also played the part of Zanga, the Moor, in Edward Young's *The Revenge*; Rolla, the Peruvian army commander, in Richard Brinsley Sheridan's *Pizarro*; and Hassan, the vindictive Moor, in Monk Lewis's *The Castle Spectre*. Because of the prejudice he faced as a black actor, he expanded his repertoire in his first few years in England to make sure he had as much work as possible. Although Aldridge enjoyed great success in the provinces, Ireland, and Scotland, he was never invited for a season at London's major theaters, as he so desired. In 1833 he succeeded Edmund Kean at Covent Garden (after Kean collapsed and then died) for only two nights, to mixed reviews. On the other hand, England's Industrial Revolution galvanized a working-class audience who admired and welcomed Aldridge for his talent (Marshall and Stock vii; Rzepka, introd. to "Obi.").

In juxtaposition to his tragic characters, Aldridge performed comic roles in afterpieces, such as the part of the drunk but clever slave, Mungo, in Isaac Bickerstaff's *The Padlock*. In fact, he often played both Othello and Mungo at the beginning of a provincial tour to demonstrate his breadth as an actor. Many critics found it curious at best that a man of African descent should be performing at one of the British national theaters. The *Spectator* wrote that "the range of characters in which Aldridge could appear must necessarily be very limited. . . . He is said to make a capital Mungo" (qtd. in Marshall and Stock 124–125). The *Morning Post* opined that his complexion was not as dark as "the representatives of Othello generally assume" and that his enunciation was "frequently broad and strikingly un-English" (22). Aldridge was simultaneously criticized for being too African and not African enough, demonstrating the narrow expectations of a British audience that saw him, despite his range as an actor, most clearly as Mungo, the slave.

Aldridge's theatrical experiments, however, appealed to his audiences on the continent and in Russia. When he performed abroad, he spoke English while the other actors spoke their native languages; thus the international audiences were obliged to focus on Aldridge's gestures and expressions, prompting "perceptive reviews from foreign critics who paid much closer attention to his interpretation and did not expect him to imitate a preconceived model" (Marshall and Stock xvi). Aldridge thus made the characters his own.

In one of his most revolutionary moves, Aldridge took on white roles, and he may well have been the first black actor to use whiteface.[5] He played a variety of Shakespeare characters, including Shylock, Richard III, Macbeth, and King Lear. Notably, as the first actor in 128 years to revive *Titus Andronicus*, Aldridge took liberties with the script, arranging to have it blended with a melodrama by an Irish playwright to render Aaron, the Moor, as a sympathetic hero rather than a villain (Lindfors, *Ira Aldridge* 349). Likewise, in Saint Petersburg he transformed the role of Shylock to a sympathetic character, reinterpreting and rewriting the ending to suit his purposes.

Aldridge's whiteface roles censor and reverse the practice of blackface common to the period. Saidiya Hartman proposes that white actors in blackface demonstrate to themselves and their audiences their possession of the black body, proposing that such "elasticity" permits "white self-exploration" while defining and maintaining whiteness (29). In whiteface Aldridge takes possession of the white body, interrogating issues of race while defining and reclaiming his own black body from white representation. In both white and black roles, Aldridge manipulated the cultural production of race.

Aldridge likewise manipulated the production of his personal identity. Most accounts of his life claim that he was born in New York, but some indicate that he was born in Maryland. His 1849 *Memoir* alternately claims that he descended from a line of princes in Senegal—a myth that theater playbills and publicity material perpetuated. He acquired a number of stage names, including "Mr. Keene, Tragedian of Colour" (1825), "F. W. Keene Aldridge, the African Roscius" (1831), and "Mr. Aldridge (A Native of Senegal) known by the appellation of The African Roscius" (1833) (qtd. in Carlson, "Race and Profit" 184). Aldridge came to British audiences with a layering of names, characters, and identities that he expertly deployed to market himself. His multiplicity of identity positioned him to evade stereotyping or typecasting while capitalizing on his skills. Moreover, his indeterminate identity opened up myriad possibilities for him professionally, personally, and socially. Aldridge's complicated identical layers suited him to the role of Jack Mansong, a likewise ambiguous and prismatic figure, and he took advantage of the representative possibilities.

Ira Aldridge used Jack Mansong's ambiguity to create a more complex character that articulated the horrors of slavery and plantation culture. The character of Jack presents an excess of identity, a suffering victim and evil villain: Karfa and Jack. Aldridge's voice made it possible for his audience to understand the motives of Karfa/Jack in ways that the silent Jack of Fawcett's pantomime could not do. Jack's African name, Karfa, links him to his preslavery past, to a homeland from which he is irreparably torn. To his mother Karfa vows to avenge that separation: "As Africa receded from my gaze I swore that the first white man who purchased Karfa's services should also feel his hate" (Murray 9). Occupying the positions of both the wronged African and the vengeful slave, Jack represents a surplus of difference that in the world of melodrama must be stripped down and expunged from the community for the restoration of order on the plantation to occur (see Cox and Van Kooy).

Jack's missing fingers, his identifying absence, mark his difference from the other slaves. His mutilated body signifies what Brooks refers to as "strangeness": a "body that defies a singular context and a national culture (29). Writing about Dion Boucicault's mid-nineteenth century drama, *The Octoroon*, Brooks suggests that this kind of strange figure is "a body without a nation, and yet like the sideshow freak, the transatlantic body in performance is repeatedly called on to forge some kind of national consciousness, at the very moment in which its figure exposes and affirms the tenuousness of nationalism and its fictions" (29). In Murray's melodrama with Aldridge as Jack, the rebel's three-fingered hand tells a story of loss and retribution, of lost nation and mutilated culture.[6] Like Jack's dismembered body that defies "singular context or national culture," the transatlantic Aldridge in the mobility that defined his career and his public identity offered alternative identifications.

Jack's dismembered body may likewise be likened to the "dismembered corpse" of drama, or as it was referred to in *The Satirist*, "The Monster Melodrama" (Cox and Gamer xvii). Murray's shift from pantomime to melodrama permits the performance to voice Jack's vengeance, a tactical move that seems strangely appropriate, given the generic excesses of the form itself. Brooks has argued that an excess in character has been borne out in "multiple, parallel, converging, and intersecting acts of surrogation" that is related to the excess of racial melodramas: "Within this context, excess should be understood as an articulation of the heterogeneous complexities of bodies and identities in nineteenth-century transatlantic culture. These racial melodramas consistently reconstitute order—presenting and exposing excessive bodies in order to finally purge them from the narrative altogether" (41). In its heterogeneity, this type of melodrama has been critically entwined with other nineteenth-century genres, including the pantomime, sentimental fiction, and minstrelsy.[7] Murray's *Obi* in particular reflects the imbricating of genres characteristic of the melodrama, enveloping as it does its previous incarnations of the narrative. Jack's vengeance, his moral ambiguity, and his "strangeness," require the purging of his body from the narrative.

Jack's "strangeness," embodied by his three-fingered hand, his rebellious spirit, and his eloquent language, separates him from his peers, a difference registered even more pointedly by Aldridge's black body on the stage among the white bodies in blackface. Jack first appears in a scene with the obeah woman—his mother—uttering promises of vengeance on white men in general and Ormond in particular: "Years have elapsed since I sacrificed the wife of the white man, a victim to the memory of my beloved Olinda, whom they tore lifeless from these arms as they dragged me from my native land; can I forget? Never" (Murray 9). Jack's speech positions him as a victim of the slave trade, driven to revenge by desperation and grief over the loss of his wife and family. This interaction becomes a crucial moment of the melodrama, because it underscores his position as simultaneously wronged and wrongdoing.

Jack's interaction with Rosa, a far cry from Fawcett's alleged hint at interracial desire, likewise demonstrates his dual status as victim and villain. Rosa's pleas for mercy elicit from him the most affecting language of the melodrama: "You whites are ever ready to enforce for one another that civilized, that Christian law of mercy which our dusky children never yet partook of" (Murray 22). Rosa appeals to his pity for an "aged father," to which Jack responds, employing language reminiscent of the rhetoric of the British Abolition Society:

> *I* had a daughter once; did they spare her harmless infancy: Where is my wife? Was *she* spared to me? No! With blood and rapine the white man swept like a hurricane o'er our native village, and blasted every hope! Can aught efface the terrible remembrance from my soul, how at their lordly feet we begged for mercy and found it not. Our women knelt, our infants shrieked in vain, as the blood-stained murderer ranged from hut to hut, dragging the husband and the father from their homes, to sell them into bondage! No more, no more! The vext spirits of my wife and child hover o'er me like a holy curse, and claim this due revenge. (22–23)

Jack's expressive depiction of the violence visited on his family, his village, and his nation brings to the fore the trauma and villainy of the European slave trade, and Aldridge would have performed these lines with the dignity of an experienced Shakespearean actor. Jack concludes this speech by raising his dagger and preparing to murder Rosa, but Quashie (who is soon joined by Sam and Tuckey) intervenes. Jack's quick demise in an unfair three-to-one fight permits him to say his piece without in fact exacting his revenge. Jack's death reinstates the social and moral order that the melodrama sought to make apparent to its audiences.

Jack's tragic story encourages audiences to sympathize with his motives for revenge while condemning him for his crimes, and Aldridge specialized in holding in tension charges of victim and criminal. But in the final scene Jack's villainy outweighs his pathos. The audience already knows that Jack had "attempted the honour" of Rosa's mother and then murdered her, and in the final scene he prepares to kill Rosa. At that very moment, Quashie jumps in to save her. In this moment of judgment, Aldridge would have portrayed Jack feelingly as a tragic antihero, destined to die for his crimes; however, the narrative perpetuates stereotypes of black men as potentially violent criminals unless they can be contained, manipulated, or reformed. The final tableau positions Quashie, Sam, and Tuckey with Ormond, Rosa, and "the other characters," grouped behind Jack, who "dies amidst the shouts of the SOLDIERS and NEGROES" (24). The colonial military and plantation system, then, enforces social control by pitting black men against one another. Like his obeah-practicing mother, Jack represents that which must be exorcised from an otherwise harmonious society.

The melodrama reduces the role of the obeah woman to a single appearance in her cave. Murray gives voice to her vengeful but entirely ineffective incantations, and her spell threatens to torture and, sicken, and kill white men:

Like a cankerous thorn in the white man's heart—
Till I pierce him and wring him in nerve and spleen

By arrows felt, but never seen.

Then by flame unbodied burn him,

Then on racking windlass turn him,

Till his sinews quiver and ache anew,

And the cold sweat falls like drops of dew,

Toil him and moil him again and again,

Sicken his heart and madden his brain;

Till strength, and sense, and life depart;

As I tear the last pulse from the white man's heart. (8)

Unequivocally malevolent, the obeah woman imagines the physical and mental torture she will inflict on the white man. Her hostile words reinforce stereotypes about African culture and rebellion on the plantation; however, she cows not even her own son with her power. Jack calls her "hag" and scorns her obeah powers as "mummery." When she exhorts him to respect her, he replies, "Thy power is in the fear of thy votaries—and fear I know not" (9). Though he accepts her charms in his obeah horn, he privileges his dagger as the only charm he trusts. The audience does not see the obeah woman again. She appears on stage only to function as an obsolete symbol of African culture and resistance in the Caribbean. Like Jack, she lives outside the boundaries of the plantation, an abject reject of plantation life.

The isolated evil duo of Jack and his mother indicate both the persistence of black resistance in Jamaica and its decline. In the melodrama Jack lives and fights alone, his reviled mother as his only associate.[8] Jack believes his isolation functions as security for him, assuming Rosa's search party will be unable to find her in his jungle nooks. "In these wild glens,—old nature's fortresses, which they fear to penetrate, I breathe again," he boasts, employing Maroon strategies of surprise attack and camouflage (22). Without associates to patrol the hideout or call out warnings, however, Jack (and his mother) fail at their endeavors. Jack's isolation marks him as the last vestige of black resistance in his fictional universe.

Jack condemns the institution of plantation slavery, but the drama leaves room for the individual planters to redeem themselves. His enslaved counterparts work together to uphold and protect the interests of their benevolent master.

Murray's colonial characters radiate warmth and good will. The staging directs the slaves to gather around Ormond "shouting, and expressing great affection for him" (5). Ormond, in turn, refers to them as "friends" and apprises them of the arrival of their friend and champion, the captain. Conversely, the slaves perceive, as the only true threat to their peaceful existence, a "savage" who terrifies them and distresses their kind master. Ormond explains to his overseer that Jack has been resistant to his kindness:

> Long had he been on the estate, and long had every art been tried to soothe his savage nature, for Heaven knows I pitied the unfortunates, and strove by kindness and humanity to mitigate their cruel lot. With Karfa (so he was then named) alone, my efforts failed; each day but added to his ferocity: crime followed crime until the villain dared to attempt the honor of my wife. The signal punishment which awaited him drove him to madness, and under shade of night he burst his bonds, broke into my chamber, and before my sight murdered my unhappy wife.

Ormond describes Jack/Karfa's ferocious criminality and escalating madness, culminating in the murder of his "unhappy wife," despite the planter's efforts to bring the rebel into the fold. Ormond, then, functions as the protector of the slaves and innocent victim of Jack's wrath. A good father, a good master, and a good employer, he treats those around him as an extended family, bullied by the "monstrous wretch" who still lurks on the margins of the plantation, presumably waiting to subject Ormond's daughter to the same fate as his wife (5).

Ormond plays the model planter, ameliorating the institution (plantation slavery) to "mitigate" the lot of the slaves who had suffered cruel lot of Karfa ("so then he was named"), before the abolition of the trade. Aldridge thus would have played Jack as figure whose past experience—as Karfa—created the "monstrous wretch" he has become (5). "It was the torment of slavery that produced such resolute 'monsters,'" Lindfors argues, and "Aldridge would have had a stake in challenging such assumptions by humanizing such villains and making their animosity toward white oppressors comprehensible" (*Ira Aldridge* 178). Murray's melodrama distinguishes the plantation Jack from the African Karfa, the planter Ormond from his counterpart white oppressors, and the Quashie and Sam from the other slaves.

If Jack represents a menace to and an outcast from plantation society, Quashie and Sam represent successfully integrated slaves. In act 1, scene 6, Quashie sings the wistful song, "Ackee, O!" from *Paul and Virginie* (11–12). Invoking the play based on the novel by Jacques-Henri Bernardin de Saint-Pierre (1787), this scene reifies the vision of a new world utopia.[9] The happy slave characters also instill Murray's *Obi* with elements of the minstrelsy, providing a low comedic element and a bucolic example of the simple pleasures of black folk on the plantation. Quashie and Sam, with their pseudo patois, embody stock "darky" figures. Good-natured family men and affectionate toward "massa," these characters promote unity among the slaves. For example, Quashie rounds up the other slaves to celebrate the wedding of Captain Orford and Missee Rosa: "Haste Haste, my merry hearts. This night good buckra man give dance and much kous kous." Quashie sends for Jonkonnu to "get him big head on, and all dansa, dansa, like mad" (11). Act 1, scene 7, begins with a celebration, the slaves singing while the burlesque Jonkonnu performs a "comic dance" (12). Ornamented with bells and feathers, the Jonkonnu represents regulated and Anglicized African and indigenous culture on the plantation, the epitome of what Hartman calls "black enjoyment" (23).

Nineteenth-century audiences were particularly fascinated by the portrayal of innocent amusements "enjoyed" by slaves at either the command or the leisure of the planter. The figure of the dancing slave on display,

Hartman explains, seem to suggest a "comfort with bondage and a natural disposition for servitude" (23). On the plantations, these amusements made "discipline a pleasure or vice versa," and they were constitutive of "harnessing the body" for successful plantation management (43).[10] Act 1 begins and concludes with celebration and song, thus emphasizing the contentment of the slaves and consequently obscuring the violence of plantation life for the audience. The overseer initiates the holiday: "Adieu to labour! Let the sugar canes take care of themselves and hey for mirth and merriment!" (4). Dismissing the sugar cane, he glosses over the hard work of the plantation and the foundation of the slave trade, sugarcoating its tyranny. By giving and taking away pleasure at his will, the planter and overseer exert control over their slaves.

Ormond confirms the purity of loyal slaves' motives by rewarding them with the promise of freedom: "My gallant hearts, your courage shall not go unrewarded; and as the first proof of my bounty, no more my slaves—be free! (Negroes shout.) Fear not [Jack's] wily stratagems—his magic art—all will fail before the arm that's nerved by freedom and by gratitude" (Murray 14). Ormond claims that "freedom and gratitude" are more powerful than subterfuge or superstition, thus invoking a secular, emancipationist discourse. The melodrama *Obi* imagines a slave society organically evolving into an orderly, hierarchical, Anglo-centric Jamaica. The loyal Afro-Jamaicans and benevolent Anglo-Jamaicans keep in place the unequal relationship of enslaved to the dominant.[11]

The characters of Tuckey and Kitty—a free black and a mixed-race house servant—complicate this otherwise neat social hierarchy by blurring the boundaries of black and white, free and enslaved. Tuckey first appears in a scene set in the planter's house. Unlike the bare-legged Quashie and Sam dressed in striped dresses, Tuckey dons a military uniform livery jacket to indicate his English-identified status as the captain's servant. Both Tuckey and Kitty speak Standard English and live in the big house rather than the huts of the slaves. Tuckey first speaks to Kitty with authority, bidding her to "Be brisk . . . my pretty maid," presumably calling on his superior rank and experience. Kitty answers haughtily, "Pray, where did you learn to forget the difference between black and white, my dingy spark?"[12] He responds, "In England, my dear, where truth to speak, though I saw many pretty damsels, I saw none that could in any way compare with you" (Murray 7). Tuckey's allusion to his life in England and his compliment pacify Kitty, who finds him not quite as "dingy" as she first thought. Jerrold Hogle has proposed that "[Tuckey] is a once-enslaved but now free black; no longer a slave but still only a servant; a spokesman for freedom but the final shooter of Jack; a playful critic of many situations (like the Fool in *King Lear*) but devoted to the safety and interests of his white master, Captain Orford" (para. 13). The Jamaica of the *Obi* melodrama presents with these characters the creolized and complicated culture of the colonial West Indies.

Tuckey's playful exchange with Kitty prompts him to reflect on more serious social issues. When she leaves the room, he says to the audience, "Ah, we poor blacks have a weary time of it, and are as much railed at as if the darkness of the skin were a sample of the colour of our hearts" (Murray 7). His subsequent song, "Possum up a Gum Tree," celebrates the wiliness of the oppressed, comparing a free but still-exploited black man to an opossum chased up a tree by a raccoon who manages to escape the situation. As both Jeffrey N. Cox and Jerrold Hogle note, this song functions as a critique of racial hierarchies. The final verse evokes the taboo of interracial desire:

> Black boy him love Jill Jenkins,
> Tink he'll wed—t'ink he'll wed,
> His massa chide him thinking,
> Beat him head—beat him head. (7)

Tuckey's song suggests that even a free black man would be punished for the transgressive flirtation between himself and the mixed-race Kitty; his status is not entirely removed from that of his enslaved brethren. The following verse alludes to the stereotype of the black man's intemperate desire for liquor ("Black boy love his rum, too") as well as for white (or lighter) women (8).[13] Tuckey's criticism of socioracial attitudes, however, is undermined by his ultimate commitment to the plantocracy. In addition, Tuckey's song, "Opossum up a Gum Tree," carries a complex history that follows a labyrinthine path back to Ira Aldridge, a free black man who did in fact marry a white woman.

By 1830 the song "Opossum up a Gum Tree" had become part of Ira Aldridge's repertoire beyond the *Obi* plays, by way of the white British comic actor Charles Mathews. Mathews visited New York in 1822 on a tour dedicated in part to learning about and marketing black characters for his one-man sketches, and he claims to have seen the song performed by a "black tragedian in the character of Hamlet" at Brown's Theatre, on Mercer Street, which he called the "Niggers' theatre." Mathews claimed that the audience interrupted the "to be or not to be" soliloquy, mishearing "opossum" for "oppose them" (or perhaps hearing the actor correctly) and demanding the song. Mathews adopted the song into his *Mr. Mathews's Trip to America* (1824), in an alleged imitation of Aldridge, "burlesquing 'the preposterous notion' of blacks performing Shakespeare" (McAllister 158).[14] Aldridge later claimed in his memoir that Mathews invented the whole thing: "I never attempted the character of Hamlet in my life, and I need not say that the whole of the ludicrous scene as described by Mr. Mathews, never occurred at all" (11). Although Mathews specifies that he saw the "Kentucky Roscius" perform and thus not Aldridge, "the African Roscius," Aldridge profited from the misunderstanding by including the popular "Oposum" song in his own repertoire, responding to and mimicking Mathews. As Cox puts it, the "song provides a way for Aldridge to claim "a kind of metatheatrical signature, a way of signifyin[g] that this [obeah] has been made into his play" (para. 12). His performance of Mathews mimics, challenges, and appropriates English representations of African American culture. His performance of a white man performing a black man indicates his "possession" of both the white and black body.

In the role of Three-Fingered Jack, Aldridge played and revised the white man's construction of a black man. With eloquent speeches and a dignified stage presence, Aldridge moved beyond "the terrible, big ugly Mr. Bates" of Brown's African Theatre, his former theatrical home. He thus challenged nineteenth-century constructions and productions of race in England and the United States, upending racist hierarchies and "doing" his own black body the ways and for the reasons he wished. In both white and black roles, Aldridge transformed transatlantic performance culture.

Ira Aldridge deployed his layered identity. Uniting his experiences as a black actor fighting for racial equality, Aldridge mined the spaces between the archive and the repertoire—between written and embodied history. He garnered international fame and secured a space of honor at Shakespeare's birthplace for his accomplishments, despite Charles Mathews's popular opinion that black man should not perform Shakespeare. Despite also the overdetermined conclusion of Murray's racial melodrama, Aldridge's powerful portrayal of the Jamaican folk hero gave voice to the radical sentiments suggested and suppressed by the text (and genre) of the melodrama and circumscribed by nineteenth-century British theater culture.

Obi in Boston and Tempe

In July 2000 Boston University professor Chuck Rzepka produced *Obi: A Play in the Life of Ira Aldridge*, the first of a two-city, two-performance event that combined material from the nineteenth-century *Obi* plays within a narrative framework and interspersed it with academic papers. Actor-director Vincent Earnest Siders directed and narrated the first performance for the Boston Playwrights' Theatre on the Boston University campus, a small, professional theater founded in 1981 by Saint Lucian Nobel laureate Derek Walcott and with connections to the English and Theater Departments at Boston University. That September, University of Arizona professor Jerrold Hogle directed the North American Society for the Study of Romanticism (NASSR) version for primarily white academics attending the conference at Arizona State University. These performances-as-text follow the story of Jack Mansong as it moved across the Atlantic from London to Boston, from Boston inland to Tempe, and to its virtual home on the *Romantic Circles* Praxis Series (RCPS) website. The resulting multimedia event (available on website and DVD) intriguingly engages different voices and genres to at once perform and inscribe the history of "Three-Fingered Jack."[15]

The RCPS provides a fitting locale for the dissemination of a circum-Atlantic narrative, giving it a global reach. The RCPS mission statement asserts a dedication to "using computer technologies to investigate critically the languages, cultures, histories, and theories of Romanticism" and commits to "mapping out this terrain with the best and most exciting critical writing of contemporary Romanticist scholarship." In its use of new media, RCPS combines traditional written work with the dynamic collaborative energy of computer technology. The RCPS adapts a traditionalist field to accommodate a changing profession, updating romantic period scholarship for the twenty-first century.

Rzepka's *Obi* embraces the same kind of collaborative innovation and contemporization. In its amalgamation of written texts and performance culture; its use of new media to include participants from around the globe; its engagement of directors of different places and backgrounds; and its complication of seemingly straightforward narrative trajectories, it creates an example of literary and cultural creolization. The somewhat awkwardly inserted scholarly papers into the performance raise questions about the role of the academy in the face of twenty-first-century racial problems. They ask, for example, what can these white scholars say or write to fix the problems of institutionalized racism? In form and content Rzepka's project complicates white American assumptions about race and the institutions that participate in its production.

Rzepka, Siders, and Hogle worked to foster conversations among participants and audience, self-consciously addressing the historical, ideological, and theoretical problems the script confronts. The Boston and Tempe performances followed a two-part format that used key scenes from the 1800 pantomime (part 1) and from Murray's melodrama as it was performed for the Drury Lane Theatre in London (part 2).[16] The second acts emphasized the differences between the pantomime and the melodrama, highlighting the social and political transformations of the decades between them.[17] The productions repeated (with a difference) the same scenes, staged differently, especially the finales, to address the concerns and expectations of their different audiences.[18] Siders's direction of *Play in the Life of Ira Aldridge* pays homage to Aldridge, deconstructing the offensive racism of the script. Hogle shocks his audience with offensive material to emphasize the "setting of black against black" in a "deliberate picture of a large-scale white supremacy . . . educating whites out of their complacency *even on stage* by awakening them all . . . to what the horrors of slavery really meant in ways the Anglos surrounding him had not recognized before" (para. 8). Rzepka, too, addresses this "amnesia" with a project intended to "educate, celebrate, and inspire" ("Obi Now" para. 15). Like representations of Three-Fingered Jack for more than two centuries, the millennial *Obi* explores the priorities and expectations of its producers, cast, crew, and audience.

Vincent Siders's creative staging of the Boston *Obi* responds to questions raised by the inherently racist script, especially those surrounding race and its representation. He deploys against it a structure of engagement and collaboration characteristic of African American theater traditions, adopting, for example, a storytelling or griot stance and using methods such as call-and-response, community participation, and improvisation. Uniting his roles as director and narrator, he guides and performs the narrative. The performance begins with a monologue. The audience cannot yet see Siders, who sits on the darkened stage, but hears his disembodied voice telling a story about "Poppa Bear" looking for honey (Rzepka, *Obi*).

This monologue, Rzepka explains, functions as a riff on the African American tradition on folk tales, as controversially popularized by white author Joel Chandler Harris, but for, for Siders, the Poppa Bear story carries an additional register (e-mail). Siders attributes the story to his "Theater Father," his Poppa Bear, James Spruill, an African American professor of fine arts at Boston University. The two men had become good friends and collaborators, and Spruill asked him to take over the direction of the *Obi* play, which Siders, as he explains, came to see as a "hornets nest":

> One day Brother Bear was walking along when he saw Poppa Bear sitting by the side of the road with a big brown honey pot by his feet. "Brother Bear, I'm tired. It's hot, my feet hurt, I got a crick in my back, and this pot is so heavy. Would you mind being kind and bring it on home for me?" "With pleasure!" Brother Bear answered, picking up the pot and merrily continuing on his merry way as he fantasized about the goodies soon to be had. But little did he know that inside that pot was a hornet's nest. (Instant message)

In this allegory, Siders ("Brother Bear") helped Spruill ("Poppa Bear") carry the weight of a project that, despite its ostensibly sweet enticement, holds within a world of stings. However, despite the pain, Siders concludes, his "fondest memory of the evening" came just after curtain call: "I locked eyes with Poppa Bear from across the room. He bowed. I bowed back. And it was done" (instant message). The Poppa Bear story, then, serves as both a riff on Uncle Remus stories and a reflection on projects that bring together academic and African American theater communities; it reveals the "hornet's nest" of issues that surround the representation of racist history in contemporary contexts.

When the stage lights come on, the audience sees Siders sitting on the stage in a chair, holding the *Obi* script; in this scene Siders describes to the audience the problems he faced working with the *Obi* text and his initial resistance to it. In storytelling mode Siders describes his first encounter with the script for *Obi: A Play in the Life of Ira Aldridge*, and his commentary enacts elements of his Afrocentric theatrical approach. Reading aloud from the script, he calls into being the actors who perform the first act of the pantomime with the duet of Sam's and Quashie's wives:

> The white man comes, and brings his gold—
> The slaver meet him on the Bay—
> And, oh, poor negro then be sold,
> From home poor negro sails away.
> Oh, it be very, very sad to see
> Poor negro child and father part—
> But if white man kind massa be,
> He heal the wound in negro's heart.

Siders interrupts the actors, cutting them off in midsong.[19] Repeating aloud in a mocking tone the lyrics of the offending song, he holds up the script as the actors stand back, looking surprised and confused. Siders's disruption invites the audience and actors to question the lyrics that praise the kind white master for comforting his homesick slaves, healing the "wound in negro's heart." Still in character—playing himself as potential director—Siders "calls" producer Chuck Rzepka on the phone to indignantly ask him the leading question: "What were you thinking [giving me this racist script]?" In doing so, Sider baldly questions the validity of reproducing racist sentiments even for educational reasons (Rzepka, *Obi*).

Siders-as-director draws Rzepka into a discussion that brings difficult racial issues and production problems to center stage. Rzepka responds with "Obi Now," the first academic paper of the evening, performing the role of himself, a white romantic period scholar and producer of the event. The interweaving of oral and scribal traditions highlights the production's hybrid form and the tensions it generates. Acting out the concerns of the white producer and the black director for members of the Boston University community, Harvard students, and a professional African American theater community, the Boston *Obi* creates a space to explore the problems of mounting the nineteenth-century British representations of race (and racial issues) on the twenty-first-century mixed-race stage.

Siders remembers the tensions that accompanied these explorations and his efforts to "drive the point that . . . love for Romantic literature and satisfying academic curiosity were not enough." For example, he describes what he calls, "The Blackface Debate." He wanted to use blackface, but some of his colleagues worried that younger peers would be "turned off":

> I wanted to use this opportunity to shift the symbolism from one of mockery to revolution. The debate ensued long into the night. The next night I sat in the dressing room, wearing the *Obi* costume, waiting for my final entrance and still unsure what to do. Suddenly it came to me. I coated the inside of my fingers with the black grease paint, then made my way onstage. At the end of my monologue and as the scene reached its climactic peak, I stroked the three fingers from forehead to chin, leaving three black stripes, and backed off stage. . . . Reason being, I wanted to use this opportunity to shift the symbolism from one of mockery to revolution (instant message).

Self-consciously shifting an act of "mockery" to one of "revolution," Siders performed the performance of blackface, literally painting his face while on stage. In doing so, he supplements a radical "reading" of the romantic text by radically embodying stage conventions of the nineteenth century. "We had some knock down drag outs," he relates, "but out of it came a genuine understanding" (instant message).

Siders interspersed the Boston performance with seemingly improvisational or unscripted moments between acts. In these interstitial moments the performers moved in and out of character roles, extending the discussions and problems proposed by the text and provoked by the director. For example, after the action of the part 1 finale, Tuckey raises up Jack's head, and the cast freezes on the stage with arms upraised. At this silent moment the lights darken, and the booming hip-hop music of "Can't Truss it" by Public Enemy erupts. The cast members toss around the amputated head like a basketball, calling to mind contemporary sounds and images of urban life.[20] The "pick-up game" with Jack's head suggests the criticism of socioeconomic and racial problems in inner-city America. The Boston audience would have recognized the political and aesthetic implications of the hip-hop interlude, especially staged directly after and against the standard pantomime fare of the finale.[21]

Part 2 opens with another such moment. The audience "overhears" the actors discussing the difficulty of attracting cast members for the production and the related issues surrounding the representation of race:

VOICE 1: When we talked on the phone, she was game, but then she read the script.

VOICE 2: How do you want me to play this? I've never played a black man before.

VOICE 3: He's not a black man; it's a stereotype.

VOICE 4: "Now my black beauties, silence your ebony pipes." That's my favorite line.

VOICE 3: That's been cut.

The first voice seems to allude to the absconsion of a prospective cast member, likely a black woman who backed out after reading the script. The third voice (probably Siders) responds to the second voice (definitely the white woman who played Tuckey), addressing the constructed nature of race and gender and the attendant constructions of stereotyping. The fragmented nature of this conversation, in part discussing the fragmented script, underscores the problems of staging the play with any semblance of ideological coherence. These scene-between-the-scene segments welcome the audience into the inner workings of the performance, opening it up for reflection. The conversation calls attention to the performance as a text that evolves and changes as it moves through the hands and minds of those who struggle with it.

Siders rewrote the final scene, enacting his vision for the narrative and combining his roles as narrator, actor, and director.[22] At the moment when

Quashie lunges to give Jack the fatal blow, Siders interrupts the action and enters the stage dressed in the obeah woman's costume. He calls on Jack, Tuckey, Sam, and Quashie to change their actions to foster social change:

> To AUDIENCE: Enough! Enough. I read this over a thousand times. You know, it always ends the same. But, I think it's about time for a change.
>
> To JACK: Jack, rise . . . your work is not done. . . . Come forth, my friend. Your name will continue to reign in story and in legends. You will continue to be an inspiration to all of us. I thank you. For your strength, for your fortitude, for your courage—for your willingness to take that step that would eventually leave you hunted, hated, and honored.
>
> To TUCKEY: Free black! It is time you too had a change of mind. You have been offered privilege. You have seen things others have not. It is time to use that resourcefulness to assist your people in their liberation.

Siders changes the script, permitting Jack to live on as a force of inspiration and strength. He flips Tuckey's script too, urging him to break his alliance with the white colonial structure that employs methods of divide and conquer and to instead join Jack in the common project of liberation.[23] Siders participates in that very project, disrupting the nineteenth-century texts and proposing alternatives to them. Moreover, in through the Boston Playwrights' Theatre, he works with members of the Boston University community to change the ways that academia and community theater respectively work. Like the obeah woman whose dress he dons, he functions as a conduit between worlds.

Finally, Siders-as-obeah-woman directs Sam and Quashie to "take back the tale of Three-Fingered Jack" to the plantation, to reclaim and amend it. Invoking obeah, he announces that the rebel escaped by way of magic: "How suddenly he disappeared, slipped through your fingers. Once again, the magic of obeah" (Rzepka *Obi*). Siders-as-director, likewise directs his cast and audience to "take back the tale," suggesting that they rewrite their history and rethink their future. He explains his theory about the ritual of theater as a way to transcend time and space: "For me theatre is ritual, and in this case, an opportunity to reshape time, space, and minds. At this moment the past, present, and future converged. The present was used to shift the past in order to shape the future. Ira was a revolutionary. Still, because of his time, there were limitations. Dressed as [the] Obi [woman] I assumed the power to give voice to Ira in the present day" (instant message). As actor, director, master of ceremonies, griot, visionary, and revolutionary, Siders—like Aldridge—"does his body differently" (Brooks 8).

In September 2000 Jerrold Hogle directed the second part of the production, now titled *Obi; or, Three-Fingered Jack (1800–1830): Selections with Commentary*. Hogle tailored the performance for the expectations of a mostly white academic audience attending a romanticism conference in a (very white) college town outside of Phoenix. This location posed challenges in casting, particularly in drawing racially diverse actors, and it resulted in an all-white cast except for the black single actor (Walter Becher) playing Jack. Though Hogle remarks that he created "a deliberate picture of a large-scale white supremacy," he also acknowledged the struggles of attracting black cast members to the production (para. 7). With no little consideration, Rzepka and Hogle addressed the representation of racial identity by using masks to indicate the race of the characters to avoid the offensive use of blackface to speak to the construction of race. In terms of cast and audience, then, the Tempe *Obi* reproduced the conditions of Aldridge's performance. As Catherine Burroughs rightly has noted, Hogle valuably contributes to the current theorizing of romantic drama by highlighting "this tension between intent and reception" (384).

Hogle's essay, "Directing *Obi* in 2000," explains his directorial choices, and his reflective and culturally sensitive piece addresses the particular challenges posed by directing a performance that grapples with such offensive material. Hogle views his academic audience as more interested than Boston's in "something approaching historical recreation, a reenactment of the cultural conditions and theater conventions, as well as the ideologies and imperialism, of a period and a 'Romantic' England they had all studied for years" (para. 7). Rzepka and Hogle both acknowledge that as white producers of a nineteenth-century racial melodrama, they tread on delicate ground, and these concerns inform their theatrical methods. The Tempe *Obi* therefore approaches the performance of blackness by way of what Saidiya Hartman calls "white self-exploration" and empathy, which poses its own set of problems.

In her discussion of abolitionist John Rankin's descriptions of slavery, Hartman proposes that his identification with (his "slipping into" the captive's body) highlights the problems with the very idea of empathy: "The ease of Rankin's empathetic identification is as much due to his good intentions and heartfelt opposition to slavery as to the fungibility of the captive's body" (19). Rankin, the empathetic abolitionist, recalls Wordsworth's poet, who in the act of composition "slips" into his subject's mind for the sake of pleasure: "[It] brings his feelings near to those of the persons whose feeling he describes, nay, for short spaces of time, perhaps to let himself *slip* into an entire delusion, and even confound and identify his own feelings with theirs" (Wordsworth and Coleridge, 104). The white actor performing the black character (or the sensitive poet, in composition) permits the exploration and appropriation of the other. Hartman explains "The . . . loosening of the strictures of identity enabled by blackface mask in turn fortified a repressive and restrictive reception of blackness, which, although elastic enough to permit white self-exploration, could not trespass the parameters established to maintain racial hierarchies" (29).[24] With its largely white cast and audience and with the inherent racism of the script, the Tempe *Obi* would inevitably uphold the illusion of white "integrity or wholeness" (32). However, Rzepka's and Hogle's innovative production and direction extends what could have been a mere moment of white self-exploration into a critical ontology that revises romantic scholarship.

The NASSR *Obi* in its empathetic identification shifts Hartman's arc of "white exploration, renunciation, and *enjoyment*" (26–29) to a movement of white exploration, renunciation, and *discomfort*. Chuck Rzepka addresses the responsibility of white scholars to identify not with the enslaved but with the enslavers. He underscores the painful nature of this task, "an effort that is, in some ways, even more painful than imagining what it must have been like to be black in the slave-holding West . . . the painful effort of identification with our own forebears' bigotry, callousness, and cruelty—an indifference to suffering made all the more appalling, it seems to me, by their negligent, everyday acceptance of it" ("Obi Now" para. 8). Hogle too acknowledges this painful identification, admitting that he chose to highlight the most shocking aspects of the *Obi* play, despite their capacity to disturb or unsettle: "If a revival of *Obi* is unsettling, that is all to the good in the view of all of us who participated" (para. 17). He elaborates, "I believe that the 1800 *Obi* was similarly monumental, graphic, and insistent to its audience in cathecting all racial conflict and arguments over slavery ultimately onto the severed head of Jack . . . and through his sacrificial destruction, seeming to eradicate this teeming cacophony from the Empire with deliberate force, supposedly to the benefit of slaves and masters alike" (para. 11). Rzepka's *Obi* project urges scholars of romanticism to remember and explore the assumptions, values, and legacies of racial hierarchies that many people might wish to forget.

Rzepka's ambitious *Obi* project aimed to "make visible to us our own acts of denial in the present, our own cultural amnesia, as we watch ourselves being 'led out' into other, historically specific acts of denial" ("Obi Now" para. 10). Paul Youngquist, like Rzepka, addresses this "amnesia" of romanticism in another RCPS in 2012 (Youngquist and Frances Botkin para. 1).[25] As he remarks, "with notable exceptions, studies in British romanticism remain 'pretty white'": "It's not simply that most Romanticists, ourselves included, are middle class white folks working for institutions that traditionally privilege peoples and cultures of European descent. Nor is it simply that British culture, at least in its Romantic avatar, presumes whiteness as the (transparent) racial bias of production.

The whiteness of Romantic studies is a symptom of amnesia. It bespeaks a massive act of forgetting on the part of contemporary scholarship, an institutional disavowal of the economic conditions that help make cultural production during the Romantic Era possible" (para. 1). Venues like the RCPS help to address cultural and literary amnesia. These endeavors, like Aldridge's almost two centuries earlier, and William Brown's before that, challenge Anglo-European assumptions about race, working within and against institutions—romanticism, academia, racial melodramas—that continue to participate in the cultural production of whiteness and blackness.

CHAPTER 5

After Emancipation

MASQUERADE AND MISCEGENATION

Less than a decade after Ira Aldridge first performed the role of Three-Fingered Jack in Bristol, the emancipation of the slaves in the colonies and the ongoing debate over slavery in the United States complicated British attitudes toward race and concomitantly about empire.[1] Social unrest in the colonies and divisions among abolitionists amplified and shaped English attitudes toward slavery and "free labor" in the United States and around the world. "Anti-slavery," Richard Huzzey deftly proposes, "evolved from a question of imperial morality to a cause for moral imperialism" (40). The "end" of chattel slavery, the fatal drop of world sugar prices in the 1830s, and the adoption of free trade in the 1840s threatened Great Britain's dominance in the Atlantic world. These rapid social, political, and economic changes heightened England's commitment to maintaining its perceived racial and moral superiority over its subjects around the globe, even as these same subjects fought against it.

In Jamaica the postemancipation period generated a new set of sociopolitical problems surrounding race, class, and governance. The formerly enslaved people continued to endure harsh conditions during the four-year postemancipation apprenticeship period, contributing to a labor crisis and the importation of indentured servants.[2] These conditions provoked resistance from the oppressed working classes. In the 1865 Morant Bay Rebellion, for example, Baptist deacon Paul Bogle marched several hundred Afro-Jamaican freeholders and sugar workers in revolt against continued social and economic oppression; the government responded violently with flogging, hanging, and the establishment of martial law. The following year, partly in consequence to the rebellion and the subsequent Gov. John Eyre debacle, Jamaica became a Crown Colony, limiting the participation of black and mixed-race Jamaicans until independence (Gad Heuman 159–160).[3]

Economic and social unrest continued through the end of the nineteenth century, into the first decade of the twentieth century, and beyond. As local and foreign capitalists bought up land in Jamaica, workers scattered to large plantations, to Kingston, and abroad (Patterson 148, Burton 96). Marcus Garvey's black nationalism grew out of these conditions, and after his travels to Costa Rica, Panama, and England, he founded his pan-Africanist Universal Negro Improvement Association (Garvey and Hill).[4] By the 1930s, on the heels of global depression, Jamaican workers, many returned from working abroad, such as Garvey, agitated for political and civil rights, and in 1938 a series of violent strikes vexed production on plantations and docks across the island.[5] Some scholars identify Leonard P. Howell and his early Rasta ideology as playing a critical role in black, anticolonial resistance, arguing for its significance to the popular consciousness that led to the labor uprisings of 1938.[6] These decades culminated with the emergence of strong trade unions and nascent Creole nationalism, as the colony moved toward independence from England.

In the period between emancipation and independence, the figure of the black rebel persisted in the English and Anglo-Jamaican imaginary and consciousness as a real threat to the privileges of race and class, even as (or perhaps because) these categories broke down. Events like the Morant Bay Rebellion, Mimi Sheller argues, united black, brown, and poor white people, revealing "the fluidity of racial categories, their changing meanings over time, and their contested historical interpretation" (562–563).[7] Thomas Frost's *Obi; or, Three-Fingered Jack; A Romance*

and H.G. de Lisser's *Morgan's Daughter* use the figure of Jack to explore
the racialized consolidation of Jamaican national identity in the face of
extreme socioeconomic shifts that destabilized the power of a white colonial elite. In both novels of masquerade and miscegenation, the figure of
Jack unsettles English control over an agitated black population. Though
his insurgence fails, his threat prevails, increasingly entwining categories
of race and class.

THOMAS FROST

Thomas Frost published *Obi: A Romance* the same year the Crystal Palace
drew spectators from around the world to view England's achievements
of empire and industry; these spectacles titillated Victorian audiences and
stimulated appetites for sensation.[8] Midcentury English readers devoured
fiction that drew on popular forms such as yellow journalism, penny
dreadfuls, crime novels, melodrama, and minstrelsy.[9] The novels of
the period, as Daphne Brooks has proposed, employed conventions of
Victorian spectacular culture (spiritualism, mesmerism, and magic), owing
"much to a hybrid jumble of popular nineteenth-century show culture
ritual and diasporic religious practices" (15). Thomas Frost's "romance"
emerged at the intersection of changing attitudes and appetites, anticipating the sensation novels of the following decades.[10]

An English journalist and self-professed author of potboilers, Thomas
Frost left little impression on the literary world, though his nonfiction
met, as Peter Gurney argues, a "middle-class taste for otherness" (58).[11]
Frost's writing probed shadowy figures who inhabit the margins of society,
for example, "scores of gypsies, smugglers, and highwaymen who lived by
their own alternative, often superior, modes of justice and morality" (58).
His treatment of Three-Fingered Jack coincides with these socioaesthetic
interests as well as with his preoccupation with "carnivalesque" domains
that subvert the state (Gurney 61). In naming his account a "Romance,"
Frost invoked a genre associated with emotionally overwrought adventure,

befitting the exploits of a sexualized black bandit and his partner in crime, Julia, "the beautiful quadroon" and mistress of disguise, threshold figures who disrupt categories of race and gender.

Scholars have completely ignored *Obi; or, Three-Fingered Jack: A Romance*, a hodgepodge of illusion and subterfuge.[12] Corrupt planters assault female slaves of all shades of black and brown, these women at once the objects and products of sexual violence. Tyrannical overseers deliver ruthless lashings and orchestrate public executions, driving rebels to retaliate, exchanging black corpses for white ones in the dark of night. Mixed-race conjurors bewilder audiences, blurring the lines between reality and illusion. Jack's sexual liaisons with increasingly light-skinned women respond to English concerns about miscegenation; the number of mixed-race characters incriminate the profligate planter class in the racial demographic; and Jack's exploits challenge traditional institutions of authority.

Frost's Jack unites the romantic hero and the swaggering outlaw.[13] A striking and fearsome figure, he evokes admiration and fear in Anglo- and Afro-Jamaicans alike: "Tall, robust, and muscular, yet admirably proportioned, the negro might have stood for the model of the Farness Hercules, and his countenance expressed an energy of purpose, a decision of character, and a dauntlessness approaching audacity" (de Lisser, *Morgan's Daughter* 12). Sensitive and loyal as well, Jack's scheme to free the slaves gathers momentum upon the murder of his father, who was lashed to death by Wilson, the overseer of Jack's master, Mr. Morton. Jack's revolt founders the moment his faithless rebels spy the "redcoats and glittering bayonets" through the trees (6). Deserted by his supporters, Jack submits briefly to prison, and upon his escape he loses a finger not to a black man but to the white soldier guarding the prison. He methodically loots and kills planters, overseers, and soldiers, often directly avenging the violence visited on slaves or rebels.

Jack unleashes his wrath on the plantation system, however, his violence peaks in response to the treatment of his beloved, Cora. Jack snatches Cora directly from the lecherous hands of Mr. Morton in midassault, denying Morton the "bliss" Cora was to afford him, her "future services," and "ay, the children [she] will probably have" (12). Cora's escape with Jack deprives Mr. Morton of his property and his pleasure, marking another way that Jack assaults the institution of slavery. Mr. Morton sends bloodhounds after them, "the same means which had proved efficacious in hunting and capturing the fugitives during the Maroon war" (69). Frost's only mention of Maroons in the novel recalls Jamaica's deadly history of a colonial police force, its patterns of insurgence and counterinsurgency. Cora dies in the battle, shot by the military and mauled by hounds.

Jack's frenzied vengeance of Cora propagates Eurocentric stereotypes of the violent and hypersexual black man. In a paroxysm of grief and rage, he kills the planter Dorrington and violates his wife while the slaves, sympathetic to the outlaw, stand by and watch. He next abducts planter's daughter, Rosa Selby, and imprisons her with her suitor, Captain Orford. After cataloging the atrocities against himself and his family, Jack explains that he will not show "mercy" to the accursed race at whose hands all these horrors have been endured" (78). To Orford and Rosa he says, "It was not to mingle your sighs and tears that I brought you together, but to hear my project of revenge. I have brought this maiden here to cook my food, mix my grog, and light my pipe. You love each other. Well, you will see her forced to submit to my will—you will see me revel in her beauty— and you will be powerless to prevent the consummation of my purpose" (78). Reversing the raced sexual dynamics of the plantation, the fierce black avenger targets the honor of the white maiden. Although the morally dubious Orford manages the couple's escape, Rosa falls into the deeper danger of his predatory designs on her person and fortune. Though Jack vows that he will never kill a woman, he renews his program of violence on white men.

With few exceptions Jack targets white men in power (planters, overseers, traders, and officers), directly retaliating against crimes perpetrated against himself or his people. When, for example, forty soldiers hang and gibbet one of his own men in a spectacle aimed to "imbue his fellow slaves with awe and submission," Jack removes the corpse, and replaces it with that of the brutal new overseer on the Dorrington plantation (229). In another example, he responds to the torture and execution of two of his peers by Dorrington's son; in turn Jack kills Dorrington Jr. and, for extra effect, tosses the head into the midst of a dinner celebration for the planters. Jack's most brutal crimes reflect to the planter class and military their own methods.

The outlaw follows his own code of honor, pledging protection to any African-descended person who supports his program to "extirpate" the white race. He forms a small band of escaped slaves to live by his rules: "My hand shall never be raised against man or woman in whose veins flows one drop of African blood, unless that man or woman seeks to betray me to my enemies" (287). He holds his crew to standards of chivalry, making an example of one of his men, Juba, who tries to rape a slave woman. His protection extends to mixed-race women, who increasingly inspire his affection. As the novel progresses, his lovers Cora, Julia, and Angelina lighten in shade: Creole, quadroon, and white, respectively.[14] He seduces away from the planters the very light-skinned female population they desire, and he also potentially darkens the population, another mode of "extirpating" the white race.

Frost depicts Jack as an amalgamation of romantic sentiment, playful banter, and vengeful design, a lover and a fighter who wears a "stern expression which seldom left [his countenance] unless under the temporary influence of smiles of beauty." In one scene a fully armed Jack crashes a planter function, startling dinner guests with his Obi horn and "Herculean form." Though the men hope he has come to surrender himself, he rather comes for food, conversation, and (his own) entertainment: "I came in because I was hungry, and I could not have come at a more seasonable time, I perceive" (301). Jack and the planters eat and drink rum, discussing his crimes, which Jack considers no worse, no more unlawful, than those visited on his people by the white plantocracy. After delivering an eloquent speech about his "inalienable rights," Jack retrieves his weapons, dons his hat, and kisses the "full red lips" of the surprised white servant girl, Angelina Snuggs (299). The scene establishes Jack as a surprising combination of reason and rage, swagger and humor, and menace and machismo, like a "hero of one of [Angelina's] romances" (301).

Jack's romance with Angelina provokes her black colleague, servant Scipio Africanus.[15] In his anger and sexual frustration, Scipio assaults Angelina, plots with authorities to capture Jack, and rapes and kills a female slave. Scipio functions as Jack's foil, "one the avenger and champion of the negroes and the terror of the whites, the other the betrayer of that champion and the violator and murderer of a woman of the African race" (396). Jack kills Scipio, as he killed Juba. "The traitors of my own race are worse than the whites," he proclaims (368). Scipio's dark deeds bring into relief Jack's heroism, and his resentment represents the poisonous disunity wrought among black people by slavery.

The relationship between Angelina and Jack blurs conventions of race and class. In helping Jack escape from a group of soldiers, she secures his love and loyalty, and in turn he raises her above other women of her race, exclaiming, "You have done a better deed than I thought it in the nature of one of your race ever to do; but you are a woman, and you are a sort of slave yourself" (314). Jack sees her, therefore, as white but also not quite white because of her servant status. Her low status and socioeconomic stasis force her to rely on a parade of morally questionable men for support. After Jack's death Angelina quickly acquires a new protector, a former lover from England, "a fashionable London preacher" who has moved to Jamaica to escape a criminal investigation (405). Her character links together issues of race and class, a "sort of slave" with a tenuous station on the island.[16]

Jack's partner-in-crime and sometimes-lover Julia inhabits a likewise unstable social position, but her slave status precludes reliable male protection. The beautiful, illegitimate daughter of a "creole slave girl and the gentleman from whom Mr. Morton had purchased the estate" was raised to pleasure men, "such connections being so frequent in the West-Indies as to excite no surprise, most of the planters having a creole or quadroon mistress, and illegitimate slave children of every shade of colour" (7). Though initially Mr. Morton's willing concubine, Julia loses his favor by helping Cora escape, and he sends her away for a flogging and fieldwork. She subsequently murders Morton and joins forces with Jack: "I am suddenly exchanging a life of luxury for one of peril and hardship," she explains, "but the change is one from slavery and degradation to freedom and liberty" (32). Julia does not successfully exchange luxury for peril but rather she remains suspended between slavery and freedom, as she is between black and white.

Julia's fair skin and beauty give her limited access to privilege, and her African blood subjects her to the indignities of the enslaved. As she explains to the newly arrived Arthur Morton: "I am your uncle's slave, Mr. Morton, because he purchased me—because my mother was a slave—because the blood of the negro mingles with that of the white man in my veins" (28). At the same time, Jack blames her white blood for her treachery: "It is the accursed white blood in her veins that has made her faithless" (267). Julia's untenable situation between slave and concubine compels her to a life of crime, but her training as "dame du maison" unfits her for the outlaw's rustic life; she ultimately trades in the security of Jack's remote cave for the comforts she loves above all. Using her feminine wiles and intellect to manipulate men and acquire possessions, she thus resembles Kimberly Snyder Manganelli's conceptualization of the "tragic mulatta" as a "wanton opportunist" (19).[17] Her ambiguous race also permits her to adopt different disguises.

Julia's many disguises include a male mixed-race clerk, an "ebon" Sybil, a "veiled lady" of questionable origin, an effeminate but handsome young missionary, and, finally, a young, English lieutenant. These disguises permit her to move around Jamaica and to resist enslavement, imprisonment, and torture. She can hide in full view by transforming her gender, her race, or both. For example, she eludes arrest by dressing up as Captain Inglis, a mockery of the English/Inglis, undermining colonial authority.

Disguised as a black sorceress, Sophonisba, she uses a magic lantern to manipulate a large crowd of the "aristocracy of Spanish-Town" (237).[18] Her flexibility of identity embodies English anxieties about the erosion of British control over the colonies and the colonial class itself, even while stimulating Victorian tastes for spectacles of magic and theatricality (see Castle). In her transfigurations Julia embodies what Daphne Brooks has called the "hoax of 'race' itself, turning it for once and all into an optical, illusionistic, phantasmagoric stunt" (42). An escapologist of sorts, Julia uses illusion to keep herself in play rather than in thrall.[19]

The figure of the fraudulent black sorceress appears several times in the novel, twice performed by Julia and the third by a mulatto man dressed as a woman. The unnamed character identifies "herself" as the island's first obeah practitioner and trades rum for obeah. Jack entrusts her/him to protect a runaway slave, Hebe, who recoils at the dank cave, the old "mulatto woman," and her slimy snake. The hideous wretch attempts to seduce the young girl as she sleeps: "she had not slept long when she awoke abruptly, without knowing what had awakened her: a hand . . . passed caressingly over her bosom" (258). Disgusted and alarmed, Hebe discovers his true sex: "You are not, then, what you seem!" Revealed as an imposter, he in turn reveals that nothing is what it seems and exposes to her obeah as deception itself: "The Fetich gods and the Obi charm are alike impostures, delusions, lies" (259). Foiled in his scheme, the mulatto man wages war on Jack and helps the authorities secure the rebel's capture for the reward and prestige. With his black and white blood equally mixed, the mulatto moves between identity categories and loyalties; he acts first as Jack's ally, but he then assists the planters in tracking him. Violent and ambitious, but without power or protectors, the impotent mulatto man consolidates the worst of the colonial racial stereotypes: bounty hunter, informer, rapist, and impotent trickster.[20]

The conclusion of Frost's novel does not restore order, despite the inevitable death of Jack and Julia—it careens to its conclusion with blood, gore, and murder. The servile, recently baptized Quashie and the "grinning satellite" Sam apprehend and kill Jack, whose obeah (acquired from the defunct obeah practitioner) fails him. Quashie gives the final blow, "dividing with his cutlass the jugular and carotid arteries, the blood gushed out in a hot and crimson current, and with a slight quiver of the limbs, vitality left the body of the formidable bandit" (400). Despite the victory, the slave population remains restive: "Quashee and Sam, rejoicing in their anticipated freedom, paraded with heads erect and eyes flashing with triumph . . . but every other countenance among the slaves wore an expression of gloom" (403). Julia avenges Jack by killing Sam, and then she commits suicide, fulfilling after all the fate of Maginelli's tragic mulatta. Trailing dead planters, felled rebels, and unhappy slaves, the novel paints a gruesome and cautionary picture of plantation life.

Jack's death and the "gloom" of the enslaved people speak to the continued problem of plantation slavery in the Atlantic world, particularly in the U.S. South, which resembles most closely the former West Indian slave colony. In the decades that followed Nat Turner's 1831 slave rebellion in Virginia and Baptist preacher Sam Sharpe's rebellion in Saint James, Jamaica (1831–1832), antislavery sentiment had grown steadily in England and the U.S. North.[21] Conditions for civil war in the United States percolated midcentury. Frost's Three-Fingered Jack rehearses the language and concerns of abolitionist movements that would lead up to the Civil War. In an eloquent speech to the degenerate planters, Jack evokes the Declaration of Independence in his demand for his "inalienable rights":

I have a right to be free, or why was I not born with an iron collar around my neck and manacles on my wrists? These rights I claim in virtue of my existence; the breath which I draw is my charter. They are common to all, and they are inalienable. . . . Laws are only binding when they exist by the consent of the majority of those who live under them. This you well know is not the case in Jamaica; and when it is attempted to enforce laws without the consent and contrary to the will of the majority, the compact under which states are formed is broken, and society returns to its original elements. When this is the case, men revert to their natural rights until their civil rights are restored upon a just and equitable basis. This is what has happened in Jamaica; the coloured people are not only ruled by laws made without their consent, but are virtually excluded from all benefit of those laws. . . . All that has happened since has been the ordinary occurrences of a *civil war*— martial law and retaliations. (303; emphasis mine)

In his allusion to civil war, Jack anticipates the bloodshed awaiting Britain's former colony while also addressing the failure of emancipation in Jamaica to bestow political, civil, or economic liberties on the former slaves.

Of the very few white men who have survived the plots of Jack and Julia, the planter Mr. Selby and the clergyman Mr. Butler recognize that Jack's death will not solve the problems on the island. They agree that a combination of reform and gospel, a "progressive amelioration," would be preferable to emancipation. They acknowledge as well that continued oppression in Jamaica will provoke resistance, inviting history to repeat itself. Mr. Butler remarks, "There will some day be a revolution in Jamaica, for if we judge the future by the past, rulers will be neither wise nor virtuous enough to gradually emancipate the slaves, and take care that the development of their minds and the improvement of their morals keep pace with their progress towards freedom; and some future Three-Fingered Jack will raise the standard of revolt, avenge the wrongs, and proclaim the rights of his countrymen and become their chief" (391). Mr. Butler's criticism of the English colonials can be read as a criticism of the emancipation process in Jamaica. Frost's novel imagines the possibility of "some future Jack" to continue a history of black rebels such as Denmark Vesey (1823) and Nat Turner (1831) in the United States as well as Tacky (1760), Sam Sharpe (1831–1832), and Paul Bogle (1865) in Jamaica. Invoking transatlantic rebellion, the narrator remarks, "We relate events that occurred almost a century ago and yet slavery continues to exist in the Western world, and that, too, under the flag of a republic. . . . Go forth ye [Frederick] Douglasses and [William] Browns to awaken sympathies of the lovers of freedom in the old world" (330). Dead Jack may be, but his legacy of rebellion, Frost's novel prophesies, will continue.

By 1851 England had established itself as an antislavery society, but Britain's foreign policy of moral imperialism and economic agenda of "free labor" fostered oppression around the globe and dissatisfaction at home. Huzzey has argued that "anti-slavery ideologies were one of the principal ways that commercial, strategic and moral objectives could be combined" (174). British interventions in Brazil, India, and the Ottoman Empire paved the way for the Scramble for Africa later in the century. In England the Chartists demanded improved conditions for the working class, linking their conditions and interests with agitation for global social reform. Published the year before *Uncle Tom's Cabin* emerged, Frost's *Obi* reflects his own political sensibilities and concerns about race, class, and empire (see Meer).

Frost's *Obi* was the last "new" adaptation of the Jack story to emerge in England. Published closer to the India Mutiny than to emancipation, it conveys Frost's liberal politics and related concerns about empire. Gurney writes that Frost's account of the India Mutiny "directly challenged the complacent belief in the progressive nature of the British Empire and criticized Parliament for trying to 'under-rate the magnitude of the blow that had been struck at British domination and influence in the East'" (62). It was not until the twentieth century that the figure of Jack Mansong emerged in literary Jamaica to expose the fiction of British progress.

H. G. de Lisser's *Morgan's Daughter*

In 1930 Herbert George de Lisser first published *Morgan's Daughter*, serialized in *Planter's Punch*, an annual magazine geared toward a white Jamaican elite nostalgic for the planter lifestyle of the previous century, and it emerged in novel form in 1953. Registering the racial and political tensions born out of a decolonizing Jamaica, de Lisser's historical romance entwines and conflates the histories of pirates, Maroons, and slave rebels into a conservative endorsement of colonial rule at the very moment that a largely black working class and peasantry agitated for rights and representation.

Morgan's Daughter appropriates the story of Three-Fingered Jack for a tale about pirate-descended, Maroon-blooded Elizabeth Morgan and her plan to drive the English from the island. Elizabeth's rebellion hinges on the credibility of navy deserter John Martin's disguise as the (recently killed) Three-Fingered Jack "come back to life, sometimes as a black man, and sometimes as a white" (138). Using Martin's alleged "magic" to mobilize the "superstitious" black population—slaves and Maroons—she plots a coup that would put her and Martin in control of the island and its black masses. The legitimate government prevails, disbanding the motley crew of black, brown, and poor white rebels. In its preoccupation with color and class hierarchy, de Lisser's novel maps the problems of the decolonizing present onto the colonial past. Moreover, it reflects his allegiance to the white elite of early twentieth-century Jamaica, despite his own mixed-race heritage.[22]

De Lisser started his illustrious journalistic and literary career at the end of the Victorian period, but his political views did not progress with the times. In addition to becoming editor of the *Daily Gleaner* in his early twenties and serving on the board of the Institute of Jamaica for decades (later as its chair), he wrote over twenty novels and a series of travel guides. Editor of the *Gleaner* for nearly forty years, he also penned a column, "Random Jottings," which provided a platform for satirical commentary on topical issues. Between 1920 and 1944 he published *Planter's Punch*, a publication associated with the Jamaica Imperial Association, on whose board he served for decades, pursuing its agenda to preserve (and then federate) British Jamaica. In these roles de Lisser dominated the cultural and intellectual scene, until eventually he was driven out by more progressive intellectuals.[23] He began, as Matthew Smith puts it, "as a leading member of the first generation of brown, middle-class intellectuals, anxious to assert their identity as interpreters of their own reality" (*Liberty* 29). Though initially sympathetic to the Afro-Jamaican middle class, de Lisser's writings document his increasingly antiblack and antilabor sentiments.

By the 1920s de Lisser had associated himself with the world of the white elite, and he self-servingly expanded the term "white" to include Portuguese Jews, Lebanese immigrants, and light-skinned Afro-Jamaicans (Rosenberg 81). Leah Rosenberg explains that his social rise and "change in racial designation and political vision" resulted in part from the transformation of Jamaica from a sugar to a banana economy, a transformation in turn "influenced by a regional economic reorganization and the rise of U.S. imperial power" (67). Aside from a brief flirtation with Fabian socialism and equally brief support of Jamaican annexation to the United States, de Lisser cleaved to the priorities of the Jamaica Imperial Association, a "conservative spokesperson," his friend and biographer W. A. Roberts wrote, "when Jamaica was conservative" (104). In addition, his political views borrowed from the conservative ideology of his famously racist influence, James Anthony Froude, author of *The English in the West Indies* (1898). De Lisser's much-cited article "Marriage," for example, describes black men as unable to organize or lead: "Good humoured and impulsive, an admirable imitator when well taught but with no inventive faculty whatever. His political and social organisation is of the most primitive type, his cities are collections of huts which cannot withstand a season's rains. He has no literature, and no art. His music is of the rudest. He is sometimes brave to recklessness and sometimes a deplorable coward" (9).

This passage exposes de Lisser's colonial attitudes of superiority toward Afro-Jamaican people and culture. As the country moved toward independence, de Lisser remained convinced that it needed English control over its unruly black population, whom he believed to be incapable of self-rule. He conveyed these concerns in his swashbuckling potboiler about the famous buccaneer's mixed-race ancestor, into which he enfolded the story of Three-Fingered Jack.

Morgan's Daughter takes place in Jack's colonial Jamaica, a sugar colony exposed to internal and external challenges to English legitimacy: "In the year 1780 anything might happen in the chief commercial city of Jamaica; a rising of slaves, a sudden landing of the enemies with whom, just then, Great Britain was at war" (17). The novel makes much of England's precarious but controlled situation on the global stage: "But all was calm and peaceful now; the winds were light, the waters sparkling blue like the sky overhead; and though war raged between England on the one side and France and Spain on the other, with rumours of a coming conflict with the Dutch, the Mistress of the Seas was England, and her merchant ships could move about with comparative security" (68). The novel depicts an island protected by an efficient military that protects a thriving plantocracy, enjoying a "complacency" established in part by Jack's death earlier that year (4). However, the calm dissipates when a seemingly resurrected Three-Fingered Jack robs one of the island's wealthiest and most decorated men, Colonel Breakspeare, "a militia colonel, not regular, and a great planter and slave holder," eroding the "comparative security of the island" (43, 4).

Colonel Breakspeare represents the respectable white ruling class, uniting the professions of military and plantocracy. Over rum punch, he and Gov. John Dalling discuss the effect of Three-Fingered Jack's "return" on the slave population, though caring little about its actual welfare. Concerned only about production and security, Breakspeare resists the notion that "the slaves should be taken into any sort of consideration" (43). The men fear that any hint of Jack's renewed activities or the very suggestion that they had failed to kill him would throw the island into chaos: "He will be still more an object of superstitious reverence to the negroes than he ever was in the past; he could create rebellion after rebellion for us" (44). The gentlemen thus enlist the assistance of the shrewd Captain Thorton to contain the situation. Pompous and heavy handed, Thorton represents a "self-sufficient" and "snub nose[d] class of Englishman," committed to the colonizing project and faithful to the white elite (25).

Rebels, however, lurk within those very ranks. For example, James Hamilton, formerly a major in the continental army, joins the rebel plot. Sworn enemy of the governor, sympathizer with the American colonial- ists, and a suspected murderer, Hamilton represents the worst aspects of the military and planter class, "hard and cruel above the average of slave holders in a hard and cruel age," a disgrace to even his peers, "a licentious and careless community" who "shuddered" at his reputation (154).[24] Not entirely English, the "grim Scotsman" sullies the reputation and purity of the respectable plantocracy, revealing too the fractures within it.[25]

John "Jack" Martin, a "refugee from English justice," embodies the cor- rupt, social-climbing class of the English population in Jamaica, suggest- ing too the potential for the degeneration of white residents of the island. A London lawyer by profession, his professional crimes and gambling debts compel his flight to Liverpool, where he is impressed onto a man-o'- war as a common sailor. Flogged on the ship and treated "little better than a slave" on the plantation, he learns that as a "low down white man" he "simply does not count" (37). A storm enables his escape to the northern coast of Jamaica, where he takes work as a slave driver. Eager to escape his situation and conveniently in possession of a three-fingered hand (due to the shipwreck), he seizes the opportunity to impersonate Jack and "simply take the money from those who have it" (38). In blackface he steals the money he needs to either escape from or improve his standing on the island. In "thieving" Three-Fingered Jack, John Martin at once capitalizes on the black man's alleged crimes and avoids the repercussions of his own.

Martin's disguise as Jack emphasizes rather than obscures his unstable position as a poor white man in Jamaica. With black skin, but "aquiline nose," and knee-high boots, he stands out in dress and appearance, like something of another time and place: "Residents of the island, white or black, would have at once perceived that this man was a character entirely out of the ordinary. . . . And had they noticed that in addition to his two long guns, he carried stuck in a band round his middle a brace of pistols, they might have imagined that he was of the fraternity of the pirates or buccaneers, but for the fact that those gentry no longer existed in Jamaica" (7). At once both but also neither black outlaw and white pirate, he occupies a threshold space outside the legitimate social order, trapped by his economic situation and criminal desertion. "I had been driven out of my own country," he explains, "and was a fugitive in this one. I had been treated like a dog on an English man-o'-war; and, after all, my mother was Irish, and the Irish have never had much love for England. I was partly a rebel by blood" (38). English and not-English, "white man at war with his own race," Martin intrigues Elizabeth Morgan because she too feels like "something of an outlaw" (32, 38). Like the Welsh pirate-governor from whom Elizabeth descended, Martin strives to outsmart rather than submit to the law, mobile in his relation to it.[26]

Taking advantage of his identical mobility, John Martin adopts whiteface as well as blackface, disguising himself also as John Huntly Seymour, an English newcomer to the island. In part to impress the planter and military classes, Huntly signs up for an expedition against the Spanish Main as a "gentleman volunteer." Ambivalent about Elizabeth's plan for rebellion, he prefers to ascend to the status of the white elite rather than to "make a bid for mastery" as "king" of the black population. "He did not relish the prospect of having to live among a gang of savage blacks and a few equally savage whites," the narrator explains. "If he might not go back to England, at least he must mix with men and women of his own type in Jamaica, or, striving to do so, die" (223). He therefore resolves to take the risk in making his fortune in the war, with hopes of returning a hero worthy of marriage to Colonel Breakspeare's daughter. But he cannot outrun the law indefinitely; wanted by the authorities for his theft as "Jack," for his desertion as Martin, and for suspected espionage as Huntly, he faces criminal charges on three levels. The novel refers to the imposter alternately as Seymour, Huntly, Jack, and John, emphasizing in his excess of names and simultaneous lack of core, a deficit of social or ethical substance. Elizabeth eventually exposes his weakness, dubbing him "worse than the negro whose name and complexion you borrowed" (247). She recognizes that he lacks the courage and conviction that she shares with Three-Fingered Jack.

The titular character of *Morgan's Daughter* inherits her rebellious spirit from her mixture of pirate and Maroon ancestry, which precludes her access to white respectability. Educated in England, she nonetheless endures the "insolence so often meted out to mulatto girls." In between races and classes, and thus "rigidly excluded," she resents her social position: "dissatisfied with her lot, she was ready, when the opportunity arose, to stir up trouble and summon the slaves and maroons to revolt" (4). Embracing her buccaneer ancestry, she views herself as "something of an outlaw" like her infamous ancestor who "began as an indentured servant and rose to be governor of Jamaica" (33, 95). Elizabeth amalgamates in one character the island's fiercest historical rebels, but her status as a mixed-race woman erodes her already-dubious status as a Morgan. Huntly/Seymour comments, "This was Henry Morgan come to life again, but as a woman—and that was her weakness. As a woman with a mixture of blood in her veins, who was not treated as she felt it her right to be" (133). Her "weakness," the narrator implies, comes from her combination of pirate, Maroon, and woman—an unnatural, extralegal status. She therefore designs her plan with the hope of being "chieftainess of them all" (111) while the Maroon leaders and Seymour/Martin hold the position of governors.

Elizabeth imagines a leadership composed of brown and white men who, with her help, would keep under control the untrustworthy black masses. In other words, she envisions a "coloured ruling class," much like the professional "brown" class into which de Lisser was born but rose above.[27] To a skeptical Seymour, Elizabeth explains, "You forget the coloured people—those with both white and black blood in their veins. You forget the white men who would remain if allowed to do so. Surely these would be enough to keep the savages from getting out of hand" (97). She likewise distrusts the Maroons, judging them incapable of organization. She opines, "They needed someone to unite and organize them and to bring them to make common cause with other negroes. At present they are used to put down slave rebellions and hunt down runaway slaves. . . . They fight black against black." Elizabeth strives to replace methods of divide and rule with those of "unite and conquer," and she deploys her mixed-race uncle David—a Maroon leader—to unite the armed Maroons with the slaves (96).

De Lisser depicts his black Maroons as restive and "warlike," a threat despite their tenuous peace and seeming accommodation. Named for the leader of the 1760 failed rebellion, their leader Captain Tacky grasps for more wealth and power; however, in calling a Maroon Tacky, the novel dismisses important distinctions among leaders of black resistance in Jamaican history. De Lisser's stern and proud Captain Tacky encourages in his men the "itch of warlike excitement" and lust for "the ambush and the wild assault, the surprise of the enemies and the burning of homes and estates" (148). Tacky orchestrates for Seymour a performance of Maroon strength and skill; bursting out of the bush where they had been camouflaged, the Maroons exploded into a "cacophony" of howls and screams: "Leaping and contorting their magnificent bodies, making threating gestures with their weapons, they advanced . . . then flung their weapons at their feet" (145). De Lisser's description of the Maroons tellingly echoes that of *The History of Jamaica*, written by planter, historian, and apologist Edward Long, indicating the colonial (and racist) tenor of his political views (vol. 2).[28] However, the "war dance" confers on John Seymour respect, acceptance, and submission: "The Maroons had given [the] welcome as a rule reserved for only the highest in the land" (de Lisser, *Morgan's Daughter* 145). This ritual performs the complicated dynamic between the Maroons and the island's white residents, demonstrating the Maroon's combination of fierceness and subjection.[29] "Black, tall, and athletic," the narrator explains, "these men of the mountains" differ "essentially from the ordinary negroes" (141). De Lisser's Maroons occupy a unique position on the island: more advanced than the enslaved population but more savage than the English.

The "ordinary negroes" play little part in this novel, indicating their position at the bottom of the island's hierarchy of race and class. The novel lumps the enslaved people in groups and generalizations. Elizabeth has "no belief in the integrity of most of them" and dismisses them as ancillary to the rebellion, driven only by desperation and hunger (107). "The slaves are discontented everywhere," she confides. "In Westmoreland and St. James they are almost starving and would rise as one man if called upon to do so" (231). The Maroons, she acknowledges, will mobilize with military skills and weapons, but the slaves bring little but their dissatisfaction to the rebellion. *Morgan's Daughter* thus stratifies its population with white colonials at the top and black slaves at the bottom. But it is the middle stratum—Maroons, mixed-race folk and poor white people—that disrupts the "comparative security" of the island with their clambering for power (68).

Disgruntled and disenfranchised, Elizabeth and Martin represent the middle class of de Lisser's contemporary Jamaica. The penniless deserter and the embittered "mulatta" join forces in a battle they inevitably lose in part to the combination of Seymour's ambivalence and Elizabeth's emotional excess.[30] Only respectable white folk, the novel suggests, can represent the lower classes of poor white men, haughty brown women, and unruly black masses. By embedding the legend of Three-Fingered Jack in a tale uniting Maroons, piratical mixed-race women and "low down white men," de Lisser transfers contemporary anxieties about race and class to his historical romance (37). In thieving the story of Three-Fingered Jack, *Morgan's Daughter* empties of agency the figure of the black rebel, giving it instead to a motley crew destined to fail.

In its first publication in 1930, *Morgan's Daughter* anticipated a particularly violent decade in Jamaican colonial history, arguably the worst since the Morant Bay Rebellion of 1865, and it limns the subsequent tensions surrounding British Crown rule. The Riots in 1938 united plantation and dockworkers around the island, creating a "revolutionary brigade demanding social change" (Beckford and Witter 61). At the same time, a brown middle class emerged, giving birth to new political parties, trade unions, and leaders such as Norman Manley and Alexander Bustamante. Staunchly loyal to the respectability of English colonial rule and deeply suspicious of the motives of the middle class, the Anglo-identified Herbert de Lisser distanced himself from "upstart" brown leaders and their bids for self-government.

De Lisser likewise grew increasingly critical of Afro-Jamaican activism, such as Marcus Garvey's. He used his *Gleaner* column, "Random Jottings," to "obliterate" organizations and issues such as Garvey's Universal Negro Improvement Association (UNIA) (Cobham 7). Garvey represented one of de Lisser's greatest anxieties about Jamaican governance. A transatlantic political force, the pan-Africanist Garvey spent his life fighting for black civil rights and economic independence for the working classes; moreover, some of his ideas served as the foundation for the Rasta movement, which gained steam also in the early 1930s. Marcus Garvey's social, political, and racial ideologies conflicted directly with those embraced by the conservative de Lisser.

De Lisser's suspicion of emerging black nationalism did not escape Garvey, who wrote that "fellows" like de Lisser "are being used to keep down the Negroes of the Islands" (qtd. in Garvey and Hill 190). Biographer Tony Martin writes that Garvey accused de Lisser of creating the impression that he had Afro-Jamaicans in "as serious a state of unrest as during the Morant Bay Rebellion in 1865" (134). De Lisser indeed harshly delineated Garvey in his novel *The Jamaica Nobility* (1925) less than a decade after publishing *Revenge*, a novel that negatively depicted Bogle in fictionalizing the Morant Bay Rebellion.[31] In other words, de Lisser draws a literary line that connects the black rebels Three-Fingered Jack to Paul Bogle to Marcus Garvey; these black rebels represent for de Lisser the problems he associated with Afro-Jamaican anticolonial resistance to the nation-building project.[32]

During the politically fraught period between emancipation and independence, English authors stopped writing about Three-Fingered Jack, and Jamaican interest in the figure emerged. Writing eighty years apart within this period, the liberal-minded Frost and the conservative de Lisser used the figure of Jack to fictionalize the anxieties of a white colonial elite that struggled to maintain its grip on the island. While Frost's Victorian novel anticipates a new chapter in England's problematic history of empire, de Lisser's conservative text applies a dying Victorian sensibility to a modernizing colony moving inexorably (and for him troublingly) toward independence. De Lisser once declared that he would see Jamaican self-government over his dead body. As it happened, the very year he died, 1944, Jamaica made its first big step toward self-rule, its first general election, moving toward the two-party system that would eventually give rise to garrison politics and the "Troubles" of the 1970s and 1980s.

CHAPTER 6

Mansong

NO LONGER "NEARLY EVERYBODY WITE"

Two centuries after the spectacular procession that accompanied Three-Fingered Jack's disembodied head and hand through the island capital, Jamaicans flocked to Kingston's downtown Ward Theatre for its annual pantomime. On its fortieth anniversary (1980), the Little Theatre Movement (LTM) resurrected Jack Mansong as a hero. Ted Dwyer's *Mansong* radically revises the English *Obi* plays, and it replaces John Fawcett's "rude" procession of blackface revelers with an all-black cast performing a "majestic, resolute song of hope" (Dwyer 7).

The Ward Theatre sits on the north end of what is now called "Parade" in St. William Grant Park, named for the renowned black nationalist labor leader, and statues of political rivals (and cousins) Norman Manley and Alexander Bustamante flank the north and south ends of it. Originally a drill center and parade ground for British soldiers, the park also became a site for public floggings and hangings. From 1792 to 1799 the theater on the current site of the Ward was appropriated by the English to serve as military barracks; these military inhabitants frequently put up their own plays, sure evidence of the astonishing ways that eighteenth-century playhouses and the performances within wielded social, political, and cultural authority in Jamaica and elsewhere.[1] In the twentieth century, St. William Grant Park served as a venue for labor leaders such as Marcus Garvey (also a playwright), and the Ward Theatre launched Jamaica's two major political parties, the People's National Party (PNP; 1938) and the Jamaica Labour Party (JLP; 1943). Today the recently refurbished Ward Theatre looks over the lively park populated by crowds of vendors, "sufferers," and dominoes players. In 1980, however, Parade was one of many citywide sites of political violence, recalling no doubt the military exercises for which it was originally used.

Because of the violence surrounding the 1980 general elections in Jamaica, the Ward Theatre only barely passed muster for the staging of the annual National Pantomime. That year marked a particularly violent year in Jamaican history, and the LTM worried whether downtown would "be calm enough for the Ward to be the scene of the Pantomime as usual," following, as it had, months of social "confrontation and turmoil." The LTM committee pondered the "heavy challenge" of the decision and opted to move forward, debuting *Mansong* on Boxing Day, with "thanks to all the people who showed faith in maintaining a tradition" (Gloudon, *Chairperson*, 5). The "confrontation and turmoil" to which Gloudon refers stemmed from the bloodshed surrounding the general elections, a contest between Edward Seaga's Jamaica Labour Party and Michael Manley's People's National Party; these "tribal wars" caused the death of more than eight hundred Jamaicans, victims of politically driven gang violence. Dwyer's *Mansong* identifies these contemporary divisive struggles in Jamaica as the inheritance of a British colonial rule, and his pantomime imagines instead a postcolonial Jamaica that unites "Out of Many One People."

The Little Theatre Movement National Pantomime has become an institution that celebrates Jamaican cultural heritage, emerging out of but radically departing from the British genre. Instead of the mimed action, spectacle, and stock figures of the traditional British genre, the distinctly Jamaican pantomime employs dance, music, song, improvisation, and patois dialogue as it delivers commentary on contemporary social and political issues (E. Hill 283–284). As Little Theatre Movement cofounder Greta Fowler has explained, "the experiments with traditional Pantomime have evolved into a more mature type of West Indian play with a deeper theme, enlivened with music, colour, rhythm and dance" (1). In its creolizing methods, the LTM performed a Jamaican national identity rising out of the challenges and political residue of decolonization.

In 1911 George Bernard Shaw visited the newly built Ward Theatre and announced its need to nurture a manifestly Jamaican culture. For this project, Shaw stated, Jamaica needed an orchestra, a theater, and good architecture as well as good writers, painters, and a national library. His suggestions take for granted the spaces and places of the metropole (libraries, architecture, urban infrastructure) but also acknowledge the need for an indigenous tradition. He insisted that "the ordinary travelling companies from England and America be sternly kept out of [the theater], for unless you do your own acting and write your own plays, your theatre will be of no use; it will in fact vulgarise and degrade you. . . . Your Kingston man need be no longer a colonial" (qtd. in E. Hill 3). The Irish playwright would indeed have known something about the exigencies of the "colonial man," and his words proved prophetic for the establishment of a uniquely Jamaican genre. The Jamaican pantomime has become the most notable example of Jamaican integrated theater, becoming "identifiably Jamaican," the "most popularly supported annual theatre event in the region" (284).

Founded in 1941, Kingston's LTM initially offered the traditional pantomime fare of productions such as *Jack and the Beanstalk* and *Babes in the Wood*, but in 1943 it presented *Soliday and the Wicked Bird*, the first Jamaican pantomime. Though it returned to the English style for another decade, it next produced what has been termed the "Anancy Cycle," a series of pantomimes featuring Brer Anancy, the Spiderman trickster of the African folk tradition. The Honorable Louise Bennett (Miss Lou), Jamaica's famed and beloved theater personality, inaugurated the Anancy plays, coauthoring with director Noel Vaz *Brer Anancy and Bluebeard* in 1949. Miss Lou had started her career by reading her dialect poems at concerts in Edelweiss Park in Kingston, a venue established by Marcus

Garvey's Universal Negro Improvement Association in 1929. These public performances featured a range of activities, including elocution contests, drama, and boxing. After having seen her first LTM performance in 1947 (*Cinderella*), Miss Lou published a poem that spoke to the need for an Afro-Jamaican theatrical tradition:

It was just like movie pickcha [picture]

Pretty costume, pretty light,

Plenty songs and bans a dance an [plenty of songs and bands and
      dance and]

Nearly everybody wite! [nearly everybody is white]
      (qtd. in Morris, *Miss Lou* 5)

Miss Lou contributed to the "Jamaicanization" of the LTM, methodically replacing the predominantly "wite" company with black actors, writers, and directors.

From then on the LTM employed folk songs, proverbs, and patois, and local authors wrote for celebrity actors, such as Miss Lou and Ranny Williams, and staged productions geared toward Afro-Jamaican people and priorities. Brian Heap has dubbed the Jamaican pantomime "The People's Theatre," and he remarks that it is now "so indigenous [that] its conventions have to be interpreted to Britons" ("National Pantomime" 66). In its "indigenous" conventions, the Jamaican pantomime recalls Sylvia Wynter's designation of the term "indigenous" to refer to a cultural process of adaptation and transformation that rejects European norms ("Jonkonnu," 35–36). This process relies on engagement with folk and popular cultures.

Appealing to a collective understanding of Jamaican history and culture, the National Pantomime annually draws some seventy thousand multigenerational middle-class Jamaicans from around the island. The audience participates in the performance, sharing language, musical sensibility, and sense of humor—singing along, clapping, laughing, and calling out to the performers. Henry Fowler, husband of the LTM founder,

Greta Fowler, has written that the pantomime is "the art where all art meets. It changes to accommodate the talent available . . . created out of need to satirize our sociopolitical condition, to respond to our own music and rhythms, and to accept our language as a vehicle of communication of which we can be proud" (7). In addition, he describes the pantomime as a way of projecting "our own folk heroes in an age of imported cinema fare with Nordic heroes and heroines with whom we cannot identify" (qtd. in Reckford D1). Dwyer's *Mansong* reclaimed Jamaican folk hero Jack Mansong from an English literary and stage tradition, indigenizing the story for contemporary Afro-Jamaicans. The Jamaican pantomime, itself a revision of genre, provided an apt vehicle for this reappropriation of the black rebel.

Like most Jamaican pantomimes, *Mansong* relies on practices of the African diaspora such as storytelling, drumming, dancing, spirit possession, and call-and-response format. Opening with a Jonkonnu band and featuring songs set to beats ranging from reggae to pseudo-African, *Mansong* privileges Afrocentric over Eurocentric aspects of Jamaican culture. It introduces the manly Mansong as a brave Coromantee prince, a hero who will defeat the backra [white planter class]. Dwyer recycles the Rosa-Captain subplot of Fawcett's *Obi*, but he significantly changed the dynamic among the other characters, adding the central character of Jack's sister (and Quashie's girlfriend), Teena, to the mix. When Teena discovers that Jack has arrived on the plantation, she and Dada, the obeah man, keep her brother's identity a secret because "backra policy" divides up tribe members on the plantation. Loosely adapting the nineteenth-century British prose *Obi*, Dwyer's Jack foments a rebellion that lands him in jail; he escapes, kills the jailer, and heads for the mountains, protected by Dada's obeah. When the governor issues the proclamation for Jack's arrest, Quashie (still ignorant of Jack's true identity) vows to kill him and use the cash reward to buy freedom for himself and Teena. Dwyer changes the ending of the legend, permitting Jack to live and bonding him with Quashie in a joint vision of freedom and black power.

Dwyer's adaptation emphasizes the relationships among the black slaves, relegating the white characters to minor and often comic roles. The romance between Quashie and Jack's sister, Teena, eclipses that of Rosa and the captain. Obeah-man Dada plays a central role, functioning as the storyteller or griot on whom the slaves rely for stories and spiritual protection. Director Dennis Scott emphasizes the importance of slave history to *Mansong*: "We've told the story from the slaves' point of view, this time. What happens in the Great Houses was important. It still is. But not nearly as important or as interesting, to most of us, as what happens in the shadow of the estate, where the little people work out their lives and gossip and tell tales and share dreams" (7).[2] Scott calls attention to histories occluded from colonial records, such as Afro-Jamaican oral histories, stories that sometimes can only be imagined.

Mansong celebrates Jack as unequivocally a hero. The song "Jack Naw Jester" (Jack is no joke), reprised at various moments through the performance, for example, describes him as "Brave like a lion, / An strong like iron":

Him fear no laws;
Him bad like yaws;
Him up dere a fight for de blackman cause:
Prince of de Coromantyn.
Dis yah war him boun fe win [He's bound to win this war],
And when him dun Backra gwine run [and when he's done, Backra is
    going to run],
For de brave man Jack now mek no fun [Brave man Jack is no joke]

A strong lion (a nod to the Rasta Lion of Judah), Jack can beat the English legal system (laws), and promises to infect plantation slavery like the obeah-associated disease (yaws) that had famously halted production on the plantation. The program cover shows Jack standing tall and proud with rippling muscles and clenched fists; he stands beneath a giant tree, whose roots sprout behind his closely shaved head like dreadlocks, and he wears an obeah bag around his neck and a machete across his body. "Comedy and Tragedy" masks border the image, resembling African masks and reflecting the hero's status as a Coromantee prince. The cover, then, advertises a strong, black, African-identified man: handsome, virile, and proud.

Only Quashie dares fight Jack, and for that he acquires hero status as well. Dada refers to Quashie as next to Jack "de baddes [baddest] man bout" (16). Quashie and Jack fight for dominance on the plantation, put into opposition by oppressive systems that pit black men against one another. In offering a reward for the capture or killing of Jack, the government condones and recompenses black-on-black crime. Tuckey explains,

> [Backra] promise all kine a reward to anybody who capture or kill him, slave include. An das how Quashee and Jack buck up face to face. No wonder Quashee is a kina hero pon dis plantation. De only one fe fight Jack an chop off two a him finger.
>
> [The white men promised all kinds of reward to anybody who captures or kills him, including slaves. And that's how Quashee and Jack met. No wonder Quashee is kind of a hero on the plantation. He's the only one who fought Jack and cut off two fingers.] (15)

Quashie's determination to capture and kill Jack increases when he (wrongly) suspects the rebel's rivalry for Teena's affections. Dada tells Tuckey that the "love business" only complicates the existing "conflick" between the men. Burning with anger and sexual jealousy, Quashie relishes the fight with Jack, "Fist to fist. Man to man" (46). Teena begs Quashie to desist, explaining that the slaves need solidarity rather than violence, that it makes no sense to fight a brother freedom fighter: "Jack fight fe freedom too, Quashee. But you wan kill fe freedom? Jack one a we own people—so dat we can be free? No Quashee, dat no mak no sense" [Jack fights for freedom too, Quashie. But you want to go kill for freedom? Jack is one of our own people—so that we can be free? That doesn't make any sense] (39). Quashie and Jack, Teena points out, should be fighting together against "Backra" for freedom. Once Teena reveals Jack's identity as her brother, Dada brokers the peace between the two rivals, uniting them as African men, Ashanti and Coromantee warriors, against the British plantation system. *Mansong* thus criticizes the forces that separate rather than unite the Afro-Jamaicans.

Like other Jamaican pantomimes, *Mansong* uses topicality to address the social, political, and economic issues of the day. As Dwyer's collaborator Carmen Tipling puts it, "major issues in the public arena come to be treated skillfully in the pantomime . . . [placing] the audience right in the centre of the drama" (January 30, 2006).[3] In 1980 garrison politics, clientism, and poverty put Afro-Jamaicans into conflicts that echoed and reproduced international neoliberal dynamics. In a scene in which Dada looks into the "calabash of life," he foretells "tribal war," a shortage of foreign currency, and "hauntings" by the International Monetary Fund (43); these lines surely allude to Manley's vexed dealings with the IMF that contributed to his loss of the 1980 election.

Dada's allusions to Jamaican economic, political, and cultural crises suggest that two hundred years after Jack's capture and almost two decades after Jamaican independence, the island nation struggled against forces that manifested in violence on the streets of Kingston and around the island. The relationships between the men on the plantation in *Mansong*, especially between Jack and Quashie but also between Quashie and the overseer, Sam Power, resonate with the troubling machismo of the "shotta," or shooter of contemporary Jamaica. These resonances underscore the ways that the colonial police state and plantation slavery grew into postcolonial garrison dynamics. *Mansong* imagines a future where men like Jack and Quashie pull together for peace and love among Afro-Jamaicans.

The deeply respected Dada drives this liberatory, utopian narrative. As the storyteller and obeah man in *Mansong*, Dada uses a magic flute to transport the audience from the present to the past he recounts.

Dada plays a figure on his flute, and characters emerge from the group, turning and wheeling into the wings. When the actors reenter, they have transformed into figures from the story (Morris, "New Story Time" 16). Though Dada guides the narrative, Scott blocked *Mansong* so that the entire cast almost always remains on stage. The slaves function as the chorus, singing songs that accompany and comment on Dada's story. Traditionally, the Jamaican pantomime chorus drew from a "scratch" cast of community members rather than from a selection of trained professionals (though this has changed), demonstrating the strong link between the pantomime and the community. Indeed, as Verena Reckford wrote, Jamaican pantomime is "theater for Jamaicans, by Jamaicans, out of the Jamaican way of life" (D1). Charles Hyatt's performance as Dada garnered praise from local critics and viewers, perhaps because it spoke to different sets of shared knowledge, including memories of him in similar roles. In 1980 Hyatt was the only remaining member of the old pantomime cast; he thus emblematized the continuity as well as the innovations of LTM productions. As a community elder, Hyatt's Dada provides the leadership, and as the obeah man he embodies the spiritual center of the slave society. Speaking to and with the audience and chorus, Dada links the vernacular and the spiritual.

Moving between past and present, Dwyer employs call-and-response formations during the interludes. This musical pattern echoes traditional work songs as well as black spirituals, affirming the singers' connection to the larger diasporic community. One example features an unnamed man pulling a cart across the cane field. He sings about Jack living up in the mountain and eluding capture as well as about Quashie's effort to catch him. The other slaves sing the response: "Warrior men oh! / Warrior men oh! / African fighter / Warrior oh!" This "plaintive tune," a work song, honors both Jack and Quashie as African fighters and laments the combat between them (Dwyer 41).

Another example of the call-and-response structure speaks to the slaves' desire to claim their own story. Dada sings the lead part: "Everybody have a song / Fe Dem own song / Everybody have a story fe tell; de song may be sad, / or de story may be sad, / But a fe dem story jus the same [Everybody has his own song / Everybody has a story to tell; the song may be sad / Or the story may be sad, / But this is our own story just the same]." Responding, the chorus agrees: "So we ha fe we song / Fe we own song / We ha fe we story as well [So we have our song / Our own song / We have our story to tell]" (4). The song about storytelling underlines relationships among the characters anchored in community structure and African rituals; however, it intimates the vulnerability of historical transmission for the unlettered in a scribal culture that often writes out their individual experiences as well as collective remembering. Dwyer's amalgamation of oral and written materials plays with the tension between the two modes of transmission, the elisions and mythologizing.

Mansong explores themes of storytelling and history, bringing into relief the problems of representation from within a postcolonial culture. In the first act Dada explains to his peers the important role that Jack Mansong played in the romance between Rosa and Captain Whitehorn, and he laments the absence of the slaves' lives in backra history:

DADA: We tell we story wud a mout from gineration to gineration. But sometime mout keen slip an story tell wrong, or head keen go bad an story feget. [But] when you write it dung like Backra eena book it keen go wrong an it won't feget. . . . But Backra write story fe please demself. Oonu tink say Backra a go write dung de part dat anya we play eena de love story between Miss Rosa and de Captain. Oonu tink say dem woulda write dung de part dat Jack Mansong play eena dat love story?

[We tell the story by mouth from generation to generation. But sometimes the mouth slips and tells it wrong, or your memory becomes poor and you forget. [(But) when you write it down in a book like the white man, it can't go wrong, and it won't be forgotten]. . . . But Backra write stories for themselves. Do you think white people will write down the part we play in the love story of Rosa and the captain? Do you think they will write down the part that Jack Mansong plays?]

1ST SLAVE: No Dem naw go write it dung [No, they won't write it down].

2ND SLAVE: Jack a fe we hero [Jack is our hero].

3RD SLAVE: An dem ha fe dem hero write dung eena dem book [And they write down their own heroes in their books].

DADA: Some a oonu jus come pon dis plantation an mi see oonu a open oonu mout likehorse a yawn, a talk bout we hero Jack Mansong. But oonu know de true story an a who a go write it dung? Promise me Tuckey bwoy dat wha Backra learn you fe do, you wi use it. You up eena de Great House day close to de Backra people dem. . . . You must write down de true story of Jack Mansong dat you pickinny, pickinny kean read bout it.

[Some of you just came to the plantation, and I see that you open your mouth like a horse's yawn when we talk about our hero, Jack Mansong. But you know the true story, and who will write it down? Promise me Tuckey, boy, that when white people teach you to write, you will use it. You are up in the Great House, close to white people. . . . You must write down the true story of Jack Mansong so that your children's children can read about it.] (4)

Dada encourages Tuckey to transcribe the slaves' oral history into the language of the metropole to ensure its survival. In so doing, he both acknowledges and criticizes the authority of a British scribal tradition. Carolyn Cooper has theorized this dialectical relationship between scribal and oral discourses, or the "seemingly oppositional ideology of 'long head' and 'book,'" but she makes a claim for cultural production that "allows for both the relative autonomy of oral texts existing independently of a tradition of writing, and [their] interdependence" (*Noises in the Blood* 2). Tuckey's unique status as a house slave and then personal servant to the captain gives him access to backra culture and its tools, putting him in a position to transform it.

A betwixt-and-between character, Tuckey occupies a critical space on the plantation. His book-learning aspirations and his seeming adulation of Captain Whitehorn render him an object of good-natured teasing from his fellow slaves. His peers mock his English clothing, what they call his "jonkonnu" costume," and call him the "pet monkey of the Backra" (Dwyer 3). Tuckey defends himself, switching from Jamaican into Standard English, a rhetorical turn (institutionalized by Miss Lou) he employs throughout the performance, and he explains his clothing as part of his work for Captain Whitehorn: "Dis is not Jonnkonnu costome (Pompously). This is the uniform of the servant of an English gentleman (Ceremoniously opening book). Look, this is an Englishman and this is his servant. Capt. Edward Whitehorn is an Englishman an him wish me from now on to be his personal assistant and to accompany him every-where him go. An this is how him say I must dress" (3). Tuckey flips the script, embodying the contradictions and complexities of the Jonkonnu, a figure Peter Reed calls an "always already hybridized act" ("There Was No Resisting" 70). Wynter has referred to "Jonkonnu" as "the original 'carnival' form of Jamaica, at once mimicking and mocking the power relations on the plantation ("Jonkonnu" 43).[4] Tuckey's character playfully keeps these ambivalences in tension. Despite his pompous tone, his residence in the Great House, and his acquisition of letters, Tuckey's loyalties lie with the slaves. As Henry Louis Gates Jr. has suggested, slave narratives can make "the white written texts speak with a black voice [which] is the initial mode of inscription of the metaphor of the double-voiced" (131). In other words, as a "signifying" (rather than "pet") monkey, Tuckey can rewrite British colonial history to accommodate his own (3).

The white male characters of the custos, captain, and governor, representatives of the colonial state, echo English versions of the story that describe Jack as a violent, dangerously gallant, obeah-bearing Robin Hood:

CAPT: Jack Mansong! The vagabond has achieved extraordinary notoriety. His name is all over England. Robin Hood of the Tropical Forest! Defeat whole armies. Store up treasures. Gallant to ladies! Incredible!

> Gov: I tell you Captain, it's incredible. He is a plague. It's being rumoured
> of his being possessive of extra-ordinary powers. Protected by spirits
> they say.
> Mrs C: Obeah. Black magic. The only person who ever came close to
> harming him is a slave Quashee who chopped off two of his fingers.
> Gov: We have to offer a large reward for his capture this time.
> Custos: Yes. Put a large price on his heathen head. (18)

Dwyer depicts these characters as foolish and one-dimensional, and they mimic the comedy provided by blackface characters in nineteenth-century English pantomimes about the West Indies. *Mansong* reverses the thrust of cultural criticism with black actors playing comic white characters and speaking formal English, and the audience identifies with the patois-speaking black characters. Moreover, the governor and the custos, colonial authorities, flail and flounder. Unable to face Jack, for example, they dress as women to sneak past him. The English soldiers, too, are subject to various mishaps, such as red ants in "delicate places" and attacks by voracious mosquitoes. Jack steals the pants of one soldier and likewise "thieves" the pants of the custos, as he puts it, a "vivid testimony to the state of hooliganism, violence and indiscipline rampant" in Jamaican society, a reference to the (re)current political problems in Jamaica (18). Authority figures without pants, soldiers with ants in their pants, and officials in women's clothing: these situations rehearse a range of unmanly, hapless behaviors in the English and Anglo-Jamaican characters. *Mansong* thus depicts an ineffective, white masculinity against strong Afro-Jamaican men.

Unlike her male counterparts and critical of them, Rosa demonstrates strength of character and treats the slaves with humanity and respect. Invoking twentieth-century feminist ideology, Rosa refuses to marry for security or property. Many local men pursue her, but she has no interest in them or their fortunes (which Jack systematically steals). Rosa's mother acknowledges the inadequacy of Anglo-Jamaican men: "They lack breeding and civilized manners. A foreign man would be ideal but not many things come from foreign [from abroad] these days—most of all husbands." Fearing her own husband's imminent death, Mrs. Chapman hopes for a match to provide their family with "needed capital" and with protection for the plantation, conflating the economic problems of nineteenth- and twentieth-century Jamaica (13). The imported English captain Whitehorn offers their dubious solution.

Slightly better than his Anglo-Jamaican peers, but certainly no hero, English imperialist soldier Whitehorn amalgamates nineteenth-century colonialism with twentieth-century capitalism. Previously posted in India, the captain has decided to settle down in Jamaica and buy a nearby plantation, a move that wins Rosa's approval and betrothal. A boastful soldier and game hunter, he decides that it would be "rather sporting" to "have a shot at Jack Mansong" (18). But Jack's guerilla tactics outmatch the captain and his incompetent troops. Disguised as a tree and using Maroon tactics of "ambush," or camouflage, Jack tricks the soldiers into thinking that he has used obeah to make himself invisible to them; he then kills most of them and scatters the rest (29–39). The captain blindly swishes his sword at the air, blustering and bellowing, until Jack "clobbers" and kidnaps him (30). He remains Jack's prisoner until Rosa finds and saves him. The captain's entitlement, pugnacity, and arrogance consolidate (post)colonial attitudes toward Afro-Jamaican culture, but even with an army of men, he cannot defeat Jack Mansong. Moreover, he requires the help of a strong woman to save him.

Mansong parodies Eurocentric attitudes, particularly Captain Whitehorn's ignorance about and attitudes toward obeah. A dialogue between the captain and Dada underscores Whitehorn's ignorance and Dada's playfulness:

CAPT: Tell me Dada. What exactly is O-bee-ya and how does it work?
DADA: O-bee-ya?
CAPT: O-bee-ya. Come on my good man. Don't tell me you don't know
      anything about O-bee-ya. Your people practice it. They say Jack
      practices it and that is why it's been so difficult to capture or kill him.

DADA: Oh! You mean Obeah!

CAPT: That's it.

DADA: No captain, a don't know nutten bout Obeah, sar. But mi do
hear all kine a strange story bout it Sar.

CAPT: Like what? (26)

Acquiring the demeanor of the sycophantic slave, Dada simultaneously
resists compliance. He circumvents answering directly and responds in
a song about obeah charms that gives no real information to the captain. Whitehorn at any rate dismisses Dada's song as a "fascinating black
poem" (26). Captain Whitehorn's condescending attitude toward obeah
reflects the pantomime's comic but critical representation of the English
characters, particularly those in positions of power. The Afro-Jamaican
characters, on the other hand, respect obeah and seek its protection, or
they suffer by its consequences.

Dada's obeah protects Jack, empowers Quashie, and shifts the power
dynamic on the plantation by stripping the overseer of his memory
and power. The overseer, Sam Power, the hypermasculine villain of the
show, delights in tormenting the slaves and wielding his power over
them. Though he has backra-sanctioned authority, he does not inhabit
the ascendancy class; nor does he usefully harness its privilege, as does
Tuckey. Sam's patois speech separates him from the planters, and his whip
separates him from the slaves. Swaggering and vengeful, Sam harasses
Teena and torments Quashie, calling himself a "big man pon dis plantation" (22). Moreover, his marked aggression toward Quashie stems from
his desire for Teena. In one of the final scenes, Sam tries to steal Jack's
treasure, which he believes will transform him into a "rich Backra gentlemen." When Dada threatens him with obeah, Sam laughs at his "little
power" that "caen do nutten" and pulls out his gun, the primary tool of the
colonial state (47). Dada's obeah triumphs, and he erases Sam's memory.
The ancestral spirits (dancers in masks) chase Sam around the stage, and
Sam returns to the plantation as Quashie's humble servant (48). A defunct

symbol of colonial power, Sam represents the failure of European control over African culture on the plantation. Instead of becoming rich like backra, Sam devolves into a servant to the slaves. Sam Power's downfall marks the beginning of the new power structure on the plantation.

The concluding act introduces a significant new character: a white English author writing a book titled *The Legend of Jack Mansong: The Jamaican Robin Hood*. Seeking the "view of the people," this Standard English–speaking author asks Tuckey for a final comment. Tuckey replies in heavily jargoned Standard English: "Jack represents the historical protectarian struggle against the decadent and parasitic bourgeoisie and clearly demonstrates the revolutionary élan inherent and dormant in the bosom of the oppressed, depressed, suppressed and repressed masses that must inevitably erupt and triumph over antagonistic contradictions arrayed against the prognosticated incarnation of an egalitarian society. (All are dumbfounded and look at each other and Tuckey in amazement)" (51). Tuckey's speech marks his appropriation of European discourse or, as the captain puts it, his inclusion into the "ranks of the intellectual progressives," a sideways glance at Manley's intellectual agenda. Dada expresses his disapproval of that kind of "bookscience," suggesting that Jamaica has not yet benefited from the imposition of European academic or linguistic models (51).

Dada's censure suggests the problems that attend the unalloyed acceptance of ascendancy discourse. Tuckey's speech—anticolonial as it is—is *about* but not *for* the slaves. Disapproval aside, Dada recognizes that the author "can write fe him story about Jack, but me an you know fe we story" (he can write his story about Jack, but we know our story), thus making the distinction between the oral and written histories of Jack as well as between the English scribal traditions and Jamaican patois (50; original ending). This original conclusion endeavors (but fails) to combine them, to acknowledge both traditions, and to emphasize the creolized voice of Afro-Jamaican people rather than that of the white ruling class.

The final scene brings the slaves and backra together on the stage.[5] The governor gives Teena and Quashie their freedom, and the planter's wife, Mrs. Chapman, announces that she has decided to turn the plantation into a cooperative farm. She says, "We shall produce to feed ourselves and abolish shortages. Let's all pull together." The governor, concluding the play, reiterates these sentiments: "Come on Backra. Let's join the people and drop foot" (51; original ending). The language here, like Tuckey's jargoned speech, resonates with and satirizes the socialist rhetoric associated with the ideology of Michael Manley's recently ousted People's National Party. *Mansong* thus at once imagines and questions the reality of a racially and culturally integrated Jamaica. However, Ted Dwyer revised this finale a few weeks before the opening night, and he replaced the backra-established cooperative farm with an Afro-Jamaican vision for a new community.

In his revision of the final scene, Dwyer excised the character of the white author, the socialist rhetoric of Mrs. Chapman, and backra "dropping foot with the people" on the stage (51; original ending); these changes reflect up on the shortcomings of an outgoing democratic socialist administration and the suspicion of a new government's (Seaga's) economic plans to run a country populated by mostly black people but ruled by wealthy light-skinned people. This final scene leaves out the backra altogether and celebrates the slaves' freedom (purchased with Jack's treasure) and the establishment of a black people-powered Jamaican culture. Dada performs a marriage ceremony for Teena and Quashie, using "old time" rituals. Invoking the ancestors, he sprinkles salt, grain, and water on the ground. As he performs his incantations, the company hums an "African melody" (53, revised ending). Quashie identifies their group as a community despite their different tribes and histories:

> All we ever have pon this plantation is one annoder. We work together, suffer an cry together. Mi an Teena know how you all feel. Dis plantation mek we all one blood, one flesh. All you come. Look! Look beyon

de river, all the way to de bog cotton tree dem, pass de windmill, pass
de bridge, way beyond the cane fiel to where de sun rise each morning
over dat hill. All dat a fe we lan.

[All we have on this plantation is one another. We work together,
suffer, and cry together. Teena and I know how you all feel. This plantation makes us one blood, one flesh. All of you come. Look! Look
beyond the river, all the way to the cotton trees, past the windmill, past
the bridge, way beyond the cane field, to where the sun rises each morning over that hill. All of that is our land] (53; revised ending).

Quashie proposes a postplantation life of peace and unity to heal the
wounds of slavery, and this vision relies on their occupation of and stew-
ardship of the land: a West Indian indigeneity. Even Sam Power joins
the celebration. Quashie works to create a "new village," looking forward
into the future of freedom. Moreover, their new village gestures toward
Wynter's concept of *indigenization*, neither "part-peasant" of the plot nor
"part-slave" of the plantation, they moved away from the "interstitial"
contradictions of plantation slavery ("Jonkonnu" 35). The characters of
Dwyer's revision reject the economic and ideological site of the plantation
in favor of a new relation to the land.

Both the original and the revised conclusions to *Mansong* self-reflexively
address issues of storytelling and history. Originally, the final scene (act 2,
scene 8) begins with Tuckey crying because he thinks that Jack is dead,
because, as he explains to Dada, backra told him so. Dada and Quashie
agree that the fact (or fiction) of Jack's death matters less than his life. When
the slaves want to know whether or not Quashie really conquered Jack,
Quashie tells them that what happened up there does not really matter:

Some say mi kill Jack. Some say me no kill him. Believe wha oonu wan
believe. But dis a kean tell you mi an Jack mek we peace. Jack woulda
wan all a wi fe be like him (Holding Charm). A hope dat I can liv up to
all dat Jack stan for."

[Some say I killed Jack. Some say I didn't kill him. Believe what you want to believe. But this I can tell you: Jack and I made our peace. Jack would want all of us to be like him (Holding Charm). I hope I can live up to all that Jack stands for.] (50).

Though Quashie warns Tuckey of the vagaries and inconsistencies inherent in storytelling, he urges him to teach the story of Jack Mansong so that future generations will know to whom they should attribute their freedom. Against the revelry of Teena and Quashie's wedding, the Afro-Jamaicans celebrate the facts of Jack's life rather than the fiction of his death.

Quashie and Jack offer two different but complementary models of resistance and rebuilding. When asked if he plans to go to the mountains to "fight Backra like Jack," Quashie explains that there are other ways to fight for freedom than with a gun, choosing instead community building and education" (50). Jack declares that "the fight is over, but the struggle begins wid freedom," and Dada agrees with Quashie that Jack "caused" freedom, but that Quashie will administer it: "Yes," Dada says, "Quashee right. Is Jack Mansong cause it [freedom]. . . . Quashee and Jack Mansong is one in spirit. The two a dem a we hero" (3). Dwyer conflates the historical enemies into one hero, sending a message of unity and cultural commonality.[6] In troubled times *Mansong* sent a hopeful message that promotes "One Love."

Mansong received excellent reviews from local critics, who were impressed with the story line, music, and special effects. Mervyn Morris wrote that "the transitions are beautifully managed. . . . The interaction between 'reality' and 'story', the link we make, is underscored in the production style . . . [which] invites us actively to use the imagination, to complete the creation of what has been suggested" ("New Story Time" 16). The interaction that Morris identifies between reality and story evokes also the relationships between the present and the past, creolization and colonialism, and the oral and the written. Moreover, his reflections are suggestive of the evolutionary and improvisational nature of storytelling and history.

In August 2008 Aston Cooke mounted a nonmusical adaptation of *Mansong* at the Jamaican Youth Theatre, pictures of which can be found on his Facebook page. Cooke urged his actors (ranging in age from eighteen to twenty-two) to conduct research at the University of the West Indies library and the National Library of Jamaica to find material for their parts. For this contemporary group Three-Fingered Jack emblematizes a "rebel with a cause," a "freedom fighter who used whatever methods necessary to achieve his goals" (interview). One of Cooke's students, Rayon McLean, explains that Jack stands out in Jamaican history as a rebel who refused, like the Maroons, to accommodate the colonial state:

> We have a Jamaican saying that says, "One, one coco, full basket [One by one a coconut can fill a basket, or success takes time]." If Jack started his fight against slavery, it mostly contributed to the overall success for the abolition of the slave trade. One thing I noticed, though, all other slaves who played important parts in any rebellion, there's information on them . . . so, I concluded that all these other slaves had some amount of compromise with the state, like the Maroons who signed some kind of treaty or something like that. But with Jack there's no evidence . . . of him being in any compromise with the state, so that might have affected the availability of information on him. I guess where there's no compromise, there's no need to have it written down in history, because those who were the rulers of the information books wouldn't have documented it. (Interview)

McLean's insightful comments speak to the scant written information about Three-Fingered Jack, who lived and died outside the plantation system, with "no compromise." He speaks also to the ways that written histories tend to elide the stories that challenge hegemonic, Eurocentric narratives. Jack's unwritten story of freedom fighting nonetheless reverberates in Jamaican culture, his struggles "one coco" in a basket that continues to fill. By performing their parts for the Kingston community and by circulating an abridged version of the play to schools around the island, Cooke and his students reproduce and disseminate their adaptation of Dwyer's pantomime. When Ted Dwyer wrote *Mansong*, he aimed for an audience in need of role models to help them through troubled times. His utopian vision, however, contrasts with the continuing troubles of the island nation, suggesting too the exigencies of community building, of "imagined communities" (as Benedict Anderson would have it), under the banner of "nation."

The Jamaicanization of the National Pantomime formalized with the move of the LTM to its own building on Thomas Redcam Road in 1961, the year before independence, built on lands purchased from the government with funds raised by the annual pantomimes and donations from the public over the years. The space also houses the National Dance Theatre Company. In 1985 the LTM moved to the "company" system, replacing the "scratch cast" and "star system" with professionals. Brian Heap argues that the Pantomime Company opened up opportunities for a younger generation of performers, "particularly those graduating from the Cultural Training Centre, in which the Little Theatre Movement, as founder of the Jamaican National School of Drama, has a vested interest." The LTM thus created a space for Jamaican theater that combats the problems of "critical and academic indifference" in tandem with increasing commercialization and decreasing volunteerism ("Pantomime" 4D).

In recent years criticisms of the Jamaican pantomimes have emerged. Barbara Gloudon, who has (problematically for some critics) written many of the pantomimes, identifies the source of the problem in the lack of local scriptwriters who are willing to include "every actor, musician, technician and member of the company" in the process ("Playwriting and Pantomimes" 3C). The dearth of scriptwriters reiterates the problems raised by Tuckey in *Mansong*, the problems surrounding written representation from within an oral culture. However, before Jamaican theater was nationalized, performance happened in public places, without buildings, professionals, or public sanction. It happened in places like Garvey's Edelweiss Park, where Miss Lou started her career. The Jamaican pantomime grew out of these traditions, working with larger economic and social forces that aimed to establish and concretize an official national narrative. The needs of Jamaicans and Jamaica have evolved in the twenty-first century, however, and the pantomime has consequently declined in popularity, as Jamaicans look for new models and methods of popular self-representation. Community and experimental theater, for example, offer alternatives to the potential limitations of nationalized, institutionalized models.

The LTM stopped using the Ward Theatre for its annual pantomime in 2002, because of the poor state of the facility and surrounding area. Though the Ward recently opened as part of efforts to invigorate the area for cultural consumption, downtown Kingston remains perilously close to garrison activities in the area. The 2010 extradition of alleged Jamaican drug lord Christopher "Dudus" Coke, for example, and the downtown violence surrounding it recall past conditions that produced outlaws such as Jack Mansong. Like Jack, Coke has been called a "Jamaican Robin Hood," known to some as a vicious criminal and to others as the benefactor of oppressed people. Still others view Coke and his ilk as necessary evils in troubled times. Jamaican popular culture today continues to glorify aspects of the figure of the "Bad Man," a scenario with important connections to Jack Mansong.

Epilogue

"THE BADDEST MAN AROUND"

Three-Fingered Jack Mansong lives on in Jamaican press and popular culture. His potent legacy persists in figures like the "Rudie," the don, the dance-hall artist, and even the Rasta. Like self-emancipated black people in colonial Jamaica who refused to submit to the debilitating, degendering conditions of slavery, contemporary rebels fight the oppressive institutions of its aftermaths. The criminalization of resistance in Jamaica continues to create the conditions for extralegal modes of survival. In turn, these criminal activities can perpetuate violence against and between black men who, in fighting for survival, face the distinct possibility of imprisonment, death, or both. Narratives that glorify "badass" rebels like Three-Fingered Jack and his successors imagine alternatives to the harrowing social and economic pressures of postcolonial Jamaica.

A full 125 years after emancipation, Jamaican independence produced a tangle of political, cultural, and economic problems that even today divide descendants of white planters and their "downpressed" majority counterparts, the working-class and rural poor descendants of Afro-Jamaican slaves. Despite Jamaica's independence, vestiges of English colonialism suffuse the educational and legal systems, and additionally U.S. popular culture both pervades and exploits that of Jamaica. Occasions of state violence, the criminal justice system, the prison regime, wage slavery, and even tourism impose a neocolonial dynamic that echoes the injustices of plantation slavery. The chasms between classes persist, and in Kingston many of the dispossessed poor live in urban ghettos divided by garrison politics and clientism (the exchange of goods and services for political support or patronage). Area leaders, or "dons," have long controlled these ghettoes, their activities underwritten by the nation's two major political parties, the Jamaica Labour Party (JLP) and People's National Party (PNP), both of which traded votes for money or development projects.[1] Tribalism and political violence have racked the nation for decades, even before the 1930s establishment of the bipartisan system.[2] By the 1970s popular culture glorified the hypermasculine gangster who ruled the streets. The violence reached a climax during the 1980 general elections, the same year the LTM staged *Mansong*, celebrating the notorious outlaw Three-Fingered Jack.

That same year Lester Lloyd Coke, "Don" in Tivoli Gardens (a West Kingston JLP enclave), extended the reach of his Shower Posse (so named for showering communities with bullets), building international networks in the United States, Canada, and England to traffic guns and drugs.[3] The Shower Posse had controlled Kingston's Tivoli Gardens and associated communities for four decades, engaging in frequent and bloody conflict with the rival PNP-protected Spangler Posse. The 2010 extradition of Coke's son, the notorious Christopher "Dudus" Coke, brings to the fore transnational socioeconomic problems that have long blurred the lines between outlaw and lawman in Jamaican politics, street life, and music.[4]

Christopher Coke had run Tivoli his since his father's 1992 death, making "soldiers" out of "sufferers." He was a benevolent, brutal, and beloved patriarch, and he exposed the complexities of political violence in Jamaica, shedding light on some of the reasons that many poor communities support leadership steeped in corruption. Protected by the JLP, Coke in turn protected his communities, providing school supplies, building schools, and punishing criminal activity such as prostitution and murder. To these populations Christopher Coke was a savior known as "Dudus," "President," "General," and "Shorty." Bunny Wailer, for example, released a song, "Don't Touch di President" that portrays Dudus as a "Robin Hood from the neighborhood" (Meschino 6, 18). Dudus contributed to the musical life of the island by funding free concerts that featured some of Jamaica's most popular reggae artists. These concerts mediated the rising tensions between dance-hall artists such as Vybz Kartel (now himself in prison) and Mavado, after conflicts between their factions (Gaza and Gully, respectively) grew violent in 2009. At a memorial for one of the deceased victims of the 2010 Dudus Troubles, a sound system played a Buju Banton song that celebrated Coke's top-ranking status as "Gun Specialist." Maroon-identified reggae artist Banton hailed from Denham Town in West Kingston, and he now sits in a Georgia jail for trafficking guns and cocaine (though the gun charges were dropped). These connections highlight the nexus of drugs, crime, and music in Jamaica as well as the figure of the "big man" who inhabits the cracks, in between and at the margins of sociolegal respectability.

When the United States extradited Coke for trafficking drugs and guns, his devoted supporters attacked Tivoli police stations, prompting chaos and the declaration of a state of emergency in Kingston. Residents of Tivoli wielded signs with slogans such as "Jesus die for us. We will die for Dudus" as the police stormed the area (Spaulding). Worn down by U.S. pressure, the Jamaican government announced it would extradite Coke. Gunfire and looting progressed for several days, resulting in some seventy deaths and the eventual capture of Dudus, who was heading to the U.S. embassy to surrender. In a 2012 letter to his trial judge, Coke asked for leniency in light of his good works for the poor, sick, young, and elderly in Tivoli: "I implemented a lot of social programs for the residents of my community—programs that teach them about self-empowerment" (qtd. in Hays). Yet he is also the same man who was "so ruthless he once ordered a rival killed with a chain saw" (Hays). As one of his lawyers puts it, "there are two sides to Christopher Coke . . . and everyone only talks about one side" (Weiser). Like Three-Fingered Jack, Dudus has been called a "Jamaican Robin Hood," a figure who functions as an emblem of hope for oppressed peoples and an emblem of evil for their oppressors. For some a vicious criminal and to others a protector of the "downpressed," this ambivalent figure represents an alternative to the systemic injustices of the "shitstem." Unlike Jack, however, Dudus maintained a relationship with the two-party system that had dominated the nation for decades.

The two-party system in Jamaica has been long associated with dangerous divisions and rivalries that trickle down to the street, and it has thus created the occasion for currents of radical resistance that undermine mainstream politics. Marcus Garvey's black nationalist People's Political Party (founded just before the two major parties in 1929), for example, furnished ideological foundations for the emerging Rasta movement, disrupting Jamaica's march toward a Creole nationalism.[5] The Jamaican government criminalized the Rasta movement from the moment of its public emergence in the 1930s. Leader Leonard Howell endured repeated arrests and imprisonment, and soon after his first prison term in 1934 he established the "guerilla" commune of Pinnacle. In 1954 Jamaican government forces raided and destroyed the community. The African-identified political, social, and spiritual congregation of the Rastas for "groundation" (peaceful debate and ritual marijuana smoking) threatened the perceived respectability of the Christian state and the Creole nationalism that would culminate in constitutional independence in 1962. The Rasta movement, Anthony Bogues argues, "became *the* central force for radical popular forms," though not the only "source of subaltern rebellion" (22). And the government did its best to repress it.

Just after independence in 1962, Prime Minister Sir Alexander Bustamante infamously proclaimed, "Bring in all Rastas dead or alive—if the prisons can't hold them, then Bogue-hill Cemetery or the Mad-house can" (Junior Manning, qtd. in Barnett 6). This pronouncement heralded additional decades of state violence against Rastas. Resistance to state violence included the Bad Friday Massacres in Coral Gardens, ignited when a group of armed Rastas burned down a gas station and killed a police officer. In 1966 police stormed the Rasta enclave Back O' Wall, to which many Pinnacle residents had moved, following a conflict between a Rasta and a police officer. The state cracked down on ganja as well, adding a drug-related component to the charges against the group. JLP leader and future prime minister Edward Seaga initiated the redevelopment of Back O' Wall into Tivoli Gardens, routing and dispossessing the Rastas to establish what would become a JLP enclave and, later, the community of Dudus Coke.

Two years after the razing of Back O' Wall, another wave of violence ensued in 1968, when the Hugh Shearer government banned Walter Rodney, a radical Guyanese lecturer on African history, from the University of the West Indies campus. The subsequent series of disturbances came to be known as the "Rodney Riots." Deeply critical of the postindependence middle class, Rodney interwove Rasta and Marxist thought in his rejection of white imperialist capitalism. Dedicated to the concerns of the urban youth, Rastas, and "other religious rebels," he worked both within and outside the university to support and mobilize the goals of the Black Power movement (West, "Targeting").[6]

Despite the overt state prejudice against Rastas, Michael Manley used Rasta symbols and reggae music in his 1972 election campaign, harnessing the popularity of Bob Marley. In his efforts to mobilize (some would argue, manipulate) the black masses to his camp, Manley used, for example, the emblem of Joshua's staff and the music of Bob Marley. "Soul rebel" Bob Marley combined the politics of the "Rude Bwoy" with the spirituality of the Rasta and emerged as the most famous singer out of West Kingston.[7] Though he denounced the "politricks" of the "shitstem," the 1976 Smile Jamaica concert in Kingston embroiled him in the nation's partisan politics and gang tribalism and prompted an attempt on his life. This cluster of events was fictionalized in Marlon James's recent Man Booker Prize–winning novel, *A Brief History of Seven Killings*.

Nonetheless, two years later Marley reluctantly participated in the One Love Peace concert, an idea birthed by two rival gangsters locked in the same jail cell, Claudius "Claudie" Massop (JLP) and Aston "Bucky"

Marshall (PNP). In an iconic moment, Marley called to the stage and joined hands with Prime Minister Michael Manley and opposition leader Edward Seaga. Shortly after the concert, both gangsters were killed, and the worst of the PNP/JLP violence came to a head two years later. Although the concert did not heal political wounds, Marley widely spread his message of unity, justice, and human rights. His "militant stardom" as Paul Gilroy calls it, combined "moral, spiritual, political and commercial energies" with a global reach (*Darker Than Blue* 89).

Former wailer Peter "Steppin' Razor" Tosh embodied an angrier militancy than Marley's ultimate peaceful stance. Brandishing a guitar shaped like an M16 assault rifle, he took to the stage at the same Peace Concert and delivered a legendary, antiestablishment speech that lambasted the problems of racism, classism, police brutality, and economic policy, and he compared these conditions to plantation slavery.[8] In addition, he dedicated a song to his brethren in prison for possession. His message underscored his commitment to justice, which he declared as important as peace: "Everyone is crying out for peace, no one is crying out for justice" ("Equal Rights"). Tosh's Rastafari sympathies, particularly in relation to repatriation to Africa, his disdain for American consumerism, his black pride, and his ever-present spliff put him in direct conflict with the idealized middle-class respectability ingrained in the state.

It was, however, the Perry Henzell/Trevor Rhone film *The Harder They Come* (1972) that internationalized "Rudies," Rastas, and West Kingston, starring Jimmy Cliff as Ivan "Rudie" O. Martin.[9] Director Perry Henzell drew the character using facets of Cliff's problems with the music industry intertwined with the story of the 1940s Jamaican gangster Vincent "Ivanhoe" Martin, also known as Ryghing or Rhygin' (a variant of "raging"), whose story bears resemblance to the story of Jack Mansong.[10] Ivan's criminality grew out of the inequities of a classed and racialized police state, and the film reveals the brutality of ghetto life for the poor black residents of West Kingston. Ivan's conflicts with the state, particularly with the church, reflect the social and (Christian) spiritual forces that shape and constrict the Jamaican urban poor. Ivan channels what Carolyn Cooper has called "heroic badness," an "indigenous tradition" with origins in slave rebellions ("Sheriff" 153).[11] Ivan embodies the energy and fate of martyrs to freedom and violence. As he dies, showered by bullets, he remembers himself watching a spaghetti Western at the Rialto Theatre (a clip from an earlier sequence). This "revolutionary" film, Kamau Brathwaite writes, marked a "dislocation in the socio-colonial pentameter . . . [and] for the first time at last, a local face, a native ikon, a national language voice was hero" (*History of the Voice* 41). Ivan died a hero in his own mind, but also in the eyes of his working-class Kingston audience.[12]

Initially banned by the government, *The Harder They Come* prompted riots when the Carib Theatre sold out on its opening night. Its immediate success in Jamaica stemmed from its revolutionary use of patois, its iconization of Rastas and Rudies, its criticism of corrupt systems, its reggae rhythms, and the casting of real people off the street who filmed on locations in West Kingston. Afro-Jamaican Trevor Rhone (often unacknowledged as Henzell's collaborator) reworked Anglo-Jamaican Henzell's initial screenplay to better reflect the lives and language of working-class black Jamaicans.[13] The collaborative, kinetic, and improvisational style of filming enabled Jamaicans to participate in their own cultural production, to revise the white man's screenplay into an Afro-Jamaican event starring a "badass" black hero. Jimmy Cliff achieved national and international fame with his rendition of a cop-killing "Rude Bwoy" with the cool swagger of the blaxploitation star.

Though not a blaxploitation film, *The Harder They Come* shares (perhaps echoes) elements of the genre: the Corbucci-style antihero, ample sex and violence, a funky seventies aesthetic, and, most important, a grounding in transnational movements that politicized race and envisioned community.[14] Melvin Van Peebles's *Sweet Sweetback's Baadasssss Song* (1971) had inaugurated the genre the previous year, and for the next four years these films proliferated, starring black heroes for black audiences. Van Peebles wrote, scored, directed, and starred in *Sweetback*, and he dedicated his film "to all the brothers and sisters who have had enough of The Man"; the opening credits announce that it "stars the black community."[15] Black Panther Huey Newton viewed *Sweetback* as a "revolutionary film" and announced that it "helps put forth the ideas of what we must do to build community" (113). Characters like Ivan and Sweetback appealed to black urban audiences, creating a new standard in hero and audience, both films prompting community-style "talking back" to the screen.[16]

Many of the blaxploitation films that followed *Sweet Sweetback*, however, were produced, directed and distributed (like *The Harder they Come*) by white men. Some critics have argued that the films exploit (as the name suggests) the black body for mass consumption; however, the centrality of strong black heroes, the creative energy of black actors, the creation of black audiences, and the participation of black communities set revolutionary precedents in the cultural production of race in modern visual culture. The figure of the black outlaw, especially when sexualized, reifies white stereotypes of black men as violent, oversexed criminals; however, characters like Ivan and Sweetback expose the conditions that provoke violence and machismo, at once countering, corroborating, and complicating these stereotypes. As I have shown in the previous chapters, black actors and producers can negotiate the limits of representation imposed by an exploitative, white-dominated industry.

Quentin Tarantino notoriously vexed these issues surrounding the cultural production of race in his 2012 film *Django Unchained*. With Tarantino's trademark combination of violence, irreverence, and humor, the film offended critics with its graphic representation of slavery and repetition of the word "nigger," raising questions of appropriateness and appropriation in representations of race. Tarantino admired genre films, particularly blaxploitation films, and he self-consciously created a black Wild West in *Django Unchained*; he named his antihero, for example, after the titular character of Sergio Corbucci's spaghetti Western (1966), starring Francisco Nero as a gunfighter embroiled in a struggle between the Klan and a band of Mexican rebels. Of his film, Tarantino wrote that the subject of slavery demands the violence of his approach: "When you learn of the rules and practices of slavery, it was as violent as anything I could do—and absurd and bizarre." The controversy that Tarantino (again) set in motion with *Django Unchained* reiterates the problems attending race and representation, particularly in narratives of violence, vengeance, and valor—characteristics associated with representations of Three-Fingered Jack and with the Jamaican gangster.

Glorified in popular culture, the so-called Badman furnishes a deadly role model for Jamaican youth. In music the shift in Jamaica from reggae to dance-hall culture marked a transition that Donna Hope argues moved from the masculine and "forgivably violent" hero of the "Rude Bwoy" to the "hypermasculine" "shotta" (shooter) linked to the transnational "narco-culture and the culture of the gun" (116–117). Anthony Bogues laments the transformation of community-minded area leaders into the "Shotta Don," marking the transition from "postcolonial rebel" into a "commanding figure of vengeance" (25). Bogues looks to the Bounty Killer song "Petty Thief" as evidence of the disturbing dominance of this figure in mainstream Jamaican culture.[17] The gun-talking, gay-bashing Bounty Killer consolidates and skews Caribbean expectations of black masculinity entwined with violence and crime. And the don continues to influence street life in Jamaica, in figures like Dudus Coke.

And we have arrived again at the arrest of Dudus Coke, purportedly taken into custody on June 2010 in drag and wearing a wig. His masquerade has provoked conversations about masculinity, heteropatriarchy, and power in contemporary Jamaica. Poet Kei Miller intervened in these discussions:

[This] sentiment of "bad man nuh dress like girl" is always kind of funny—because in a country . . . where any tour of dancehall will feature a few male dance crews who always offer, on public display, the most profound and sometimes magical performances of Jamaican queerness; and in a country where bad men run across garrison communities—one hand holding onto their uzi guns, and the other lifting up the hem of their frocks so as not to trip, then we know the real truth—that bad man dress however de rass him want to dress. And that's exactly what makes them de real bad men. (Miller)

A bad man in a dress, Miller remarks, can prove his masculinity with a big gun. The armed hypermasculinity of Dudus gives him freedom to do whatever "de rass" he wants. Even in a dress, Dudus wields what Hope calls an "extreme form of masculinity" that is "qualified by traditional Jamaica's "high levels of deviance" (126).[18] In addition, his connections with mainstream party politics underwrite his illegal activity, enabling him to at once deploy and undermine state authority, even as the state simultaneously uses and polices him. These conditions have created the space for different modes and methods of survival.

These related figures of resistance I have been outlining—Rastas, Rudies, racketeers, and renegades—inhabit Jamaican history and culture, and they repeatedly and in varying levels of success, complicity, or failure interrogate the systems of exploitation out of which they erupted. The Jamaican government (in its different forms, colonial and postcolonial) has done its best to deploy for its benefit the elements it polices, using the divide-and-conquer strategies the English put into play as far back as 1655. This strategy does not always work, but it does attest to continual resistance to state control in Jamaica (and elsewhere). Jack Mansong has furnished these various groups with a mythic model of black "badassery," at once the cypher and "everyman" of stories about social, racial, and cultural oppression.

Jack's influence has reached far beyond Jamaica. His "afterlives," to borrow Diana Paton's term, have resonated around the Atlantic for more than two hundred years. Nineteenth-century British theater and fiction used Jack's story to assert the dominance of white Englishmen over Afro- (and sometimes Anglo-) Jamaicans. Nineteenth-century African Americans leveled it to insist on black rights and representation in the United States (William Brown) and in England (Ira Aldridge). Twentieth-century

Jamaican authors and playwrights have used Jack's story to explore projects of decolonization and nationhood. Twenty-first-century white academics and black theater companies have mobilized it to fight institutional racism. Finally, contemporary Maroons associate Jack with their own controversial history as warriors and rebels who fought and won a war against the British Empire.

I now return full circle to the Maroons of Jamaica, who associate Three-Fingered Jack with their unique heritage of freedom fighting, despite his perhaps questionable methods. For Col. Frank Lumsden, Jack was "the baddest man around" (interview). Col. Wallace Sterling describes Jack as "a clever man and a good fighter" (interview), reminding us that "the Maroons always love a good fight." In times of slavery and beyond, he explained, conditions give rise to Robin Hood–style renegades:

> People like [Jack] will come about from time to time, and you have to look at this society as it existed back then, because sometimes one of the mistakes that we make is that we try to take incidents that happened 100, 150, or 200 to 300 years, or 500 years ago and try to put it into today's perspective, when the conditions that rise to the incident is not necessarily as it exists now. . . . And, you know, Jamaica wasn't the kind of country that we know it to be. It was a country that was dominated by plantation owners. . . . So, when you live in a society like that, things could happen. Three-Finger Jack Mansong could maybe . . . look at himself like the Robin Hood of Britain. (interview)

Colonel Sterling sees the tensions between Jack and the Maroons as the byproduct of a plantation system that pitted Afro-Jamaicans against one another. Moreover, he views contemporary non-Maroon Jamaican resentment about the treaty as the persistence of that dynamic. Therefore, he proclaimed, "We need a change." The treaty, he reminded the audience at the 2015 Charles Town International Maroon Conference, happened 275 years ago. "It's time to move on," he urged, "because only united can Jamaica move forward" (remarks).

Colonel Lumsden likewise disseminated a message of peace and unity for Jamaicans. He promoted in his own community, across Jamaica, and around the globe positive ways to harness aspects of Maroon warrior culture for spiritual growth, for example, African drumming and dancing, Brazilian capoeira, and even wrestling. In his vision for an "indigenous community without borders," he sought to create a global model of collective sustainability, ecological justice, and cultural persistence. Many Jamaicans, Maroon and non-Maroon alike, share his vision. In contemporary Jamaica, for example, "conscious reggae" musicians, artists, athletes, writers, and activists—men and women—continue to demonstrate Jamaica's strength, endurance, and bravery: strong bodies and minds offering role models without ambiguity or guns. Three-Fingered Jack robbed and killed for his freedom, using guerilla methods that impressed even fierce Maroon warriors. Freedom fighting, however, takes different forms.

Acknowledgments

I have tracked the story of the badass rebel Three-Fingered Jack, finding permutations in the archives of London, Boston, New York, Spanish Town, and Kingston. I have also followed Jack's footsteps in rural Jamaica, listening to people from the parishes of Saint Thomas and Portland, from within Maroon communities, and across the Cunha Cuhna Pass. This book owes so much to so many. A fellowship from the National Endowment for the Humanities supported a year of research, writing, and community engagement in Jamaica. The Fulbright Scholar Program permitted me to live and teach at the University of the West Indies in Mona. A Franklin Grant from the American Philosophical Association, gave me additional time in the Maroon communities of Charles Town and Moore Town. The Towson University Faculty Development Research Committee funded two grants, one at the exploratory phase and one further along the project. In addition, the Towson University College of Liberal Arts and the Department of English supported this work, and I'd like to thank Dean Terry Cooney and English Department chair George Hahn for their funding and encouragement. Also at Towson University Deana Johnson helped sort out countless administrative problems, even long distance, and Susan Weinginger provided invaluable support with aplomb. I appreciate, too, the help of librarians and archivists at the National Library of Jamaica and the Jamaica Archives in Spanish Town,

Jamaica, and I give special attention to Bernadette Worrell and Yvonne Fraser-Clarke at the NLJ, examples of patience and professionalism.

I owe special thanks to the friends and colleagues who have helped me to think through my ideas. Fellow Gonzo researcher and "souljah" Paul Youngquist has read almost every word, and with great generosity he has helped me navigate difficult ideas, people, and places. I thank Jeff Cox, too, for taking time he didn't have to read and make suggestions on big chunks of the manuscript. Michael Gamer's thoughtful reading of my prospectus and kind letters of support likewise contributed to the completion of this project. At Towson University I have had the good fortune to work with smart, interesting colleagues: Geoff Becker, David Bergman, Chris Cain, Clarinda Harriss, Lana Portolano, and Jan Wilkotz. I especially thank Jennifer Ballengee for bringing to life our Towson writing group and Erin Fehskens and Chris D'Addario for participating in it. I am indebted also to Natalie Zacek and the lively participants of the NEH Summer Institute: "Slaves, Soldiers, Rebels: Currents of Black Resistance in the Tropical Atlantic, 1760–1888." Michelle Dionne Thompson supplied an extra set of eyes and careful attention to detail. I owe my identity as a scholar to the mentorship of my dissertation adviser Gene Ruoff, who fully supported my movement away from canonical romanticism into Caribbean and Transatlantic studies, and his guidance continues to delight. A. Lavonne Brown Ruoff has likewise helped me through the long haul. I owe special thanks to Thomas W. Choate for helping to fund and conceptualize this project, but, more importantly, for always being there for me.

Conversations and camaraderie have also sustained this endeavor. I am eternally grateful to Towson colleague Jonathan Vincent and Rachel Cobb Vincent for their unwavering support and encouragement at the intellectual, creative, and professional levels—in Baltimore and in Jamaica. I appreciate the peaceful sails and fire pits hosted by Sonia Shah and Mark Bulmer. Erin Goss was there for the early years, enjoying snow days and Scrabble games. I owe more than I can say to Kevin Coelho and Lindsay

Wood for their loving care of Charlie Botkin while I traveled to Jamaica and beyond. Denise Mackey Klancic, Lorena Kazmierski, John Lessner, Rich McCormick, and Tom Turnbull have helped and delighted me through the years in many ways. The staff of Charmington's Cafe literally fueled my work.

Friends and colleagues in Kingston, Jamaica, have created for me a second home. I thank the late and truly remarkable Col. Frank Lumsden for his years of friendship and guidance: he helped me learn to listen to and work with people at a different tempo. Michael Lumsden, Marcus Goffe, and Rich Lumsden have been pillars of support, particularly during the difficult year that followed Frank Lumsden's passing. My role in the organization of the Charles Town International Maroon Conference has changed the scope and tenor of my work. I wish to thank the Charles Town Maroon Council, Col. Wallace Sterling of Moore Town, Chief Michael Grizzle of the Flagstaff/Trelawny Maroons, Roy Anderson, Oji Adisa, and Faithy Peterkin for welcoming me into and teaching me about Maroon culture. I honor here Gloria ("Gaa'ma Mama G") Simms for her friendship, mentorship, and spiritual example; she taught me the most important lesson about the way I work: "Tunyahan mek fashion."

So many wonderful people have welcomed me into their Jamaican homes and communities: Alan and De Ross, the late Miguel DeLeon with Penny and Megan DeLeon, Uwe Kumst, Omar Francis, Alison Perkins, Birte Timm, Heidi Savery, and Evan Williams. I owe general uplift to Dub Club, Red Bones, and Jamnesia for their music and life-sustaining vibes. I would not have survived without the nourishment so graciously provided by Ahmet "Ossie" Osman, Shaneka Johnson, and the crew at the Wine Shop. Without great drivers (and gentlemen) such as Ashman "Ashie" Ransford and Neville Greene, I never would have made it anywhere.

The careful hands of many people have guided this project, and I am delighted that my project has a home in the Critical Caribbean Studies series of Rutgers University Press. I offer sincere thanks to executive editor Kimberly Guinta for acquiring the manuscript as well as for her ongoing support and kindness. I am indebted to the series editors for their helpful recommendations that made this project a better book. The anonymous reviewers, too, offered incisive, constructive criticism that helped me reframe the project. The editorial and production team at Rutgers University Press, particularly editorial assistant Kristen Bonanno and senior production coordinator Anne Hegeman, provided painstaking, time-consuming labor. I am immensely grateful to copyeditor Susan J. Silver for her diligence and good humor as she nimbly performed (and vanquished) a gargantuan task. Thanks also go to Elspeth Tupelo of Twin Oaks indexing.

Finally, I want to thank for their support my family members: my brother Abbey; my nephew, Allie; and my stepmother, Sally Botkin, as well as the Cohen family on the East Coast and the Dorins and Rubin-Bermans on the West Coast. Charlie Botkin gave me unconditional love, and his calm but spirited presence brought me peace when I most needed it. Finally, I honor the members of my family who have already joined the ranks of the ancestors: my father, Albert; my brother Michael; my mother, Carol; and my sister, Rose.

Notes

INTRODUCTION

1. Runaway slaves were sometimes referred to as "Maroons," from the Spanish term for "wild or untamed," a term originally used to describe escaped cattle. In Jamaica they lived in remote areas in the mountains, where they practiced subsistence agriculture and developed tactics of guerilla warfare. Their 1738–39 treaties with the English (see chapter 1) designated them special subjects of the Crown; however, the terms of the treaties also dictated that they returned runaway slaves. I use "maroons" to refer to pretreaty maroons and "Maroons" to refer to posttreaty Maroons. For accounts of Maroon history, see Bilby, *True-Born Maroons*; Brathwaite, *Development of Creole Society*; Brathwaite, *Wars of Respect*; Campbell; Carey; Besson; Craton, *Testing the Chains*; Kopytoff, "Maroons of Jamaica"; Linebaugh and Rediker, *Many-Headed Hydra*; Robinson; Price; Wilson, *Island Race*; Zips; A. Thompson; and N. Roberts. See also early Anglo-Jamaican accounts of Maroons, such as Long, vol. 1; Dallas; and B. Edwards.

2. Though the newspaper did not elaborate, later accounts attribute his nickname to the result of an earlier fight with the Maroon who eventually killed him. (However, to be "three" fingered in Jamaican vernacular means to be a thief.)

3. The *Royal Gazette* located Jack's hideout in Saint David's parish, and later historians specify that he lived in a cave on Mount Lebanus in Saint Thomas in the east, with other hideouts at Cane River and Cambridge Hill (Aravamudan, introd. to *Obi* 12).

4. Obeah is a difficult term to define. Bilby and Handler define it as a "catchall term" that "encompasses a wide variety and range of beliefs and practices related to the control or channeling of supernatural/spiritual forces by particular individuals or groups for their own needs, or on behalf of clients who come for help" (154–156).

Paton proposes that "colonial-lawmaking and law-enforcing practices" contributed to the increasing reification and production of obeah as a "singular, unitary, phenomenon" ("Obeah Acts" 2). See also Watson, "Mobile Obeah," as well as Rodriques, Murison, and Gerbner in a special issue of *Atlantic Studies*.

5. For a useful version of Fawcett's *Obi* with the musical score, see Hoskins, introd. to *Obi*.

6. *Obi; or, Three-Fingered Jack* was produced in Kingston at the Theatre Royal on September 16, 1862. A benefit performance for its producer, J. Thompson, it was supported by amateurs. But records about this play and its reception do not exist, nor did it play again for the rest of the century (E. Hill 101).

7. In 1934 Williams wrote his Boston University dissertation in cultural anthropology, "Psychic Phenomenon of Jamaica." The Jesuit ethnographer did fieldwork in Jamaica, and his text includes the story of Three-Fingered Jack.

8. Dwyer's *Mansong* was produced by the Little Theatre Movement at the Ward Theatre in Kingston, Jamaica, and directed by Dennis Scott from December 1980 to March, 1981. Manuscripts can be found in LTM Pantomime Programmes, 1970–1984, on the third floor of the Pantomime Collection in the National Library of Jamaica.

9. In early 2015 Jamaican transplant to Toronto Julian King self-published *Three-Fingered Jack: The Spirit of Jamaica*. He writes, "Maybe after this is read, some scholastic soul will step up and validate . . . Jack's true existence" (loc. 2). One can inquire about King's Afrocentric tale of black justice over white tyranny tale by messaging him on his Facebook page (www.facebook.com/groups/588702077868970/).

10. Some of the oral histories in Bilby's *True-Born Maroons* call the same spot "Three-Finger Jack a Woman Tumble." Bilby's interviewees emphasize Jack's theft, his fall down the ravine, and his wife's escape (310). Few sources mention Jack's wife, and we have but scant documentation of her existence—a different story yet to be told.

11. The five-and-a-half-mile Cuhna Cuhna Pass trail connects Hayfield and other parts of Saint Thomas with Bowden Pen and the Rio Grande Valley in Portland, via the main ridge of the Blue Mountains. For information about the Blue and John Crow Mountains National Park, contact the Bowden Pen Farmers Association at www.facebook.com/Ambassabeth/. For additional information, contact the Jamaica Conservation and Development Trust at www.jcdt.org.jm.

12. Paton distinguishes between the representation of free and enslaved Afro-Jamaicans in the *Obi* texts; see "Afterlives." See also the introduction of Aravamudan, *Obi*. Much of the recent scholarship comes from Rzepka's special issue on *Obi* for the *Romantic Circles Praxis Series*, which includes articles by Rzepka, Cox, Hogle, Hoskins, Buckley, and Lee; this project (2002) filled the gap opened up by A. Richardson's seminal article and Rzepka's "Dark Interpreter." See also more recent scholarship by O'Rourke, Reed, Swydky, Warner et al., and Gibbs.

13. See, for example, Aravamudan's *Tropicopolitans*, Roach, and Gilroy's *Black Atlantic*.

14. See Linebaugh and Rediker, Dayan, and Baucom. In addition, Bilby's *True-Born Maroons* uses oral histories in a seminal study of Jamaica's Afrocentric Maroon culture, permitting these voices precedence in his history. Scott and Laughlin look beyond what they call the "dead end of the nationalist project in the Anglocreole Caribbean" toward "new space for thinking" ("Criticism as a Question").

15. Goudie's study argues that the early American republic had a "paracolonial" relationship with the West Indies that either "negates" or "affirms" its "creole complex." American national identity, he posits, hinges on obfuscating the U.S.-West Indian relationship economically and culturally, and as a result the West Indies serve as a "shadow double" (5, 13, 103). In addition, Reed's *Rogue Performances* and Dillon examine Atlantic World stage productions. Watson's *Caribbean Culture* and Youngquist's *Romanticism and the Atlantic* consider the before-neglected West Indian perspectives in their studies of the Atlantic world.

16. Nanny was named a national hero alongside Sam Sharpe, a devout Christian who tried (but failed) to lead a nonviolent rebellion, qualities that perhaps balanced out Nanny's rebelliousness and obeah. See Sharpe's discussion of Nanny's ascension to national hero as well as Brathwaite's *Wars of Respect*.

17. Despite some concerns about Nanny's status as an obeah woman and a Maroon, Sharpe explains, she served Manley's vision as a "role model for Jamaican women" at a historical moment (1975) that the young nation celebrated its Afro-Creole heritage of resistance and that the United Nations declared International Women's Year (17–20). The inclusion of Nanny to the list of national heroes indicates the rising attention of women's issues during that period.

18. Citing Burton, they note also that it resulted from deliberate attempts to change the gender makeup of the enslaved population (3). See also Knight; Knight and Crahan; Spillers; Lewis, *Culture*; and Burton.

19. In fact, debate surrounds most of the national heroes, and practical problems (such as the dearth of visual records) complicate representation of the more controversial, and darker-skinned, national heroes such as Nanny or Paul Bogle. These images, Poupeye, director of the National Gallery of Jamaica, explains, have been creatively constructed, using part imagination, part familiar images, and part oral histories (conversation). See Brathwaite, *Wars of Respect*; and Sharpe for discussions of images of Nanny.

20. Omari "Afrikan" S. Ra (born Robert Cookhorne) identifies as a political artist whose work grew out of his response to the 1980 general elections and then the 1985 Grenada invasion. His work is informed by the militant politics of Peter Tosh, and his abstract style broadcasts deliberate ambiguity ("Omari Ra"). In 2004 he

produced an acclaimed group of paintings of heads of men (including Jack and Tacky) that evoke Toussaint-Louverture and Dessalines; these images also depict self-representations of the artist, and they capture the spirit of the Haitian Revolution with reference to voodoo, rebellion, and self-affirmation ("Omari Ra").

21. In her discussion of national heroes and visual culture, Dacres has noted the central image in the reconstruction of a collective Jamaican national identity is male (130). She focuses on Edna Manley's 1965 statue *Bogle* and the ambivalence surrounding his controversial history, "related to the ambivalent national impulse to construct the authenticity of the new nation on black folk culture (131). Uncertainty indeed swirls around images of Paul Bogle, a free black deacon who led the last large-scale rebellion in Jamaica. See Sheller; and Bilby, "Image and Imagination," for more on Paul Bogle.

22. Ross documents competing notions of black masculinity during the Jim Crow period. Neal argues that contemporary black men are compelled to move away from the figure of the "Strong Black Man" and toward the conception of "New Black Man," committed to community, family, and diversity. See also R. Richardson, who examines the problematic and limited representations of black masculinity in terms of geography, specifically in the American South. Wallace argues that the "monocularistic gaze" of Western white people has constructed dichotomous stereotyping about black masculine identity.

23. Early work on Caribbean masculinities has discussed the problems involving depictions of men as powerful, promiscuous, and derelict in parenting (Lewis, "Man Talk," and Barrow). Parry discusses "sexual prowess," noting too that feminism has contributed to the erosion of male authority (qtd. in Hope 7). Mohammed argues that economic shifts for women have changed the priorities for and representations of men ("Like Sugar in Coffee"). See also Shepherd et al. on Caribbean men and education; see Chevannes, *Learning*, for a conversation about the socioeconomic problems facing Afro-Jamaican men and boys. Reddock's collection *Interrogating Caribbean Masculinities* offers an insightful overview, particularly Beckles's article, "Black Masculinity."

24. See Haynes for her discussion of what she calls the "crisis school of Caribbean hypermasculinity" (93).

25. Stephens in *Black Empire* examines radical Afro-Caribbeanist influence on the transnational "masculine imaginary" of the twentieth century, arguing that their work inhabits a black transatlantic space between the Caribbean and the United States.

26. In *The Archive and the Repertoire* Taylor refers to scenarios as "meaning making paradigms that structure social environments, behaviors, and potential outcomes" that imagine alternative conclusions (28).

27. For two American responses to these issues, see hooks and Coates.

28. Puri puts her work in conversation with disciplines outside of her own field of literature to comment on the relationship of her work in Grenada to cultural studies, area studies, anthropology, cultural geography, and memory and trauma studies ("Finding the Field," 59). See also her monograph, *Granada Revolution*.

29. I am particularly inspired by D. Thomas's exploration of historians such as Diana Paton, Vincent Brown, and Trevor Burnard, alongside novelists such as Marlon James, Margaret Cezair-Thompson, Michelle Cliff, and Edwidge Danticat in her project of archiving violence.

30. One could argue that authors, playwrights, and storytellers who imaginatively create stories about Jack engage in what Glissant calls "creative marronage," distinguishing between the political and historical resistance that "takes its strengths from a combination of geographical connectedness, memory" and "all the canny detours, diversions, and ruses required to deflect the repeated attempts to recuperate this cultural subversion" (xxii–xxiii). Cooper plays with these ideas with her concepts of "verbal" and "erotic" marronage (*Noises in the Blood* 4). Cummings interestingly frames queerness and marronage as transnational discourses "marked by an ongoing engagement with the paradoxes and tensions of belonging and non-belonging" to reassess ways that they have been applied to the reading of Caribbean cultural contexts (169). See also G. Thomas's discussion of Wynter's "Black Metamorphosis" and Césaire's use of "le verbe marronner." Also, see Fehskens on the concept of "creative marronage" in Abani's *Graceland*.

31. For Diana Taylor this binary moves between written texts or documents (archive) and oral traditions, practices, or rituals (repertoire). The *scenario* conjures up physical location; generates critical distance between actor and character; allows "reversal, parody and change"; involves multiplicity of forms; forces "participants, spectators or witnesses to 'be there' as part of the transfer"; and reactivates rather than duplicates (28–32).

32. See Bennett's "Jamaica Language"; Brathwaite's *Arrivants*; and Wa Thiong'o's *Decolonising the Mind*.

33. Lovelace, *Dragon Can't Dance*; Césaire, *Tempest*; and Cliff, *No Telephone to Heaven*.

CHAPTER 1 — DIVIDE AND CONQUER

1. Kopytoff writes that when Maroons today refer to "First Time" Maroons, they refer to the people who won the treaties rather than to those who escaped from the plantation ("Charter" 52).

2. See Paton, "Afterlives," on Quashie's transformation from Maroon to slave (52).

3. See Pestana and S. Taylor's *Western Design*.

4. In McNeill's estimation, half of Cromwell's troops were dead and half the survivors sick from "Yellow Jack" (yellow fever) within six months of invasion, while West African-born blacks were immune to the virus (10).

5. This group was called also the Carmahaly, the Vermaholis, and the Vermahalles (Campbell 25).

6. Zips agrees with Colonel Lumsden about the heroism of the Maroons, considering theirs as a "history of resistance" rather than a "history of domination" (vii).

7. Though Aravamudan in his introduction to Earle's *Obi* suggests that Congos would be Coromantees, I propose that the Congos would be Bantu-speaking Africans from Congo or Angola.

8. See Schuler's discussion of the ethnicities of slave rebels in Jamaica in the eighteenth century. She explores the tensions among the Creoles and Africans on the island. Though most rebellions and Maroons on the island were associated with the Akan-speaking Coromantees, other ethnic groups populated Jamaica as well. For example, many Bantu-speaking Congos of central-western Africa were brought to the Americas, but they were scattered about the region. More Congos arrived on the island during the postemancipation period (380).

9. Coromantee was a landing place on the Gold Coast (modern Ghana), but in the Americas it came to refer to a cultural rather than an ethnic identity; the Coromantees spoke Akan or Twi. See Eltis et al. and Burnard (4).

10. Though Jack's group allegedly pledged to kill every Creole it met, the supplement to the *Royal Gazette* refers to his second in command, Caesar, as a Creole (vol. 2, no. 67: 458).

11. My search of the *Royal Gazette* from 1780 to 1781 did not yield an advertisement posted by a specific person or estate for the capture of Jack/Bristol, but the advertisement for Caesar appeared many times. In addition, my search of the manifest of the Rozel estate (which is spelled differently in different contexts) held no slave called Jack.

12. Moseley published his first edition in 1799, but in his second edition (1800), he replaced the story of Jack with that of a tiger. See D. Lee, "Grave Dirt," for an interesting discussion of the tiger.

13. See Aravamudan's introduction to Earle's *Obi*, Craton's *Invisible Man*, and Paugh for further discussion of yaws and its outbreak in Jamaica.

14. Tacky's Rebellion prompted the "Act to Remedy the Evils arising from Irregular Assemblies of Slaves," which deemed obeah a crime and limited the privileges of enslaved people. See Paton, "Witchcraft."

15. A 1789 document based on slave testimony states that slaves sought obeah for good as well as evil, for predicting the future, advising, and curing various disorders (Bilby and Handler 158).

16. My sincere thanks to Paul Youngquist for his reference and transcription of Stevens's *Crisis*.

17. In addition to killing Tacky, Captain Davy also injured a ship's captain in an event described by Dallas (129) and mentioned by Moseley, who writes, "Sam was Captain Davy's son, he who shot a Mr. Thompson, the master of a London ship at Old Harbour" (201).

18. Assembly of Jamaica, journal, December 22, 1781, Spanish Town, National Library of Jamaica, Kingston.

19. The eighth message posts the request from Reeder's son, Nathanial Beckford, and his Charles Town peer, Cockburn (Assembly of Jamaica, journal, November 11, 1816, National Library of Jamaica):

> That John Reeder, late a Charles-Town maroon, deceased, the father of the petitioner, had a pension from the assembly on account of his services in killing Three-Fingered Jack.
>
> That the said John Reeder was interred at the sole expense of the petitioner, to the amount of 27£.0s.7d.

20. Assembly of Jamaica, journal, November 11, 1816, National Library of Jamaica.

21. See the *Hereford Journal*, November 20, 1816; and the *Chester, Cheshire, and North Wales Advertiser*, November 15, 1816.

22. The *Oxford English Dictionary* defines Quashie as a "generic name for a black person, esp. one considered as credulous and insignificant." The first notation cites Long's *History of Jamaica*, vol. 2. Planters first coined the term, according to Beckles, to represent their "ideological characterization of enslaved black men" ("Black Masculinity" 233).

23. See Bhabha (89–90), for a discussion of the concept of "mimicry" in culture clashes between natives and aliens.

24. Bilby traces the divisions between Maroons and *obroni* (non-Maroon Jamaicans) in part to the story of Nanny and her sister, the myth of "two sister pikni" (*True-Born Maroons* 110–121). The story goes that Nanny and her people resisted slavery and escaped to remote areas, where they lived according to Akan traditions. Nanny's sister and her descendants, however, submitted to slavery. From this division two related cultures emerged and split further as their populations grew and developed.

25. Colonel Lumsden states, "Look at Tacky. Tacky was a Kromanti Chief, and he gathered around him Kromantis, and one of his stated goals was to destroy Maroons. Now, when the Maroons sent for him to come in and talk, he wouldn't have any of that. And so, the Maroons decided that they were going to take him down" (interview).

CHAPTER 2 — "JACK IS A MAN"

1. Unless otherwise specified, I use the tenth edition of Burdett's *Life and Exploits*. For a thorough list of the prose versions and their adaptations, see Paton "Histories."

2. Paton, for example, argues that "representations of Jack could be adapted and adopted by those on all sides of the slavery debates," and she finds that those who treat Jack the least sympathetically are the most ideologically coherent ("Afterlives" 3). Swydky suggests Jack's history "should be read as part of a broader history of misrepresenting black resistance and independence in the Caribbean" ("Rewriting the History").

3. From Sonnet III of *Poems Concerning the Slave Trade* by Robert Southey and Erasmus Darwin, *The Botanic Garden: A Poem in Two Parts* (qtd. in Aravamudan, introd. to *Obi* 67).

4. The proclamation, which Earle cites verbatim, specifically refers to Jack's "desperate gang" (154–155), though the novel disbands Jack's crew early on and situates him as isolated from everyone except for his mother, his friend Mahali, and the obeah man.

5. B. Edwards was an English-born politician, Jamaican planter, and renowned antiabolitionist. He was a fellow of the Royal Society in 1794, became a member of Parliament in 1796, and wrote a history of Haiti the following year, which was absorbed into his larger *History, Civil and Commercial*. As secretary of the African Association, Edwards edited the African travel journals of Mungo Park.

6. This passage comes from Matthew 27:24–25 (King James Version). "When Pilate saw that he could not prevail, but rather that a tumult was beginning, he took water and washed his hands before the multitude, saying, 'I am innocent of the blood of this just man. See ye to it.' Then answered all the people and said, 'His blood be on us, and on our children.'"

7. Park wrote of the Feloops: "They are even said to transmit their quarrels as deadly feuds to their posterity, insomuch that a son considers it as incumbent on him, from a just sense of filial obligation, to become the avenger of his deceased father's wrongs" (13).

8. Tacky's Rebellion erupted in the Parish of Saint Mary in June 1760; therefore, the timing coincides with Harrop's youth, two decades before Harrop's tangle with Three-Fingered Jack. Advised by a powerful obeah man, Tacky's Rebellion was allegedly composed of dominantly Coromantee Africans. Brown estimates that five hundred black people were killed or killed themselves, and another five hundred were transported. This estimation suggests to me that Earle alludes to Tacky's Rebellion, the revolt that prompted Harrop to sail to Africa.

9. See also Bohls's discussion of the "staginess" (64) or "persistent theatricality" (74) in Monk Lewis's journal. She argues that in the colonial context the formal

distance between subject and object intimates also "the geographical and cultural distance between colony and metropole" (63).

10. Wilson calls this echo of Englishness "tentative and contingent" (*Island Race* 17).

11. Aravamudan rightly proposes that this passage was inspired by Aphra Behn's description of her eponymous hero (introd. to *Obi* 72).

12. In turn, Salih explains, this narrative demotion effectively seals off the "homo-erotic, miscegenetic possibilities that have been opened up by Stanford" (82).

13. See Watson's "Mobile Obeah" (244–245). See also Wisecup and Jaudon (134). For exciting new discussions of obeah, see the five essays published in the special issue of *Atlantic Studies*, edited by Wisecup and Jaudon.

14. Though Earle identifies him as a resident of "Scots Hall, Maroon Town" (156), he could not have been a Maroon because he was enslaved.

15. See Beckles on the usage of "Quashee" for the "typical" male slave ("Black Masculinity" 233).

16. The *OED* defines "Moorish" as "Originally: a native or inhabitant of ancient Mauritania, a region of North Africa corresponding to parts of present-day Morocco and Algeria. Later usually: a member of a Muslim people of mixed Berber and Arab descent inhabiting north-western Africa (now mainly present-day Mauritania), who in the 8th cent. conquered Spain."

17. In Park's narrative Mansong is the king of Bambarra rather than a warrior from Simbing. Other than this rather significant change, Burdett cites Park almost verbatim. Burdett is the first to call Jack "Mansong."

18. In a section titled "Observations about the State and Sources of Slavery in Africa," Park writes,

> In a country, divided into a thousand petty states, mostly independent and jeal-
> ous of each other; where every freeman is accustomed to arms, and fond of mili-
> tary achievements; where the youth who has practiced the bow and spear from
> his infancy, longs for nothing so much as an opportunity to display his valour, it
> is natural to imagine that wars frequently originate from very frivolous provo-
> cation. When one nation is more powerful than another, a pretext is seldom
> wanting for commencing hostilities. Thus the war between Kajaaga and Kasson
> was occasioned by the detention of a fugitive slave: that between Bambarra and
> Kaarta by the loss of a few cattle. (241)

19. See Kryza on Mungo Park.

20. In arguing that the English abolition of slavery would not solve its problems in Africa, Park writes,

> It [slavery] probably had its origin in the remote ages of antiquity, before the
> Mahomedans explored a path across the desert. How far it is maintained and

supported by the slave traffic, which for two hundred years, the nations of Europe have carried on with the native of the Coast, it is neither within my province, nor in my power, to explain. If my sentiments should be required concerning the effect which a discontinuance of that commerce would produce on the manners of the natives, I should have no hesitation in observing, that, in the present unenlightened state of their minds, my opinion is, the effect would neither be so extensive or beneficial, as many wise and worthy persons fondly expect. (247)

21. Park links the Moor's strength to their literacy but finds their zealous commitment to Islam a liability. The "rigid Mohammedans," he explains, "possess, with the bigotry and superstition, all the intolerance of their sect." The Moorish man, he remarks, embraces "every opportunity of displaying his superiority over such of his countrymen as are not distinguished by the same accomplishments." Park finds the Moors' knowledge of letters too limited to offer much of an advantage over their brethren and finds them "perhaps the most bigoted, ferocious, and intolerant of all the nations on the earth" (133).

22. Diouf compellingly argues that African Muslims, combining military skill and *marabout* (occult) knowledge, served as leaders in slave revolts, such as those led by the Jamaican Boukman and the Haitian Makandal (145–154). Sultana locates the first Maroons in Jamaica as African Muslims who came with the Spanish, and she suggests too that the Windward Maroons, including Nanny and Cudjoe, followed the Muslim faith. In addition, not entirely as convincingly, she links Moor and Maroon etymologically (163).

23. Diouf writes that *marabouts* were involved in making protective and offensive amulets, noting that because the Muslim factor in the West Indies has been ignored, "any religious leader of African origin has been linked to voodoo or obeah" (147, 53)

24. For an interesting comparison, see Neff.

25. For example, in the following passage Burdett replaces "The King of Bambarra" with "Mansong" and "scattered over the whole kingdom of Kaarta" with "became a scene of desolation": "The King of Bambarra finding that Daisy wished to avoid a pitched battle, placed a strong force at Joko, to watch his motions; and separating the remainder of his army into small detachments, ordered them to over-run the country, and seize the inhabitants before they had time to escape. These orders were executed with such promptitude, that in a few days, they were scattered over the whole kingdom of Kaarta" (Burdett 10; Park 88–89).

26. The name Amaal, a female name meaning "hope" or "longing," appears twice in the Quran.

27. Dallas tells another account of Davy working with Sam Grant in 1774, and Grant helped take down Jack. This overlap suggests the extent to which the Maroons formed a policing network with familiar leaders (38–39n24).

28. Paton explains also that the obeah laws in Jamaica focused on the "pretense" or "assumption" of the practice rather than on its supernatural power. This vocabulary, related to witchcraft laws in England, discredits obeah as it criminalizes it ("Obeah Acts" 5).

29. Both Paton and Swydky comment on the relevance of the Maroons to Burdett's narrative. Paton argues that the representation of Maroons disrupt the assumption that Caribbean blacks are "located firmly as slaves" ("Afterlives" 52). Swydky maintains, however, that the "cameo" role of the Maroons "distorts" and "ignores" the important role free blacks played on the island ("Rewriting" para. 34).

CHAPTER 3 — STAGING *OBI*

1. For this chapter I use the Woodfall 1809 edition of *Songs, Duets, and Choruses*, because it replicates the wordbook sold in the theaters (including the advertisement and prospectus). I refer to this text as *Obi* or Fawcett's *Obi*. The third edition of *Obi; or, Three-Finger'd Jack; A Serio-Pantomime in Two Acts* (Fawcett 1800) is available in Aravamudan's Broadview edition of Earle's *Obi; or, The History of Three-Fingered Jack* as well as in facsimile form in Hoskins's introduction to the Stainer and Bell volume. The Duncombe and Moon edition of *Obi* (c. 1825) is available on Rzepka's *Praxis* issue in *Romantic Circles* (2002) and is the most accessible and comprehensive: www.rc.umd.edu/praxis/obi/.

2. Dutton was in particular concerned with the public's increasingly "vitiated" taste for pantomimic drama. He hoped to see drama restored to its "pristine splendor and dignity" (16).

3. Cox, for example, finds moments in the play that "work against its overarching conservative message" (para. 7). Paton "Afterlives" suggests that the plantation scenes undermine the play's antislavery message. More recently, Gibbs has argued that it "elicited multivalent reactions: anti-slavery sympathy, anti-colonial sentiment, and constructions of Jack as a neoclassical hero" (627). See also Hogle; Hoskins, "Savage Boundaries"; Swydky; A. Richardson; and Rzepka "De Quincey's 'Three-Fingered Jack.'"

4. Moody has argued for the revolutionary potential of illegitimate genres in their use of chaotic or monstrous intermingling of plots, characters, and actors with material borrowed from written texts, images, and musical scores, "forging the conventions and iconography of theatrical illegitimacy" (80).

5. O'Brien examines eighteenth-century English entertainment culture to discuss the pantomime as a malleable medium to negotiate and legitimate cultural values. Worrall theorizes the racial significations of Harlequin's black mask to suggest that the use of blackface works "within a spectrum of contemporary expedient theatrical practices" that reveal complex and socially contested understandings of race (38). Like Cox and Worrall, Reed, in *Rogue Performances*, explores the figure of the

harlequin to discuss the intersection of race and class identity in the Caribbean; he imagines blackface "rogues" as potential threats to the existing social order. See also Carlson's exploration of Mungo, the comic black servant, as a register of the cultural politics of theater in the late eighteenth-century seemingly proabolition theater. She argues that this figure foregrounds "low" forms of stagecraft with marginalized figures, proposing that nonspeaking, illegitimate components of theater "voice" liberation ("New Lows" 139).

6. Cox and Van Kooy write that characters such as Jack reflect "charismatic strength" but are also "thoroughly othered," marked "as non-Christian disrupters of domestic and other social and political orders as threatening black figures . . . seen as outside the ideological boundaries that define the British Empire (466). As Moody suggests, the pantomime keeps in tension rather than resolves the ideological oppositions (88).

7. As Gibbs argues, "Blackface rebels were plastic figures in whom playwrights could sublimate ideological contention over slave revolts as a site of, on the one hand, retributive violence and on the other democratic rights and liberation" (628).

8. Like Cox, Reed suggests the radical potential or "liberatory possibilities of this figure" ("There Was No Resisting" 76).

9. See Dellarosa for a discussion of the spectacular "Grand March and Process" (162–163).

10. Linking responses to *Obi* to the revolts of Toussaint in Saint Domingue and Gabriel in Virginia, Gibbs argues that the variations of the *Obi* pantomime were "contributors to and barometers of . . . the disparate political and cultural pressures of London and Philadelphia" (626). While the London versions prompted a range of responses, she proposes, in Philadelphia in 1801, the New Theatre staged *Obi* as a seasonal spectacle that emphasized Jack's character as "savage" and "malevolent" (653).

11. See Dubois, Gaspar, Geggus, Genovese, and Egerton for discussions of these rebellions in the Americas.

12. French emigrant from Saint Domingue Victor Pelissier adapted the score for the New York debut and subsequent American versions, and he included several songs from *Obi* in his repertoire for years. See Hoskins, introd. to *Obi*; and Gibbs.

13. The early U.S. *Obi* reflects what Goudie calls the paracolonial relationship in ambivalent position to European colonialism and the West Indian colonies (5).

14. McAllister proposes that it was Euro–New Yorkers, such as the editor Mordecai M. Noah, who dubbed the venue the "African Theatre." He suggests too that Brown referred to his "African Company" to mimic the works of the Royal African Company and also to embrace its African persona (74, 104).

15. The name ostensibly came from Noah, whose description located the hospital called the African Grove.

16. See Dillon for her deft discussion of the "quintessential" figures of the black dandy, American Zip Coon, and Caribbean "Actor-Boy" (210–211).

17. See Warner and colleagues and McAllister for full discussions of these tensions.

18. Warner and his coauthors suggest that "it is not hard to imagine that the play—or part of it—was staged there [Brown's theater] in the fall of 1821" (7).

19. The speaker too, as Dillon notes, "deconstructs" binaries of whiteness and blackness by refashioning blackness as primeval redness: "We, in the image of primeval, man / Are what our fathers were when live began; / From virgin earth's red breast red Adam rose; / And we are red,—not black, like bats and crows" (qtd. in Warner et al. 2). Dillon thus rightly suggests that the Maroon Chief "serves to perform an indigenizing of New World Africans" (244).

20. The anticolonialist *King Shotaway* dramatizes this 1795 insurrection, led by Carib chief Joseph Chatoyer with the help of French forces. The insurrection failed, and the rebels were deported to Roatan. Their descendants, the Garifuna, live in Belize and Honduras (Dillon 241, 308).

21. McAllister and Warner and his colleagues note that the rioters were associated with Stephen Price, the manager of the Park Theatre and also associated with the circus. Many of the rioters were circus workers. Though *Advocate* editor Noah criticized the arrogance of the New York blacks, Brown did not suspect him.

22. See Geggus for his discussion of the use of voodoo rituals in slave uprisings.

23. For example, one South Carolina news story reported that a plot leader was to take the governor's daughter as his reward, and this article made its way to the New York *American* and *Spectator*. The newspaper accounts, according to McAllister, used the "white female/black male liaison as a reason behind the insurrection" (247).

24. In McAllister's view, Mr. Bates "performing Fawcett's intensely silent 'bad' Jack could send shivers through any disquieted Euro-New Yorker" (128). Alternately, George Thompson proposes that if Obi/Jack were "presented as compassionate as well as courageous he could well have had the audience's sympathy"; he deduces that the plot is "most likely to have shown Jack returning good for evil by rescuing the planter's wife from some peril" (135).

25. *Tom and Jerry* had opened at the Adelphi earlier that year and was immensely popular. The plot features two British men who tour London with their friend, Bob Logic. The trio attends masquerade balls as well as black slum taverns, where they meet a variety of characters, including Sal and Bob. In London the beating scene prompted young patrons to dress up as their heroes and harass police officers. The street violence spread to New York, demonstrating that life could imitate art in frightening ways.

26. See McAllister's discussion of the Afro-Dutch street festival in upstate New York (111–113). See also Dewulf.

27. This spectacle, as McAllister writes, could have generated either "great sympathy or empathy" in patrons as well as "stimulated feelings of guilt and indignation among white patrons and intensified feelings of anger and resentment among blacks" (121).

28. Reading Equiano against Ben Franklin, Goudie proposes that the *Interesting Narrative* counters the West Indian negation of the *Autobiography*: "At the same time they lay bare the deep and disturbing affiliations between the slave colonies of the West Indies and the embryonic states of the "not quite 'free' paracolonial republic" (36).

CHAPTER 4 — BEING JACK MANSONG

1. The playbill mistakenly gives Murray the first initial "J." Rzepka has noted that the Northampton playbill of 1830 points to Murray's authorship of the melodrama version; his (misspelled) name, "W. H. Murrey," is listed as author of the later Dicks edition; and his personal association with early performances of the melodrama is indicated by his appearing in the role of Captain Orford in the dramatis personae for the Oxberry Weekly Budget version (1843). (email) For this article, I use the Thomas Hailes Lacy edition, cited hereafter as Murray. This version is available at the National Library of Jamaica and includes the dramatis personae followed by the script. It can also be accessed through Rzepka's special issue of the *Romantic Circles Praxis Series*, titled *Obi*.

2. Paul Robeson, black actor, singer, and political activist, was the first black actor since Ira Aldridge to play the role of Othello in a major production company.

3. In his seminal account, A. Richardson calls Jack an "openly rebellious ex-slave" who exposes European barbarism and hypocrisy (181). Rzepka likewise calls attention to Jack's antislavery speeches that expose the "atrocities" perpetuated by the slave traders in Africa ("Obi Now" para. 6). Cox argues that despite the play's moralizing context, "in Aldridge's hands this play could become a vehicle for protest" (para. 11). O'Rourke, too, suggests that Aldridge's presence links Jacobin discourses to the English abolitionist movement, and he identifies *Macbeth* as a major precursor for the 1830 *Obi*, particularly because of the role of the witches. Many of these same critics have acknowledged the more conservative aspects of *Obi*, such as its "racist characterization" (Cox para. 9), the "exploitation of melodramatic conventions" (A. Richardson 189), and its antiabolitionist "plantation pastoral" (Paton, "Afterlives" 43).

4. Irish critic Maurice Lenihan wrote in the Clonmel *Advertiser*: "The House of Representatives of Sainte Domingue passed a unanimous vote in 1828 complimenting him on his successful progress in contradicting the assertion that his race is incapable of mental culture and bestowed upon him a commission in the Haitian

army with the rank of Captain, and Aide-de-Camp Extraordinary to this Excellency the [then] President Boyer. This honour was delivered to Mr. Aldridge through the Consul in London" (qtd. in Marshall and Stock 80).

5. Lindfors states that a black actress in Scotland played Polly in the *Beggars' Opera* and Juliet in *Romeo and Juliet* without makeup ("Mislike Me Not" 349).

6. He worked also within what Dillon calls the framework of the "performative commons" (16–17).

7. Brooks writes that "minstrelsy borrows as much from melodrama as melodrama borrowed from minstrelsy in the production of a spectacular and 'suffering' black body" (30). See also Lott and Hartman. Hartman writes that "The terror of pleasure—the violence that undergirded the comic moment in minstrelsy—and the pleasure of terror—the force of evil that propelled the plot of melodrama and fascinated the spectator—filiated the coffle, the auction block, the popular stage, and plantations recreations in a scandalous equality" (32).

8. Fawcett's pantomime, for example, gives Jack a loose band of followers, "Negro Robbers," who hang out in the obeah woman's cave waiting for her blessing. These nameless, ragtag groupies pledge their loyalty to Jack and respect and fear him as their leader. Jack "crosses their foreheads" in a ritual meant to "prevent their betrayal," and he seems to be always a few steps ahead of them (1). The robbers are armed but not particularly dangerous, and Murray writes their faint presence out of his adaptation.

9. *Paul and Virginie* introduces a French colony in which the European settlers and the Mauritius natives live a peaceful and harmonious life.

10. These characters reinforce the racial hierarchy expected by the audience. Hartman explains, "the transubstantiation of abjection into contentment suggested that the traumas of slavery were easily redressed and, likewise, the prevalence of black song confirmed blacks' restricted sentience and immunity to sorrow" (23).

11. See Doyle on what she terms "the Anglo-Atlantic gothic text," whereby the political violence of the Atlantic appears in traces (215).

12. Hogle has suggested that Kitty is a mixed-race free black; however, I cannot find any evidence in the text to support this claim. The text does not specifically identify her as mixed-race either, but both her language and her sexual interest suggest her light skin. (Thanks to Jeff Cox for helping me think this through.)

13. Hogle has proposed that this moment "would have been unprecedented in the history of *Obi* and quite rare before the 1820s in performances of this song" and that this indicates a shift in attitude between the earlier and later versions of *Obi* (para. 14).

14. Different versions of the song circulated around the United States in the nineteenth century, often as blackface minstrelsy, for example, "Possum up a Gum Stump," an even more racist rendition than Mathews's.

15. Rzepka compiled these papers, plain text versions of the *Obi* pantomime and melodrama, and video clips of the Boston performance for the *Romantic Circles Praxis Series* (edited by Rzepka).

16. Siders and Hogle used the same scenes for the first part, sandwiched between musical choruses: Rosa's introduction to the captain; Tuckey's mimed announcement of the captain's wounding (and the captain's return to the plantation); the overseer's request of the slaves to capture Jack; Quashie's mournful duet with his wife and her solo lament; the cross-dressed Rosa singing to a drunken Jack; and the execution of Jack by Quashie, Sam, and Tuckey followed by the celebration of the plantation.

17. These scenes of the second part emphasize the dilemmas of the white and black characters: the dialogue between the planter and overseer about the problem of Jack; Tuckey singing "Opossum up a Gum Tree"; the meeting between Jack and his obeah-woman mother in her cave; and Jack's demise by the plantation group.

18. Another significant change involves the scene between Tuckey and Kitty as well as the opossum song verse choices. See Hogle for a thorough description of the differences between the Boston and Tempe productions. He outlines the directorial decisions for both halves of the play, the pantomime, and the melodrama acts.

19. Hogle directed the slave characters to dance "with Arcadian gaiety" before interrupting them and having them rise from "abject" positions. He writes that he could "count on our NASSR audience to catch the harsh irony in this approach while associating it with both the British racial attitudes prior to Parliament's abolition of the slave trade in 1807 and the popular theatre conventions of the time" (para. 7).

20. The politicized band Public Enemy openly addressed the social problems of black communities in the urban United States.

21. Although hip-hop has roots in the African griot tradition and has since spread globally, it started in the United States and is associated with the political and aesthetic agenda of black American youth. Early hip-hop has been credited with helping to reduce inner-city gang violence by replacing physical violence with dance and art, but it has met with resistance for its celebration of violence and its association with gang activity.

22. Though Siders had no knowledge of or access to Dwyer's Jamaican pantomime, the two men similarly changed the conclusion (instant message; see chapter 6).

23. Hogle writes, "the black-against-black problem in this play was resolved in favor of a redirected, communal, and African American sense of time, reconstructed both from and against *Obi* to redress the imbalances that Anglo accounts of Western history have too often left in force" (para. 15).

24. Lott argues in part that blackface "mediated, and regulated, the formation of white working-class masculinity using strategies of sympathy and derision" (86).

25. Some exceptions include Carey and Kitson; Ellis; Fulford and Kitson; D. Lee, *Romantic Imagination*; and Youngquist, *Romanticism and the Atlantic*.

CHAPTER 5 — AFTER EMANCIPATION

1. For excellent discussions of racial attitudes during the Victorian period, see Huzzey, Brody, Manganelli, and Nowatzki. These texts investigate the complication and blurring of racial categories, the "impossibility of producing fixed, pure and stable identities of any sort" (Brody 12).

2. See Burton for an excellent discussion of this period.

3. See also Heuman and Burton.

4. Garvey dedicated his life to improving the working and living conditions of black people around the world. After spending time working in Costa Rica and Panama, he returned to Jamaica briefly in 1912 before traveling to work and live in London. Upon his 1914 return to Jamaica, he founded the UNIA, next taking his political ideals to the United States. With his future wife Garvey founded the *Negro World Newspaper* in Harlem in 1817. As part of his pan-African agenda, Garvey also founded the Black Star Shipping Line, a business under which auspices he was accused and convicted of trumped-up mail-fraud charges. Subsequently deported back to Jamaica, Garvey persisted in his political activities. After a speech that criticized corrupt judges, he served another prison sentence for contempt of court in 1928.

5. See Burton, Patterson, Mintz and Price, and Holt for discussions of the movement from plantation to peasantry.

6. Howell, too, spent time abroad in a trajectory similar to Garvey's. Howell ended up in a mental institution; he is still considered by many to be the "First Preacher" of Rasta. See R. Hill, H. Lee, and Bogues.

7. See Sheller for a fascinating conversation about the Morant Bay Rebellion and the blurring lines of race. See also Cobham; and Bilby, "Image and Imagination," for analyses of the rebellion and its relationship to issues of race. Dacres likewise offers insight about the figure of Bogle and masculinity.

8. Merrill examines images of American slavery presented at the Great Exhibition by fugitive slaves as performative interventions.

9. Nowatzki has proposed that the conventions of blackface minstrelsy influenced Victorian depictions of black people, registering a "hardening in British racial attitudes," a gradual decline in abolitionist sentiments, and a corresponding shift within minstrelsy (44).

10. Harrison and Fantina's collection offers an excellent overview of the genre. See also Bratlinger's seminal essay.

11. No critical attention attends Frost's *Obi*, and very little information exists about the author, other than his own memoirs. Gurney refers to the radical working-class Chartist as a "picaresque proletarian" prone to "play[ing] around with questions of identity" (66).

12. The only two extant print copies reside at the British Library and the Huntington Library.

13. The sexual register and dark humor of Frost's Jack prefigure the black rebel of the recent decades, the "badass" protagonist of blaxploitation films or Quentin Tarantino movies (see the epilogue).

14. Frost calls Cora "Creole," which in this time means having been born on the island. The narrator describes her, though, as the offspring of a mulatto and a quadroon.

15. Scipio Africanus was the Roman general who defeated Hannibal. The nomenclature "Africanus" refers to his victories in his African campaign.

16. Angelina would have been a sympathetic character to a Victorian middle-class readership. See Peak for a useful discussion of servants and class in the Victorian sensation novel. Angelina loses her position because of her "detected frailty" and her "criminal" abetting of Jack, but their interracial relationship, though taboo, was not illegal (Frost 366). Brody explains that interracial relationships in England were much more common among working-class people, and the lack of antimiscegenation in England, unlike America, made these relationships more common in English Victorian fiction. Rife with sexual misconduct, terminated pregnancies, stillborn children, and blackmail, Angelina's lurid history would have also appealed to Victorian tastes for scandal and sensation.

17. Manganelli coins the term "transnational mulatta" to refer to the mixed-race West Indian woman, a "contradictory stereotype" that "represented this figure as a deceptive adventuress, a monogamous devourer of pleasure, and a skillful housekeeper" (18). She argues that in fiction published after the revolution, the transnational mulatta is transformed from an "unruly body" who "embodied the fears and fantasies of life in the colonies" to an "imperiled heiress" who "is enveloped in a more controlled domestic narrative that replaces her agency with dependence upon patriarchal authority" (19). Brody coins the term "mulattaroon" because no word in the English language accommodates this "figment of the concept of pigment" (16).

18. Sophonisba is the name of a Carthaginian noblewoman who poisoned herself rather than suffer the humiliation of a Roman triumph. This suicide foreshadows Julia's, which concludes the novel.

19. See Gurney for his discussion of Frost's obsession with escapology. See also Brooks on the escape artist.

20. For an excellent discussion of the morally ambiguous position of the "much-maligned informer," see Cooper's *Noises in the Blood* (13). Critical discussions of mulattos usually discuss female mulattos and emphasize her tragic nature. Conversations about male mulattos also focus on the "tragic element" of a desire for whiteness, representing him as a victim of his divided inheritance. Dauts, for example, views the mulatto man as connected to the image of the French Revolution as a "family conflict," whereby the mulatto man strives to kill his white father. She explores stereotypes of mulatto men as depressed, suicidal, and fratricidal due to a "lack of identity" or to an "innate biological corruption," adding that they can also present as weak, degenerate, and cunning; these characters are driven by "mulatto vengeance" (2).

21. In 1831 preacher Nat Turner led a group of slaves and free black people in what was to become the bloodiest slave rebellion in U.S. history. It resulted in the death of some fifty white people, followed by the death of over two hundred black people by white militia and mobs. Sam Sharpe's efforts for peaceful resistance fell through, and around fourteen Anglo-Jamaicans died, while more than five hundred slaves lost their lives, most of them as a result of the trials after. Armed rebellion and seizing of property spread mostly through the western parishes, but the uprising was put down by the first week in January.

22. The de Lisser family in Jamaica was connected with the Portuguese business and finance community there, and his father's side of the family also had some African blood. For a discussion of de Lisser's social position, see Cobham. See also W. Roberts.

23. See Cobham, Rosenberg, and W. Roberts for discussions of de Lisser's intellectual life and writings. See also Smith, "H. G. and Haiti," for his discussion of de Lisser's "Land of Revolutions," an eleven-essay series about Haiti that questions the relevance of imperialism in the region.

24. The novel mentions the American Revolution with some regularity, suggesting de Lisser's contemporary concern about the growing involvement of the United States in the region. Though he briefly dabbled in support for this involvement, by 1930 his loyalties were firmly ensconced once more with England. *Morgan's Daughter* likewise makes frequent mention of Haiti. See Martin for his insights on de Lisser's relationship to Haiti.

25. A hurricane puts an end to Hamilton's estate and involvement in the rebellion, swallowing his plantation and the people on it: "The judgment of God had fallen upon Hamilton at last" (de Lisser, *Morgan's Daughter* 173).

26. A Welsh privateer, buccaneer, and admiral in the British navy, Henry Morgan worked within and against the law his whole career. He had served with Venables and Penn but became the leader of a group of buccaneers based in Port Royal.

Morgan owned vast lands in Jamaica and eventually became governor. Mackie points to the frequent association of Morgan with Jamaican outlaws enmeshed in criminal activity (26, 39). See also Exquemelin on buccaneers.

27. De Lisser struggled against the thin line between "brown" and "near white" in his own life (see Cobham).

28. De Lisser's language closely echoes that of Long, who writes,

They all joined in a most hideous yell, or war-hoop, and bounded into action. With amazing agility, they literally ran and rolled through their various firings and evolutions. . . . They fire stooping almost to the very ground; and no sooner is their piece discharged, than they throw themselves into a thousand antic gestures, and tumble over and over, so as to be continually shirting their place; the intention of which is, to elude the shot, as well as to deceive the aim of their adversaries. . . . When this part of their exercise was over, they drew their swords; and, winding their horn again, they began, in wild and warlike capers, to advance towards his excellency. . . . They next brought their muskets, and piled them up in heaps at his feet, which some of them desired to kiss, and were permitted. (qtd. in Wilson, "Performance of Freedom" 46)

29. See Wilson, "Performance of Freedom," for an interesting discussion of the Maroons in eighteenth-century Jamaica. She argues that the war dance enacts the "threat and privilege" that characterizes the Maroons, recalling "a historical victory that encapsulated different notions of time, space, and possession, and reminded spectators of the superior deployments of violence and peacemaking that made the Maroons formidable adversaries as well as loyal subjects" (47).

30. When Elizabeth discovers Seymour's affection for Joyce Breakspeare, she reports him to the authorities. She does so to force his hand and fulfill his role in the rebellion.

31. De Lisser's historical romances in particular reflect his suspicion of black leadership and condemnation of black rebellion. These views emerge particularly in *Revenge* (about the Morant Bay Rebellion) and *The White Witch of Rose Hall*. See Birbalsingh, Dawes, and Cobham for overviews of de Lisser's historical romances.

32. See Chevannes for a discussion of Garvey and his influence on Rasta movements. He discusses the Rastas' eventual rejection of Revival, Kumina, and Bongo, religions founded by enslaved Africans that use African religious practices, such as obeah ("Ships").

CHAPTER 6 — *MANSONG*

1. The Parade theater-building site housed three different structures: the Kingston Theatre in 1776 (destroyed by fire); the second in 1840, renamed the Theatre Royal in 1842 (destroyed by earthquake); and the Ward, built in 1912. See E. Hill, *Jamaican Stage*.

2. Scott dedicated his life to the arts: as a poet, playwright, dancer (in the Jamaican National Dance Theatre), actor (he played Lester Tibideaux in the *Cosby Show*), editor (of the *Caribbean Quarterly*), and teacher.

3. Whereas the nineteenth-century patent theaters wished to repress any hint of political reference, the Jamaican pantomime is inherently political in its agenda for national solidarity.

4. N. Edwards delineates the critical divide between Brathwaite's approach to creolization (based on assimilation) in "Contradictory Omens" (qtd. in N. Edwards 23) and Wynter's concept of indigenization as advanced in "Jonkonnu." Wynter identifies indigenization as the process "whose agent and product was Jamaican folklore, folksong, folk-tales, folk dance." Moreover, she sees this process as the outcome of a cultural pattern: "The development of this pattern, where the slave became part-slave in relation to the European plantation, and part-peasant in relation to the plot of land on which he fed himself and his family, was, in Jamaica, the crucial factors in the indigenization process" ("Jonkonnu" 35).

5. This scene introduces a variation of what Brathwaite has called the "Creole-society model" of the Caribbean. Brathwaite's model argues that Africans and Europeans who settled in the Caribbean contributed a distinctly Creole culture that was neither African nor European (*Development* 71). However, Bolland argues that this model neglects the issue of class.

6. Jack's decision to stay in the remote areas of the mountains and help runaway slaves locates him as a small-m maroon, as does his earlier practice of ambush; however, the elision of the (big-*m*) Maroons from the script glosses over the additional register of tensions among the island's black population.

EPILOGUE

1. See Jaffe's "From Maroons to Dons" for an interesting discussion of the complicated roles of violent and legal pluralisms in "multiple sovereignties" in colonial and postcolonial Jamaica (47).

2. The two-party system emerged out of the political violence of the 1930s, following the pressures of global depression, falling sugar prices, and unemployment, as workers returned from abroad. In the early 1930s Alexander Bustamante founded the Jamaica Labour Party, and Norman Manley established the People's National Party; these men competed for political dominance for the next quarter century (see chapters 5 and 6).

3. Coke's famed Shower Posse network was responsible for thousands of drug-related deaths in Kingston and New York in the 1980s. The Shower Posse had contacts with cells in the United States (Miami, Los Angeles, Kansas City, and Chicago) as well as in London and Toronto; it trafficked in "ganja" and crack cocaine.

Gunst's *Born Fi' Dead* explores the politically underwritten gang culture in Jamaica and its spread to New York. See also Sives for her examination of electoral violence in Jamaica.

4. See D. Thomas, *Exceptional Violence*, for her intriguing study of violence and cultural reparations in Jamaica.

5. See Chevannes, "Ships," for a clear discussion of the intersections and major departures of Garvey and the Rastas.

6. After his ejection from Jamaica and until his death in Guyana in 1980, Rodney continued to contribute to an emerging black intellectual movement in the Caribbean. Some believe that the Rodney Riots played a role in the failure of the Jamaica Labour Party to take the next election (West, "Seeing Darkly").

7. See Stephens, "Babylon's 'Natural Mystic,'" for an excellent discussion of Marley.

8. See Mackie for her insightful discussion of the Peace Concert in her article that links Rastas, Maroons, Pirates, and "Rude Boys."

9. The "Rudie" or "Rude Bwoy" arose from 1960s Jamaican street culture. White defines the figure as "that person, native, who is totally disenchanted with the ruling system; who generally descended from the 'African' elements in the lower class and who is now armed with ratchets, other cutting instruments and with increasing frequency nowadays, with guns and explosives" (39).

10. In the late 1940s outlaw Rhygin' grappled with the law for almost a decade, styling himself after spaghetti Western outlaws and adopting the names "Captain Midnight" and "Alan Ladd." In 1948 he escaped from prison, and he wreaked havoc for the next six weeks, robbing and killing those who crossed his path; he distributed photographs of himself as a gun-slinging cowboy and achieved folk hero status, an element Henzell adopted in his film. The authorities advertised a £200 reward (the same amount first advertised for Jack) for his capture, dead or alive. After a highly publicized manhunt, the police finally caught up with him and shot him to death on Lime Cay. Thousands of viewers, police and civilians, came to the waterfront to bid him farewell (Walker; Collins).

11. "Badmanism" Cooper explains, "is a theatrical pose that has been refined in the complicated socialisation processes of Jamaican youth, who learn to imitate and adapt the sartorial and ideological 'style' of the heroes and villains of imported movies" ("Sheriff" 153).

12. This seemingly inevitable conclusion underwent revision, however, in Henzell's London stage musical version in 2006. In this production the entire cast performs a final number with a resurrected Ivan, much as the 1980 *Mansong* and the 2000 *Play in the Life* resurrect Three-Fingered Jack. This revision demonstrates the ways the heroic outlaw figure can be recycled for different audiences and different agendas. See Dalleo for his discussion of the play.

13. A white Jamaican, Henzell, though a "conscious brethren," needed the help of Rhone for success, but their work together ended in bitterness. The troubled Henzell/Rhone collaboration reflects the tensions of the politically turbulent, culturally and racially charged historical moment. Collins reveals that Rhone found the original screenplay "a misapprehension of black urban Jamaican experience [and], he basically started from scratch to draft a script that would reflect the realities he understood as a black Jamaican" (60). Together they found locations and assembled a cast largely from people off the street.

14. Reggae historian Roger Steffens claims that Henzell took over the film's distribution after marketing it as a blaxploitation film failed (qtd. in McLellan).

15. The hero, a brothel-raised sex show performer (named for his sexual prowess and large penis), suffered police brutality alongside a Black Panther, and he beats the arresting officer unconscious.

16. Ongiri has argued that *Sweet Sweetback*, marketed for a mainstream audience, perpetuated a view of black masculinity as "threatening, sexually potent, and extremely dangerous at the same time that it allowed an African American audience to enjoy the opportunity to identify with that threat and imagine the possibilities of its potential. . . . [It] calls into question the limits of both the revolutionary and repressive possibilities of visual culture, while highlighting its importance as a continued site for struggle" (185).

17. The problematic figure of Bounty Killer's "petty thief," Bogues proposes, represents a collapse of both hegemony and "subaltern radical counter-hegemony" (26). One might also call Three-Fingered Jack a "petty thief," especially since his moniker undoubtedly refers at least in part to his many acts of violent theft.

18. "The fact that patriarchy reifies masculinity," Hope writes, "means that in a post-colonial capitalist society like Jamaica, different markers of masculinity become more important as signifiers in the quest for identity." This aggressive form of masculinity, she concludes, offers a way for men of the lower classes to navigate the spaces between their "lived experiences and hegemonic expectations" (127).

Works Cited

Aldridge, Ira. *Memoir and Theatrical Career of Ira Aldridge, the African Roscius.* Onwhyn, 1849.

Anderson, Benedict. *Imagined Communities: Reflections on the Origins and Spread of Capitalism.* Verso, 1991.

Aravamudan, Srinivas. Introduction to *Obi; or, The History of Three-Fingered Jack.* By William Earle. Broadview, 2005.

———. *Tropicopolitans: Colonialism and Agency.* Duke UP, 1999.

Bailey, Barbara. "The Search for Gender Equality and Empowerment of Caribbean Women." *Gender in Caribbean Development*, edited by Patricia Mohammed and Catherine Shepherd, U of the West Indies P, St. Augustine, 1999, pp. 108–145.

Barnett, Michael, ed. *Rastafari in the New Millennium.* Syracuse UP, 2012.

Barrow, Christine. "Caribbean Masculinity and Family: Revisiting 'Marginality' and 'Reputation.'" *Caribbean Portraits: Essays in Gender Identity*, edited by Christina Barrow, Randle, 1998, pp. 219–234.

Baucom, Ian. *Specters of the Atlantic: Finance Capital, Slavery, and the Philosophy of History.* Duke UP, 2005.

Beckford, George, and Michael Witter. *Small Garden, Bitter Weed: Struggle and Change in Jamaica.* Maroon, 1980.

Beckles, Hilary. "Black Masculinity in Caribbean Society." *Interrogating Caribbean Masculinities: Theoretical and Empirical Analyses*, edited by Rhoda Reddock, U of the West Indies P, 2004, pp. 225–243.

———. "The Constructions of Caribbean Masculinity," pamphlet, *Black Masculinity in Caribbean Slavery*, January 11–13, 1996, University of the West Indies, Trinidad, HT871.v421996, Wand Occasional Paper, Special Collections, University of the West Indies, Mona.

Behn, Aphra. *Oroonoko: Or the History of the Royal Slave.* Penguin Classics, 2004.

Bennett, Louise. "Jamaica Language." *The Norton Anthology of English Literature: The Twentieth Century and After.* Vol. F, 9th ed., edited by Stephen Greenblatt, Jahan Ramazani, and Jon Stallworthy, Norton, 2012, pp. 2723–2724.

Besson, Jean. *Transformation of Freedom in the Land of the Maroons: Creolization in the Cockpits Jamaica.* Randle, 2016.

Bhabha, Homi. *The Location of Culture.* Routledge, 1990.

Bible. King James Version. 2007. www.kingjamesbibleonline.org/. Accessed February 20, 2017.

Bilby, Kenneth. "Image and Imagination: Revisioning the Maroons in the Morant Bay Rebellion." *History and Memory,* vol. 24, no. 2, Spring 2012, pp. 41–72.

———. *True-Born Maroons.* U of Florida P, 2008.

Bilby, Kenneth, and Jerome Handler. "Healing and Protection in West Indian Slave Life." *Journal of Caribbean History,* vol. 3, no. 2, 2004, pp. 153–183.

Birbalsingh, Frank. *Passion and Exile: Essays in Caribbean Literature.* Hansib, 1988.

Black, Clinton V. *Tales of Old Jamaica.* Collingswood, 1966.

Bogues, Anthony. *Black Heretics, Black Prophets: Radical Political Intellectuals.* Routledge, 2003.

Bohls, Elizabeth A. "The Planter Picturesque: Matthew Lewis's *Journal of a West Indian Proprietor.*" *European Romantic Review,* vol. 13, no. 1, 2002, pp. 63–76.

Bolland, O. Nigel. "Creolisation and Creole Societies: A Cultural Nationalist View of Caribbean Social History." *Caribbean Quarterly,* vol. 44, nos. 1–2, 1998, pp. 1–32.

Brathwaite, Kamau. *The Arrivants: A New World Trilogy.* Oxford UP, 1988.

———. *Contradictory Omens: Cultural Diversity and Integration in the Caribbean.* Savacou, 1974.

———. *The Development of Creole Society in Jamaica, 1770–1820.* Rev. ed. Randle, 2005.

———. *History of the Voice: The Development of Nation Language in Anglophone Caribbean Poetry.* New Beacon, 1984.

———. *Wars of Respect: Nanny and Sam Sharpe.* API for the National Heritage Week Committee, 1976.

Bratlinger, Patrick. "What Is Sensational about the Sensation Novel?" *Nineteenth-Century Fiction,* vol. 23, no. 1, 1982, pp. 1–28.

Brody, Jennifer DeVere. *Impossible Purities: Blackness, Femininity, and Victorian Culture.* Duke UP, 2012.

Brooks, Daphne. *Bodies in Dissent: Spectacular Performances of Race and Freedom, 1850–1910.* Duke UP, 2006.

Brown, Vincent. *The Reaper's Garden: Death and Power in the World of Atlantic Slavery.* Harvard UP, 2010.

Buckely, Peter. "Obi in New York: Aldridge and the African Grove." *Obi*, edited by Chuck Rzepka. Special issue, *Romantic Circles Praxis Series*, edited by Orrin Wang. U of Maryland, 2002.

Burdett, William. *Life and Exploits of Mansong, Commonly Called Three-Finger'd Jack, the Terror of Jamaica in the Years 1780 and 1781: With a Particular Account of the Obi; Being the Only True One of That Celebrated and Fascinating Mischief So Prevalent in the West Indies.* 3rd ed. Neil, 1800.

———. *A New and Tenth Edition of the Life and Exploits of That Daring Robber, Three-Finger'd Jack, a Rebellious Slave, Who Was Brought from Africa, and Shortly Became the Terror of Jamaica, Including a Full and Accurate Description of That Fascinating Charm Called Obi, Practiced, with Such Mischievous Consequences, by the African Negroes in the West Indies.* 10th ed. Neil, n.d.

Burnard, Trevor. *Mastery, Tyranny, and Desire: Thomas Thistlewood and His Slaves in the Anglo-Jamaican World.* U of North Carolina P, 2004.

Burrell, Ian. "Move over Bob Marley: Peter Tosh Is Finally Getting the Recognition He Deserves." *Independent*, September 14, 2013.

Burroughs, Catherine. Review of *Obi; or, Three-Finger'd Jack (1800–1830)*. *European Romantic Review*, vol. 12, no. 3, 2001, pp. 381–389.

Burton, Richard. *Afro-Creole: Power, Opposition, and Play in the Caribbean.* Cornell UP, 1997.

Calendar of State Papers Colonial, America and West Indies. Vol. 37, *July 1730*, ed. Cecil Headlam and Arthur Percival Newton. His Majesty's Stationery Office, 1937. *British History Online*, www.british-history.ac.uk/cal-state-papers/colonial/america-west-indies/vol37/pp155–165. Accessed February 17, 2017.

———. Vol. 40, *1733*, ed. Cecil Headlam and Arthur Percival Newton. His Majesty's Stationery Office, 1939. *British History Online*. www.british-history.ac.uk/cal-state-papers/colonial/america-west-indies/vol40/pp179–197. Accessed February 17, 2017.

———. Vol. 41, *1734–1735*. Her Majesty's Stationery Office, 1953. *British History Online*. www.british-history.ac.uk/cal-state-papers/colonial/america-west-indies/vol41/pp402–412. Accessed February 17, 2017.

———. Vol. 9, *1675–1676*, edited by W. Noel Sainsbury. Her Majesty's Stationery Office, 1893. *British History Online*. www.british-history.ac.uk/cal-state-papers/colonial/america-west-indies/vol9/pp129–139. Accessed February 17, 2017.

Campbell, Mavis C. *The Maroons of Jamaica, 1655–1796: A History of Resistance, Collaboration and Betrayal.* African World, 1988.

Carlson, Julie. "New Lows in Eighteenth-Century Theatre: The Rise of Mungo." *European Romantic Review*, vol. 18, no. 2, 2007, pp. 139–149.

———. "Race and Profit in the English Theatre." *Cambridge Companion to British Theatre, 1730–1830*, edited by Jane Moody and Daniel O'Quinn, Cambridge UP, 2007, pp. 175–188.

Carey, Beverly. *The Maroon Story: 1490–1880*. Agouti, 1997.

Carey, Brycchan. "The Slavery Website," http://www.brycchancarey.com/slavery. November 2000.

Carey, Brycchan, and Peter Kitson. *Slavery and the Culture of Abolition: Essays Marking the Bicentennial of the British Abolition Act of 1807*. Brewer, 2007.

Castle, Terry. "Phantasmagoria: Spectral Technology and the Metaphorics of Modern Reverie." *Critical Inquiry*, vol. 15, no. 1, 1988, pp. 26–61.

Césaire, Aimé. *A Tempest*. TCG Translations, 2002.

Chevannes, Barry. *Learning to Be a Man: Culture, Socialization, and Gender Identity in Five Caribbean Communities*. U of the West Indies P, 2001.

———. "Ships That Will Never Sail: The Paradox of Rastafari Pan-Africanism." *Critical Arts: A South-North Journal of Cultural and Media Studies*, vol. 24, no. 4, 2011, pp. 565–575.

Cliff, Michele. *No Telephone to Heaven*. Plume, 1996.

Coates, Ta-Nehisi. *Between the World and Me*. Spiegel and Grau, 2015.

Cobham, Rhoda. "The Literary Side of H. G. de Lisser." *Jamaica Journal*, vol. 14, no. 4, 1984, 2–9.

Collins, Loretta. "The Harder They Come: Rougher Version." *Small Axe*, vol. 13, no. 1, 2003, pp. 46–71.

Cooke, Aston. Jamaican Youth Theatre Facebook page. www.facebook.com/media/set/?set=a.187669381284067.53468.187296141321391&type. Accessed February 20, 2017.

———. Personal interview. June 16, 2009.

Cooper, Carolyn. "I Shot the Sheriff." *Open Fire: Understanding Gun Culture*, edited by Charles Fruehling Springwood, Berg, 2007, pp. 153–164.

———. *Noises in the Blood: Orality, Gender, and the "Vulgar" Body of Jamaican Popular Culture*. Duke UP, 1995.

Cox, Jeffrey N. "Theatrical Forms, Ideological Conflicts, and the Staging of Obi." *Obi*, edited by Chuck Rzepka. Special issue, *Romantic Circles Praxis Series*, edited by Orrin Wang. U of Maryland, 2002.

Cox, Jeffrey N., and Michael Gamer, editors. *The Broadview Anthology of Romantic Drama*. Broadview, 2003.

Cox, Jeffrey N., and Dana Van Kooy. "Melodramatic Slaves." *Modern Drama*, vol. 55, no. 4, 2012, pp. 459–475.

Craton, Michael. *Searching for the Invisible Man: Slavery and Plantation Life in Jamaica*. Harvard UP, 1978.

———. *Testing the Chains: Resistance to Slavery in the British West Indies*. Cornell UP, 1978.

Csengei, Ildiko. *Sympathy, Sensibility and the Literature of Feeling in the Eighteenth Century*. Palgrave, 2012.

Cummings. Ronald. "(Trans)Nationalisms, Marronage, and Queer Caribbean Subjectivities." *Transforming Anthropology*, vol. 18, no. 2, 2010, pp. 169–180.

Cundall, Frank. "Three-Finger'd Jack, the Terror of Jamaica." *West India Committee Circular*, vol. 45, nos. 815, 815, 817, 1930, pp. 9–10, 36–37, 55–56.

Dacres, Petrina. "'But Bogle Was a Bold Man': Vision, History, and Power for a New Jamaica." *Small Axe*, vol. 13, no. 1, 2009, pp. 112–134.

Dallas, R. C. *The History of the Maroons, from Their Origin to the Establishment of Their Chief Tribe at Sierra Leone*. Vol. 1. Longman, 1803.

Dalleo, Rafael. "Performing Postcoloniality in the Jamaican Seventies: *The Harder They Come* and *Smile Orange*." *Postcolonial Text*, vol. 6, no. 1, 2011, http://postcolonial.org/index.php/pct/article/view/1213/1124.

Darwin, Erasmus. *The Botanic Garden: A Poem in Two Parts*. London, 1791.

Dauts, Marlene. *Tropics of Haiti: Race and the Literary History of the Haitian Revolution in the Atlantic World, 1789–1865*. Liverpool UP, 2015.

Dawes, Kwame. "An Act of 'Unruly' Savagery: Re-writing Black Rebellion in the Language of the Colonizer H. G. de Lisser's *The White Witch of Rosehall*." *Caribbean Quarterly*, vol. 40, no. 1, 1994, pp. 1–12.

Dayan, Joan. *Haiti, History, and the Gods*. U of California P, 1995.

De Lisser, Herbert George. "Marriage." *Jamaica Times*, August 25, 1900, 9–10.

———. *Morgan's Daughter*. Macmillan Caribbean, 1980.

Dellarosa, Franca. "'No Fear the Obi Bag': A Cross-Atlantic Hybrid for the British Stage." *Literary and Cultural Intersections during the Long Eighteenth Century*, edited by Marianna D'Ezio, Cambridge Scholars, 2008, pp. 145–167.

Dewulf, Jeroen. "Pinkster: An Atlantic Creole Festival in a Dutch-American Context." *Journal of American Folklore*, vol. 126, no. 501, 2013, pp. 245–271.

Dillon, Elizabeth Maddock. *New World Drama: The Performative Commons in the Atlantic World, 1649–1849*. Duke UP, 2014.

Diouf, Sylvianne. *Servants of Allah: African Muslim Enslaved in the Americas*. New York UP, 1998.

Doyle, Laura. *Freedom's Empire: Race and the Rise of the Novel in Atlantic Modernity, 1640–1940*. Duke UP, 2007.

Dubois, Laurent. *Avengers of the New World*. Harvard UP, 2009.

Dutton, Thomas. *The Dramatic Censor; or, Monthly Epitome of Taste, Fashion, and Manners*. Vol. 3. Roach and Chapple, 1801.

Dwyer, Ted. *Mansong*. Produced by the *Little Theatre Movement* at the Ward Theatre, Kingston, Jamaica, directed by Dennis Scott. December, 1980–March, 1981. Third Floor, Pantomime Collection, National Library of Jamaica.

Earle, William. *Obi; or, The History of Three-Fingered Jack: In a Series of Letters from a Resident in Jamaica to his Friend in England*. Thomas, 1804.

Edwards, Bryan. *The History, Civil and Commercial, of the British Colonies in the West Indies*. White, 1793.

Edwards, Norval. "'Talking about a Little Culture': Sylvia Wynter's Early Essays." *Journal of West Indian Literature*, vol. 10, no. 1, 2001, pp. 12–38.

Egerton, Douglas R. *Gabriel's Rebellion: The Virginia Conspiracies of 1800 and 1802*. U of North Carolina P, 1993.

Ellis, Markman. *The Politics of Sensibility: Race, Gender, and Commerce in the Sentimental Novel*. Cambridge UP, 2004.

Eltis, David, et al. *The Transatlantic Slave Trade: A Database on CD-ROM*. Cambridge UP, 1999.

Exquemelin, Alexandre O. *The Buccaneers of America*. Dover, 2000.

Eyre, Lawrence Alan. "Jack Mansong: Bloodshed or Brotherhood?" *Jamaica Journal*, vol. 7, no. 4, 1973, pp. 9–14.

Fawcett, John. *Songs, Duets and Choruses in the Pantomimical Drama of Obi; or, Three-Finger'd Jack (Performed at the Theatre-Royal, Haymarket) to Which Are Prefix'd Illustrative Extracts and a Prospectus of the Action; Invented by Mr. Fawcett, and Got Up under the Direction of Mr. Farley*. 11th ed. Woodfall, 1809.

Fehskens, Erin. "Elvis Has Left the Country: Marronage in Chris Abani's *Graceland*." *College Literature*, vol. 42, no. 1, 2015, pp. 90–111.

Fowler, Greta. "Years of Pantomime." *Sunday Gleaner*, December 14, 1975.

Fowler, Henry. *The LTM: Showcase for Jamaican Talent*. Program for *Bruckins*. Little Theatre Movement, Kingston, 1981.

Frost, Thomas. *Obi; or, Three-Fingered Jack: A Romance*. E. Lloyd, Salisbury-Square, Fleet Street, 1851. Reprint, British Library Digital Historical Collection.

Fulford, Tim, and Peter Kitson. *Romanticism and Colonialism: Writing and Empire, 1780–1830*. Cambridge UP, 2005.

Garvey, Marcus, and Robert Hill. *The Marcus Garvey and Universal Negro Improvement Association Papers*. Vol. 11, *The Caribbean Diaspora, 1910–1920*. Duke UP, 2011.

Gaspar, Barry David. *The French Revolution and the Greater Caribbean*. Indiana UP, 2003.

Gates, Henry Louis, Jr. *The Signifying Monkey: A Theory of Afro-American Literary Criticism*. Oxford UP, 1988.

Geggus, David Patrick. *The Haitian Revolution: A Documentary History*. Hackett, 2014.

Genovese, Eugene. *From Rebellion to Revolution: Afro-American Slave Revolts in the Making of the New World*. 2nd ed. Vintage, 1981.

Gerbner, Katharine. "'They Call Me Obea': German Moravian Missionaries and Afro-Caribbean Religion in Jamaica, 1754–1760." *Obeah: Knowledge, Power, and Writing in the Early Atlantic World*. Special issue, *Atlantic Studies*, vol. 12, no. 2, 2015, pp. 160–178.

Gibbs, Jenna. "Toussaint, Gabriel, and Three Finger'd Jack: 'Courageous Chiefs' and the 'Sacred Standard of Liberty' on the Atlantic Stage." *Early American Studies: An Interdisciplinary Journal*, vol. 12, no. 3, 2015, pp. 626–660.

Gilroy, Paul. *The Black Atlantic: Modernity and Double Consciousness*. Howard UP, 1993.

———. "Could You Be Loved? Bob Marley, Anti-politics and Universal Sufferation." *Critical Quarterly*, vol. 47, no. 4, 2005, pp. 226–245.

———. *Darker Than Blue: On the Moral Economies of Black Atlantic Culture*. Harvard UP, 2010.

Glissant, Édouard. *Poetics of Relation*. Translated by Betsy Wing. U of Michigan P, 1997.

Gloudon, Barbara. *From the Chairperson*. Program for *Mansong*. Little Theatre Movement, Kingston, 1980.

———. "Playwriting and Pantomimes." *Sunday Gleaner*, January 22, 1995, 3C–4C.

Gomez, Michael. *Black Crescent: The Experience and Legacy of African Muslims in the Americas*. Cambridge UP, 2005.

Goudie, Sean. *Creole America: The West Indies and the Formation of Literature and Culture in the New Republic*. U of Pennsylvania P, 2006.

Gunst, Laurie. *Born Fi' Dead: A Journey through the Jamaican Posse Underworld*. Holt, 1995.

Gurney, Peter. "Working-Class Writers and the Art of Escapology in Victorian England: The Case of Thomas Frost." *Journal of British Studies*, vol. 45, no. 1, 2006, pp. 51–71.

Handler, Jerome, and Kenneth Bilby. *Enacting Power: The Criminalization of Obeah in the Anglophone Caribbean, 1780–2011*. U of the West Indies P, 2013.

"Harder They Come Remake Set for 2012." *Kingston Gleaner*, April 11, 2011, 21.

Harris, C.L.G. "The Maroons: Praised and Condemned." *Daily Gleaner*, July 23, 1967, 7.

Harrison, Kimberly, and Richard Fantina, editors. *Essays on a Scandalous Genre*. Ohio State UP, 2006.

Hartman, Saidiya. *Scenes of Subjection: Terror, Slavery, and Self-Making in Nineteenth-Century America*. Oxford UP, 1997.

Haynes, Tonya. "Sylvia Wynter's Theory of the Human and the Crisis School of Caribbean Heteromasculinity Studies." *Small Axe*, vol. 49, 2016, pp. 92–112.

Hays, Tom. "Jamaican Drug Lord Faces Sentencing in U.S. Case." *San Diego Union-Tribune*, March 11, 2012.

Heap, Brian. "National Pantomime: As Jamaican as a Good Rice and Peas!" *Skywritings*, vol. 90, December 1993–January 1994, pp. 64–66.

———. "Pantomime: The People's Theatre." *Sunday Gleaner*, January 24, 1993, 1D, 4D.

Henzell, Perry, and Trevor Rhone. *The Harder They Come*. Directed by Perry Henzell. Screenplay by Perry Henzell and Trevor Rhone. Island Films, 1971; originally licensed by International Films, 1972.

Heuman, Gad. *The Killing Time: The Morant Bay Rebellion Jamaica*. U of Tennessee P, 1994.

Hill, Errol. *The Jamaican Stage: 1655–1900*. U of Massachusetts P, 1992.

Hill, Robert. "Dread History: Leonard P. Howell and Millennial Visions in Early Rastafari Religion in Jamaica." *Epoch: Journal of the History of Religions*, vol. 9, 1981, pp. 30–71.

Hogle, Jerrold. "Directing *Obi* in 2000." *Obi*, edited by Chuck Rzepka. Special issue, *Romantic Circles Praxis Series*, edited by Orrin Wang. U of Maryland, 2002.

Holt, Thomas. *The Problem of Freedom: Race, Labor, and Politics in Jamaican and Britain, 1832–1938*. Johns Hopkins UP, 1992.

hooks, bell. *We Real Cool: Black Men and Masculinity*. Routledge, 2003.

Hope, Donna. "Dons and Shottas: Performing Violent Masculinity in Dancehall Culture." *Social and Economic Studies*, vol. 55, nos. 1–2, 2006, pp. 115–131.

Hoskins, Robert. Introduction to *Obi; or, Three-Finger'd Jack*. With Eileen Southern. Stainer and Bell, 1996.

———. "Savage Boundaries: Reading Samuel Arnolds' Score." *Obi*, edited by Chuck Rzepka. Special issue, *Romantic Circles Praxis Series*, edited by Orrin Wang. U of Maryland, 2002.

Huzzey, Richard. *Freedom Burning: Anti-slavery and Empire in Victorian Britain*. Cornell UP, 2012.

Jaffe, Rivke. "From Maroons to Dons: Sovereignty, Violence and Law in Jamaica." *Critique of Anthropology* vol. 35, no. 1, 2015, pp. 47–63.

"Jamaican Drug Lord Sentencing Delayed." *Huffington Post*, May 16, 2012.

Kamugisha, Aaron. "Sylvia Wynter's 'Black Metamorphosis': A Discussion." *Small Axe*, vol. 49, 2016.

Ken, David Wong. Personal interview, June 20, 2016.

King, Julian Anthony Christopher. *Three-Fingered Jack: The Spirit of Jamaica*. Amazon Digital Services, 2014, www.facebook.com/julion.king.9?fref=ts.

Knight, Franklin. *The Caribbean, the Genesis of a Fragmented Nationalism*. Oxford UP, 1978.

Knight, Franklin W., and Margaret Crahan. *Africa and the Caribbean*. Johns Hopkins UP, 1979.

Kopytoff, Barbara Klamon. "Colonial Treaty as Sacred Charter of the Jamaican Maroons." *Ethnohistory*, vol. 26, no. 1, 1978, pp. 45–65.

———. "Maroons of Jamaica: An Ethnohistorical Study of Incomplete Polities, 1655–1905." PhD diss., University of the West Indies Special Collections, 1973.

Krug, Jessica. "Constructs of Freedom and Identity: The Ethnogenesis of the Jamaican Maroons and the Treaties of 1739." *PSU McNair Scholars Online Journal*, vol. 1, no. 6, 2005, http://pdxscholar.library.pdx.edu/mcnair/vol1/iss1/6.

Kryza, Frank T. *The Race for Timbuktu: In Search of Africa's City of Gold*. HarperCollins, 2011.

Lambert, David. *White Creole Culture, Politics, and Identity during the Age of Abolition*. Cambridge UP, 2005.

Lee, Debbie. "Grave Dirt, Dried Toads, and the Blood of a Cat: How Aldridge Worked His Charms." *Obi*, edited by Chuck Rzepka. Special issue, *Romantic Circles Praxis Series*, edited by Orrin Wang. U of Maryland, 2002.

———. *Slavery and the Romantic Imagination*. U of Pennsylvania P, 2004.

Lee, Helene. *The First Rasta: Leonard Howell and the Rise of Rasta*. Hill Books, 2003.

Lewis, Linden. *The Culture of Gender and Sexuality in the Caribbean*. UP of Florida, 2003.

———. "Man Talk, Masculinity, and a Changing Social Environment." *Caribbean Review of Gender Studies*, vol. 1, 2007, pp. 2–22.

Lewis, R. Anthony, and Robert Carr. "Gender, Sexuality and Exclusion: Sketching the Outlines of the Jamaican Popular Nationalist Project." *Caribbean Review of Gender Studies*, vol. 3, 2009, https://sta.uwi.edu/crgs/november2009/index.asp.

Lindfors, Bernth. *Ira Aldridge: The Early Years, 1807–1833*. Vol. 1. U of Rochester P, 2011.

———. "'Mislike Me Not for My Complexion . . .': Ira Aldridge in Whiteface." *African-American Review*, vol. 33, no. 2, 1999, pp. 347–359.

Long, Edward. *The History of Jamaica*. 3 vols. Cambridge UP, 2010.

Lott, Eric. *Love and Theft: Blackface Minstrelsy and the American Working Class*. Oxford UP, 1995.

Lovelace, Earl. *The Dragon Can't Dance*. Reprint, Persea, 2003.

Lumsden, Frank. Personal interview. June 10, 2009.

Lumsden, Keith. Personal interview. June 11, 2009.

Mackie, Erin. "Welcome the Outlaw: Pirates, Maroons, and Caribbean Counter cultures." *Cultural Critique*, vol. 59, Winter 2005, pp. 24–62.

Manganelli, Kimberly Snyder. *Transatlantic Spectacles of Race: The Tragic Mulatta and the Tragic Muse*. Rutgers UP, 2012.

Marshall, Herbert, and Mildred Stock. *Ira Aldridge: The Negro Tradition*. Howard UP, 1993.

Martin, Tony. *Marcus Garvey, Hero: A First Biography*. Majority, 1983.

Masouri, John. *The Life of Peter Tosh: Steppin' Razor*. Omnibus, 2013.

McAllister, Marvin. *White People Do Not Know How to Behave at Entertainments Designed for Ladies and Gentlemen of Colour*. U of North Carolina P, 2003.

McCurbin, Eric ("Worries"). Personal interview. June 30, 2016.

McFarlane, Adrian Anthony. "The Epistemological Significance of 'I-an-I' as a Response to Quashie and Anancyism in Jamaican Culture." *Chanting Down Babylon*, edited by Nathaniel Samuel Murrell, Temple UP, 1998, 107–124.

McLean, Rayon. Personal interview. June 16, 2009.

McLellan, Dennis. "Perry Henzell, 70: His Movie 'The Harder They Come' Brought Reggae to the World." *Los Angeles Times*, December 2, 2006.

McNeill, J. R. "Yellow Jack and Geopolitics: Environment, Epidemics, and the Struggles for Empire in the American Tropics, 1650–1825." *OAH Magazine of History*, April 2004, 9–13.

Meer, Sara. *Uncle Tom Mania: Slavery, Minstrelsy, and Transatlantic Culture in the 1850s*. U of Georgia P, 2005.

Merrill, Lisa. "Exhibiting Race 'under the World's Huge Glass Case': William and Ellen Craft and William Wells Brown at the Great Exhibition in Crystal Palace, London, 1851." *Slavery and Abolition*, vol. 33, no. 2, 2012, pp. 321–336.

Meschino, Patricia. "Jamaican Musicians Rally to Support Alleged Drug Kingpin, Dudus Coke." *Billboard*, June 18, 2010.

Miller, Kei. "Bad Man Nuh Dress Like Girl." Facebook blog, June 24, 2010. www.facebook.com/note.php?note_id=471431418568&id=167074302410&ref=mf.

Mintz, Sidney, and Sally Price. *Caribbean Contours*. Johns Hopkins UP, 1985.

Mohammed, Patricia. "Like Sugar in Coffee: Third Wave Feminism and the Caribbean." *Social and Economic Studies*, vol. 52, no. 3, 2003, pp. 5–30.

Mohammed, Patricia, and Catherine Shepherd, editors. *Gender in Caribbean Development*. U of the West Indies P, Saint Augustine, 1999.

Moody, Jane. *Illegitimate Theatre in London: 1770–1840*. Cambridge UP, 2007.

Morris, Mervyn. *Miss Lou: Louise Bennett and Jamaican Culture*. Andrews UK, 2014.

———. "New Story Time." *Sunday Sun*, January 4, 1981.

Morrison, Toni. *Playing in the Dark: Whiteness and the Literary Imagination*. Harvard UP, 1992.

Moseley, Benjamin. *A Treatise on Sugar: With Miscellaneous Medical Observations*. 2nd ed. 1799. Nichols, 1800.

Murison, Justine. "Obeah and Its Others: Buffered Selves in the Era of Tropical Medicine." *Obeah: Knowledge, Power, and Writing in the Early Atlantic World*. Special issue, *Atlantic Studies*, vol. 12, no. 2, 2015, pp. 144–159.

[Murray, William H.]. *Obi; or, Three-Fingered Jack, a Melodrama in Two Acts*. Thomas Hailes Lacy. New British Theatre (Late Duncombe's), no. 469, Lacy, c. 1854.

Neal, Mark Anthony. *The New Black Man*. Routledge, 2009.

Neff, D. S. "Safie/Saphie: Mungo Park's *Travels in the Interior Districts of Africa* and the De Lacey Episode in *Frankenstein*." *ANQ: A Quarterly*, vol. 21, no. 1, 2008, pp. 45–50.

Neita, Hartley. "Exploiting Our Legends." *Jamaica Gleaner*, August 12, 2008.

Newton, Huey. *To Die for the People: The Writings of Huey P. Newton*. Edited by Toni Morrison. Readers and Writers Press, 1995.

Nowatzki, Robert. *Representing African Americans in Abolitionism and Blackface Minstrelsy*. Louisiana State UP, 2016.

O'Brien, John. *Harlequin Britain: Pantomime and Entertainment, 1690–1760*. Johns Hopkins UP, 2004.

OED (Oxford English Dictionary). Oxford UP. /www.oed.com/. Accessed February 23, 2017.

Ongiri, Amy Abugo. *Spectacular Blackness: The Cultural Politics of the Black Power Movement and the Search for a Black Aesthetic*. U of Virginia P, 2009.

O'Rourke, James. "Revising *Obi; or, Three-Finger'd Jack* and the Jacobin Repudiation of Sentimentality." *Nineteenth-Century Contexts*, vol. 28, no. 4, 2006, pp. 285–303.

Park, Mungo. *Travels in the Interior of Africa*. 1799. Black, 1858.

Parry, Odette. *Male Underachievement in High School Education in Jamaica, Barbados, and St. Vincent and the Grenadines*. Centre for Gender and Development Studies/Canoe, 2000.

Paton, Diana. "The Afterlives of Three-Fingered Jack." In *Slavery and the Cultures of Abolition: Essays Marking the Bicentennial of the British Abolition Act of 1807*, edited by Brycchan Carey and Peter Kitson, Brewer, 2007, pp. 42–63.

———. "Histories of Three-Fingered Jack: A Bibliography"; "The Slavery Website" by Brycchan Carey, June 27, 2008. www.brycchancarey.com/index.

———. "Obeah Acts: Producing and Policing the Boundaries of Religion in the Caribbean." *Small Axe: A Caribbean Journal of Criticism*, vol. 13, no. 1, 2009, pp. 1–18.

———. "Witchcraft, Poison, Law, and Atlantic Slavery." *William and Mary Quarterly*, vol. 69, no. 2, 2012, pp. 235–264.

Patterson, Orlando. *Slavery and Social Death: A Comparative Study*. Harvard UP, 1985.

Paugh, Katherine, E. "Yaws, Syphilis, Sexuality, and the Circulation of Medical Knowledge in the British Caribbean and the Atlantic World." *Bulletin of the History of Medicine*, vol. 88, no. 2, 2014, pp. 225–252.

Peak, Anna. "Servants and the Victorian Sensation Novel." *Studies in English Literature*, vol. 54, no. 4, 2009, pp. 835–851.

Peebles, Melvin Van. *Sweet Sweetback's Baadasssss Song*. Directed by Melvin Van Peebles. Yeah Production Company, April 23, 1971.

Pestana, Carla Gardina. "English Character and the Fiasco of the Western Design." *Early American Studies: An Interdisciplinary Journal*, vol. 3, no. 1, 2005, pp. 1–31.

Poupeye, Veerle. Conversation, 2016.

Price, Richard, ed. *Maroon Societies: Rebel Slave Communities in the Americas*. Johns Hopkins UP, 1979.

Puri, Shalini. "Finding the Field: Notes on Caribbean Cultural Criticism, Area Studies, and Forms of Engagement." *Small Axe*, vol. 17, no. 2, 2013, pp. 58–73.

———. *The Granada Revolution in the Caribbean Present: Operation Urgent Memory*. Palgrave, 2014.

Ra, Omari "Afrikan" S. *Excavation: Head of Jack Mansong*. Artist's possession, n.d.

———. "Omari Ra." Blog by the National Gallery of Jamaica. https://nationalgalleryofjamaica.wordpress.com/2010/01/24/omari-s-ra-afrikan-b-1960. Accessed July 20, 2015.

Reckford, Verena. "The Evolution of Pantomime in Jamaica." *Jamaica Daily News*, November 14, 1974, D1, D4.

Reddock, Rhoda. *Interrogating Caribbean Masculinities: Theoretical and Empirical Analyses*. U of the West Indies P, 2004.

Rediker, Marcus, and Peter Linebaugh. *The Many-Headed Hydra: The Hidden History of the Revolutionary Atlantic*. Beacon, 2001.

Reed, Peter. *Rogue Performances: Staging the Underclasses in Early American Theatre Culture*. Palgrave, 2007.

———. "Staging Circum-Atlantic Revolt in *Polly* and *Three-Finger'd Jack*." *Theatre Journal*, vol. 59, May 2007, pp. 241–258.

———. "'There Was No Resisting John Canoe': Circum-Atlantic Transracial Performance." *Theatre History Studies*, vol. 27, 2007, pp. 65–85.

Review of Short Articles, Notes, and Reviews, vol. 21, no. 1, 2008. pp. 45–50.

Richardson, Alan. "Romantic Voodoo: Obeah and British Culture, 1797–1807." *Sacred Possessions*, edited by Margarite Fernández Olmos and Lizabeth Paravisini-Gebert, Rutgers UP, 1997, pp. 171–194.

Richardson, Riche. *Black Masculinity and the U.S. South: From Uncle Tom to Gangster*. U of Georgia P, 2007.

Roach, Joseph. *Cities of the Dead: Circum-Atlantic Performance*. Columbia UP, 1996.

Roberts, Neil. *Freedom as Marronage*. U of Chicago P, 2015.

Roberts, Walter Adolphe. *Six Great Jamaicans*. Pioneer Press, 1951.

Robertson, James. "Cromwell and the Conquest of Jamaica." *History Today*, vol. 55, no. 5, 2005, pp. 15–23.

Robinson, Carey. *The Fighting Maroons of Jamaica*. Collins and Sangster, 1969.

Rodriques, Janelle. "Obeah(man) as Trickster in Cyrnic Williams' *Hamel, the Obeah Man*." *Obeah: Knowledge, Power, and Writing in the Early Atlantic World*. Special issue, *Atlantic Studies*, vol. 12, no. 2, 2015, pp. 219–234.

Rosenberg, Leah. *Nationalism and the Formation of Caribbean Literature*. Palgrave, 2007.

Ross, Marlon. *Manning the Race: Reforming Black Men in the Jim Crow Era*. New York UP, 2004.

Royal Gazette. Supplements, vol. 2, nos. 50–88, April 1–December 30, 1780; vol. 3, no. 93, January 27–February 3, 1781. Microfiche available at Special Collections, U of the West Indies, Mona.

Rzepka, Chuck. E-mail message. September 4, 2010.

———. Introduction to *Obi*, edited by Chuck Rzepka. Special issue, *Romantic Circles Praxis Series*, edited by Orrin Wang. U of Maryland, 2002.

———. *Obi: A Play in the Life of Ira Aldridge, the Paul Robeson of the Nineteenth Century*. Performed at Playwrights' Theater, Boston University, MA, July 18, 2000; and Eighth Annual Conference of the North American Society for the Study of Romanticism, Tempe, AZ, September 14, 2000, DVD.

———. "Obi Now." In *Obi*, edited by Chuck Rzepka. Special issue, *Romantic Circles Praxis Series*, edited by Orrin Wang. U of Maryland, 2002.

———. "Thomas De Quincey's 'Three-Fingered Jack': The West Indian Origins of the 'Dark Interpreter.'" *European Romantic Review*, vol. 8, no. 2, 1997, pp. 117–138.

Salih, Sara. "Putting Down Rebellion. Witnessing the Body of the Condemned in Abolition-Era Narratives." *Slavery and Cultures of Abolition: Essays Marking the Bicentennial of the British Abolition Act of 1807*, edited by Brycchan Carey and Peter Kitson, Boydell and Brewer, 2007, pp. 64–86.

Schuler, Monica. *Alas, Alas, Kongo: A Social History of Indentured African Immigration into Jamaica, 1841–1865*. Johns Hopkins UP, 1980.

Scott, Dennis. *From the Director*. Program for *Mansong*. Little Theatre Movement, Kingston, 1980.

Scott, David, and Nicholas Laughlin. "Criticism as a Question." *Caribbean Review of Books*. November 2008. http://caribbeanreviewofbooks.com/crb-archive/18-november-2008/"criticism-as-a-question"/.

———. "Preface: Sylvia Wynter's Agnostic Imitations." *Small Axe*, vol. 49, 2016, pp. vii–x.

Sharpe, Jenny. *Ghosts of Slavery: A Literary Archeology of Black Women's Lives*. U of Minnesota P, 2002.

Sheller, Mimi. "Hidden Textures of Race and Historical Memory: The Rediscovery of Photographs Relating to Jamaica's Morant Bay Rebellion of 1865." *Princeton University Library Chronicle*, vol. 72, no. 2, 2001, pp. 532–567.

Shepherd, Verene, Bridget Breton, and Barbara Bailey, eds. *Engendering History: Caribbean Women in Historical Perspective*. St. Martin's Press, 1995.

Siders, Vincent Earnest. Instant message, Facebook. November 8, 2014.

Simms, Gloria (Mama G). Personal interview. June 15, 2012.

Sives, Amanda. *Elections, Violence and the Democratic Process in Jamaica, 1944–2007*. Randle, 2010.

Smallwood, Stephanie, E. *Saltwater Slavery: A Middle Passage from African to American Diaspora*. Harvard UP, 2007.

Smith, Matthew. "H. G. and Haiti: An Analysis of Herbert G. de Lisser's 'Land of Revolutions.'" *Journal of Caribbean History*, vol. 22, no. 2, 2010, pp. 183–200.

———. *Liberty, Fraternity and Exile: Haiti and Jamaica after Emancipation*. U of North Carolina P, 2014.

Southey, Thomas. *Poems concerning the Slave Trade*. Bristol, 1797.

Spaulding, Gary. "The Sacrifice: Souls Lost for the 'Cause.'" *Gleaner*, May 30, 2010.

Stephens, Michelle A. "Babylon's 'Natural Mystic': The North American Music Industry, the Legend of Bob Marley, and the Incorporation of Transnationalism." *Cultural Studies*, vol. 12, no. 2, 1998, pp. 139–167.

———. *Black Empire: The Masculine Global Imaginary of Caribbean Intellectuals in the United States, 1914–1962*. Duke UP, 2005.

———. E-mail. Received by Kim Guinta, October 27, 2015.

Sterling, Wallace. Personal interview. June 12, 2009.

———. Remarks to the Seventh Annual Charles Town International Maroon Conference. June 23, 2015.

Stevens, James. *Crisis of the Sugar Colonies*. Hatchard, 1802.

Sultana, Afroz. *Invisible Yet Invincible: Islamic Heritage of the Maroons and the Enslaved Africans in Jamaica*. Macauley, 2012.

Swydky, Lissette. "Rewriting the History of Black Resistance: The Haitian Revolution, Jamaican Maroons and the 'History' of Three-Fingered Jack in English Popular Culture, 1799–1830." *Circulations: Romanticism and the Black Atlantic*. Special issue, *Romantic Circles Praxis Series*, edited by Paul Youngquist and Frances Botkin, 2011. www.rc.umd.edu/praxis/circulations/HTML/praxis.2011.youngquist .html. Accessed February 20, 2017.

Tarantino, Quentin. "Quentin Tarantino Tackles Old Dixie by Way of the Old West (by Way of Italy)." *New York Times Magazine*, September 27, 2012.

Taylor, Diana. *The Archive and the Repertoire: Performing Cultural Memory in the Americas*. Duke UP, 2003.

Taylor, S.A.G. *The Western Design: An Account of Cromwell's Expedition to the Caribbean*. Reprint, Solstice Production, 1965.

Thomas, Deborah. "Caribbean Studies, Archive Building, and the Problem of Violence." *Small Axe*, vol. 41, 2013, pp. 27–48.

———. *Exceptional Violence: Embodied Citizenship in Transnational Jamaica*. Duke UP, 2011.

Thomas, Greg. "*Marronnons*/Let's Maroon: Sylvia Wynter's 'Black Metamorphosis' as a Species of Marronage." *Small Axe*, vol. 49, 2016, pp. 62–78.

Thompson, Alvin O. *Flight to Freedom: African Runaways and Maroons in the Americas*. U of the West Indies P, 2006.

Thompson, George. *A Documentary History of the African Theatre*. Northwestern UP, 1998.

Thornton, John. *Africa and Africans in the Making of the Atlantic World*. Cambridge UP, 1998.

Thurloe, John, Esq. *A Collection of the State Papers of John Thurloe*. Volume 1, *1638–1653*. Edited by Thomas Birch, Gyles, 1742. *British History Online*. www.british-history.ac.uk/thurloe-papers/vol1. Accessed February 16, 2017.

Tipling, Carmen. Personal interview. January 30, 2006.

Tosh, Peter. "Equal Rights." *Equal Rights*. Columbia Records, 1977.

Walker, Karyl. "The Story of Rhygin: The Two-Gun Killer." *Jamaica Observer*, October 21, 2007.

Wallace, Maurice. *Constructing the Black Masculine: Identity and Ideality in African American Men's Literature and Culture, 1775–1995*. Duke UP, 2002.

Warner, Michael, Natasha Hurley, Luis Iglesias, Sonia Di Loreto, Jeffrey Scraba, and Sandra Young. "A Soliloquy 'Lately Spoken at the African Theatre': Race and the Public Sphere in New York City, 1821." *American Literature*, vol. 73, no. 1, 2001, pp. 1–46.

Wa Thiong'o, Ngũgĩ. *Decolonising the Mind: The Norton Anthology of English Literature; The Twentieth Century and After*. Vol. F, 9th ed., edited by Stephen Greenblatt, Jahan Ramazani, and Jon Stallworthy, 2012, pp. 2737–2741.

Watson, Tim. *Caribbean Culture and British Fiction in the Atlantic World, 1780–1870*. Cambridge UP, 2011.

———. "Mobile Obeah: A Response to 'Obeah: Knowledge, Power, and Writing in the Early Atlantic World.'" *Obeah: Knowledge, Power, and Writing in the Early Atlantic World*. Special issue, *Atlantic Studies*, vol. 12, no. 2, 2015, pp. 244–250.

Weiser, Benjamin. "In a 7-Page Note, Drug Lord Asks a Judge for Leniency." *New York Times*, September 21, 2011.

West, Michael. "Seeing Darkly: Guyana, Black Power, and Walter Rodney's Expulsion from Jamaica." *Small Axe*, vol. 12, no. 1, 2008, pp. 93–104.

———. "The Targeting of Walter Rodney." *Solidarity*. www.solidarity-us.org/node/136. Accessed February 20, 2017.

White, Garth. "Rudie, Oh, Rudie." *Caribbean Quarterly*, vol. 13, 1967, pp. 39–44.

Williams, Joseph J. "Psychic Phenomenon of Jamaica." PhD diss., Boston University, 1934.

———. *Voodoo and Obeahs: Phases of West India Witchcraft*. MacVeagh Dial, 1932.

Wilson, Kathleen. *The Island Race: Englishness, Empire and Gender in the Eighteenth Century*. Routledge, 2002.

———. "The Performance of Freedom: Maroons and the Colonial Order in Eighteenth-Century Jamaica and the Atlantic Sound." *William and Mary Quarterly*, vol. 66, no. 1, 2009, pp. 45–86.

Wisecup, Kelly, and Toni Wall Jaudon. "Introduction: On Knowing and Not Knowing about Obeah." *Obeah: Knowledge, Power, and Writing in the Early Atlantic World*. Special issue, *Atlantic Studies*, vol. 12, no. 2, 2015, pp. 129–143.

Wordsworth, William, and Samuel Taylor Coleridge. *Lyrical Ballads: 1798 and 1802*. Edited by Fiona Stafford, Oxford UP, 2013.

Worrall, David. *Harlequin Empire: Race, Ethnicity, and the Drama of Modern Entertainment*. Pickering and Chatto, 2007.

Wynter, Sylvia. "Jonkonnu in Jamaica: Towards the Interpretation of Folk Dance as a Cultural Process." *Jamaica Journal*, vol. 4, June 1970, pp. 34–48.

———. "We Must Learn to Sit Down Together and Talk about a Little Culture: Reflections on West Indian Writing and Criticism." *Jamaica Journal*, vol. 2, no. 4, 1968, pp. 23–32; vol. 3, no. 1, 1969, pp. 27–42.

Youngquist, Paul. "The Afro-Futurism of DJ Vassa." *European Romantic Review*, vol. 16, no. 2, 2005, pp. 183–194.

Youngquist, Paul, and Frances Botkin. "Introduction, Black Romanticism: Romantic Circulations." *Circulations: Romanticism and the Black Atlantic*. Special issue, *Romantic Circles Praxis Series*, October 2011.

Zips, Werner. *Black Rebels: African-Caribbean Freedom Fighters*. Translated by Shelley L. Frisch. Randle, 1999.

Index

abolitionism: and British attitudes toward slavery, 70, 116, 127; and Brown's theater, 78–79, 81–82; in Earle's *Obi*, 48–49, 52–53, 58; and empathetic identification, 113; and Fawcett's *Obi*, 70, 78–79; and Frost's *Obi*, 125–126; in Murray's *Obi*, 90; Park on, 61, 185–186n20

academic papers in productions of *Obi*, 104–105, 108–109

African American theater communities: and Rzepka's *Obi*, 106–109. *See also* Brown's theaters

African Association, 61, 184n5

African culture: in *Mansong*, 142; in Murray's *Obi*, 98; in Park's *Travels*, 61–62

African Grove Pleasure Garden (Brown's theater), 79, 80, 92

Africans, ethnic groups of: Congos, 32, 33, 182n7, 182n8; Coromantees, 33, 182n8, 182n9, 183n25, 184n8; Feloops, 50–51, 184n7

African Theatre. *See* Brown's theaters

African tribal wars: in Burdett's *Life*, 60–61, 67; in *Mansong*, 144–145

Afro-Jamaicans. *See* assimilated Afro-Jamaicans; black masculinity; rebels, black; Tuckey (free black character)

Aldridge, Ira, 3, 16, 89–104; after Brown's theater closed, 87–88; career of, 90–94; and Charles Mathews, 103; contribution of to Murray's *Obi*, 89–90, 190n3; honored by Sainte Domingue, 190–191n4; in Mansong role, 94–97, 100, 104; personal identity of, 94, 103–104

American identity, 79, 83

American Theatre (Brown's theater), 79, 83–84

"Anancy Cycle" of Jamaican pantomimes, 140–141

Anglo-Jamaicans. *See* white West Indians

antihero figure, 17, 90, 97

appropriation, 1, 113, 128, 131, 135, 153, 167

Aravamudan, Srinivas, 6, 39, 49, 70, 182n7, 185n11

archives and counterarchives, 18, 19

Arnold, Samuel, 71, 72

Asante Oath, 31

Assembly of Jamaica, 28, 41–42, 49–50, 54–55, 183n19

assimilated Afro-Jamaicans: in Burdett's *Life*, 60; in Earle's *Obi*, 50, 56; in Fawcett's *Obi*, 73; in Murray's *Obi*, 99, 100, 101–102. *See also* Quashie (slave name of Reeder)

Back O' Wall, 163–164

backra (white planter class), in *Mansong*, 142, 147–148, 154

badassery and "bad man" figure, in Jamaican popular culture, 12–14, 159, 160–169, 198n11

Banton, Buju, 162

About the Author

FRANCES R. BOTKIN is a professor of English at Towson University, where she teaches British romanticism, Caribbean literature, and gender studies. She has published articles on Maria Edgeworth, William Wordsworth, Sydney Owenson, and Jack Mansong. She has also edited, with Paul Youngquist, a special issue in the *Romantic Circles Praxis Series*, "Black Romanticism: Romantic Circulations," and they are currently compiling a collection of academic essays, creative work, and other intellectual endeavors about Maroons and Marronage. Though she lives primarily in Baltimore, Maryland, Dr. Botkin spends several months of the year in Kingston and Charles Town, Jamaica, where she helps to organize the Charles Town International Maroon Conference.